A LITTLE WALK ON SKIS

A LITTLE WALK ON SKIS

From the Mediterranean to Austria along the Alps off piste

by

Peter Wilberforce Smith, F.R.C.S.,

Past President of the Alpine Ski Club
and
Chairman of the Touring Section of the Ski Club of Great Britain

and

Beryl Wilberforce Smith, M.D., M.R.C.P.

Dickerson, Surlingham, Norfolk

Published by Dickerson, The Common, Surlingham, Norfolk

© B. E. Wilberforce Smith 1987

ISBN 0 904405 29 X
British Library Cataloguing in Publication Data
Wilberforce Smith, Peter
 A little walk on skis
 1. Skis and skiing—Alps
 I. Title   II. Wilberforce Smith, Beryl
 796.93   GV854.8.A45

Jacket design, maps and line drawing: Suzie Hanna
Cartoon: Hugh Morren
Editor: Monica Dickerson

Typesetting by Monica Dickerson, Surlingham, and Typeshare Limited, London
Printed by Colourprint, Fakenham, Norfolk
Distributed by Cordee, Leicester

Contents

Chapter I. The Idea   1

We decide to make a start.

Chapter II. 1970: Year 1.   A Little Walk on Skis   7

The Maritime and Cottian Alps
Beryl loses part of her safety binding and we discover the inadequacies of some of the maps.
The study of the formation and behaviour of snow gives clues to planning our course.
We sleep in comfort and we pass nights in squalid surroundings.
We encounter moufflons, chamois, marmots and other Alpine wild life.

Chapter III. 1971: Year 2.   The Year of Cloud   65

The Graian and Pennine Alps
We fry and sizzle in hot sunshine, negotiate a pass in mist, walk in a circle in a white-out, and encounter an electric storm on a glacier.
We watch illegal games of Moro, find a mountain *"Marie Celeste"*, and see the highest vineyard in Europe.
We are accompanied by Anthony Gueterbock, Geoffrey Buckley and John Lewis.
We ponder on the formation of glaciers and ice avalanches and experience an example of altitude sickness.

Chapter IV. 1972: Year 3.   The Year of Frustration   116

The Pennine and Lepontine Alps
We are accompanied by Philip Booth and Jeremy Whitehead.
We sleep in a monastery, on churn covers, and surrounded by nudes.
We celebrate Jeremy's birthday and see the head sources of the three most important rivers in Europe.
I get bitten by a St. Bernard dog, Jeremy narrowly misses ski-ing over the edge of a hundred-foot ice-cliff, and we all come face to face with a soldier loading a mortar.

Chapter V. 1973: Year 4.   The Year of Progress   139

The Lepontine, Adula and Silvretta Alps
Philip Booth, Jim Mason and Richard Brooke join us for parts of our route.
We encounter several different weather phenomena such as plates of ice and horizontal snow, and assess wind direction and wind slab.
We hear Romansch and learn something about the history of Switzerland while delayed by incessant snow.
We meet a girl terrified by gaping crevasses, an avalanche-rescue dog, a traffic jam of skiers and a host of old friends.

Chapter VI. 1974: Year 5.　The Year of Disappointment　　180

　　The Silvretta Alps and the Ötztal
　　We travel alone and sample a variety of mountain huts.
　　We lose our hut slippers and find new friends, but Beryl catches a cold and we have to
　　return to England.

The Narrative is taken over by Beryl

Chapter VII. 1975 & 1976: Years 6 & 7.　The Years of Disaster　　193

　　The Stubai
　　We are snowbound for three days and then ski together for the last time.
　　Avalanches destroy our plans and we join a discussion on dry snow airborne avalanches.
　　Peter has to be taken by helicopter to Innsbruck Hospital and undergoes surgery. He
　　recovers, but dies a week before we were due to resume the traverse.

Chapter VIII. 1977: Year 8.　The Year of Endeavour　　208

　　The Stubai
　　I try to resume the traverse, and Anthony Gueterbock agrees to lead a small team
　　including David and Marjorie Richardson and Vanda Boyd.
　　We have to plough through deep snow and we practise crevasse rescue.
　　The snow continues to fall and we try an alternative route, but we have to abandon the
　　attempt.

Chapter IX. 1978: Year 9.　The Year of Fulfilment　　218

　　The Zillertal, Venediger and Gross Glockner Groups
　　Richard Brooke and Fred Jenkins lead, while Jonathan Wallis, Robin Chapman and Eric
　　Farnsworth join us for parts of the way.
　　Snow and avalanche warnings again force a change of plan, and we are caught in a
　　complete white-out.
　　We descend one of the finest ski runs, but narrowly escape first a wet-snow slab-
　　avalanche and then a wind-slab avalanche.
　　The gas cylinder nearly sets fire to the hut, we come up against a snow wall, and we have
　　to build a snow-hole for the night.

Chapter X. 1968:　Epilogue　　243

　　The Venediger and the Hohe Tauern
　　We finish the traverse before we have begun it.
　　Archie Mackenzie, Geoffrey Buckley and Peter Capps are with us for parts of the way.

List of Illustrations

Plate 1. Valley of *Les Merveilles* from outside the hut

Plate 2. Passo del Nire. We cut the last few steps with an ice-axe. It was here that I had my first experience of the inadequacy of the 1:50,000 French maps. The picture shows the typical bunched-up peaks in the area 12

Plate 3. Passo di Mont Colomb: our first wild little pass lay golden in the early morning sun 14

Plate 4. The disintegration of a snowflake 18

Plate 5a. Powder Snow 21

Plates 5b & c. Firn snow: compacted by sun and wind. It has a dull sheen. The animal track which initially compressed the snow in the powder stage remains proud. 22
Spring crust: it is frozen hard and only the surface will soften in the sun

Plate 6. *Skavla:* windswept snow. The "step" is on the windward side, and provides useful information about the direction of the prevailing wind. 23

Plate 7. Mont Ghilie: a slippery traverse on wind-blown ripples of *Skavla* 24

Plate 8. A Cornice: the prevailing wind had come from the south-west and the snow had settled as an overhanging canopy on the leeward side. 25

Plate 9. Col de Mercera. In between us lay a steep gorge 26

Plate 10. The Chastillon Hut: its attractive appearance contrasted with the squalor within 28

Plate 11. Mont Mounier. The first signs of bad weather—bands of cirrostratus and "fish" clouds approaching from the south or south-west 29

Plate 12. Lower ominous clouds of altostratus begin to cover the whole sky and surrounding peaks bringing snow with them 30

Plate 13. Underside of skis, showing Skin rolled back; Harscheisen (ski crampon); and Binding to tether ski to boot 31

Plate 14. So *this* is the hotel "with running water" 34

Plate 15. Pic des Très Evéchès on the way to the Col Pourriac; the gorge opened into a wide bowl bounded by a fine cirque of mountains 36

Plate 16. Col Pourriac: plates of hoar frost covered the snow reflecting the sun like a mirror, giving it a blinding silvery sheen 44

Plate 17. Chiappera: Monte Castello, a great spire of rock some thousand feet high guarded the village like a sentinel 45

Plate 18. Saretto: the village incinerator 51

Plate 19. Two views of the Aiguille du Chambeyron: as seen from a distance from the Col d'Oronaye; and as we saw it from below, with the shattered ridges of red granite high above our heads 52

Plate 20. Col de Noire: it was corniced, but there was no difficulty in steering a course between the frozen crests 55

Plate 21. Anthony holding a ski caked with snow: it clung tenaciously to the soles of the skis and prevented them from sliding forwards 57

Plate 22. The Pic de Rochebrune: on our way we passed to the right of it down the valley to Les Fonts 58

Plate 23. The joy of the descent lured us too far down and we had an uncomfortable climb to get out of the stream bed 61

Plate 24. Col des Acles. High up was a ridge of red dolomite fashioned into battlements and turrets: we named it "the Castle" 62

Plate 25. I caught sight of the first Stone Marten I had ever seen. I examined his tracks, but what a thrill it was to have seen the author of this signature. 69

Plate 26. We must have walked into a windscoop like this 73

Plate 27. Outside the Peclet hut. We were awoken by the dismal cry *"Il neige!"* Angrily and irrationally I felt the speaker was half responsible 74

Plate 28. Séracs: sugar cubes of blue-green ice. The striations register each snowfall like the rings of a tree trunk 77

80

Plate 29. *Bergschrund* or *Rimaye:* a crevasse where the glacier meets the rocks; in this case it was covered with snow — 82

Plate 30. The disordered jumble of séracs and crevasses which form an ice-fall — 83

Plate 31. We had a long way to go to Tignes over the Col de Premou (on the left) — 85

Plate 32. An ice avalanche. These blocks and séracs had fallen from the hanging glacier — 86

Plate 33. From the Glaieretta Glacier we had our first view of Mont Blanc — 91

Plate 34. The entire range of the Pennine Alps known as the *Haute Route* which we would be crossing in three days' time — 93

Plate 35. The Grand Col Ferret with the ridge of the Grande Jorasses on the right — 95

Plate 36. Guarding the pass was a huge cornice streaming with water — 97

Plate 37. The Rosa Blanche: it was now much nearer and within an hour we stood below its final slopes — 101

Plate 38. The Dix Hut: surely the hut could not be up there — 103

Plate 39. A crevasse: these may descend hundreds of feet into the glacier — 105

Plate 40. The Vignette hut is built on a rocky ridge above an impressive drop to the glacier below—not a place for sleepwalking — 107

Plate 41. Col d'Eveque: dawn was just breaking — 108

Plate 42. The descent from the Col d'Eveque into the Arolla Valley — 109

Plate 43. Col de Mont Brulé. As we set off clouds began to tower behind the Col and cascade towards us — 110

Plate 44. The Tsa de Tsan glacier clings to the side of the mountains to form a semi-circular bowl — 111

Plate 45. The Allalinhorn, Alphubel and Taschhorn above the Saas Valley — 119

Plate 46. Skavla: ripples of wind-swept snow on the pass below Monte Leone — 124

Plate 47. Marmot tracks: one little fellow seemed to lead the way — 126

Plate 48. The Steinenjoch. We were glad of a rest as we had been frying in the sun for the past three hours — 127

Plate 49. Bivouac in the cheese-making room — 129

Plate 50. The gendarmes, perched like a row of policemen waiting to topple over and arrest us — 131

Plate 51. The Sabbione Glacier: it ended abruptly as a sheer ice-cliff such as I had seen only in Arctic waters — 132

Plate 52. The Gries Glacier burned silvery in the late afternoon sun — 136

Plate 53. A steep gully led up to the Cadlimo Hut; a track of footsteps was already there — 142

Plate 54. The Cadlimo Hut: the winter entrance through an upstairs window — 143

Plate 55. Piz Medel: the reward from the summit — 146

Plate 56. The Diesrut Pass: as we neared the crest our figures eclipsed the sun — 148

Plate 57. Cumbals: real skulls were perched in recesses above the church door—a reminder of man's limited span of life — 152

Plate 58. Richard Brooke at the tree line where the snow petered out — 153

Plate 59. The white patch in the centre distance is a sea of cloud or *Nebelmeer:* people living in the valley do not appreciate the weather conditions above the clouds — 155

Plate 60. The summit of the Rheinwaldhorn: this is why I love mountains — 156

Plate 61. The north-facing glacier which leads up to the Rheinwaldhorn is the Lenta Glacier. The gaping crevasses unnerved the young woman — 157

Plate 62. I examined tree stumps to determine the direction of the prevailing wind — 161

Plate 63. Windslab avalanche: showing the line of cleavage and smooth underlying surface where there was no anchorage — 161

Plate 64. Bivio: an old haunt of ours. It was like coming home — 162

Plate 65. View into the Bregaglia from Piz Lunghin (Bivio) — 163

Plate 66. The print of the eagle's wing as it swooped down to a baby hare and flew off with it — 164

Plate 67. The tracks of chamois and hare — 164

Plate 68. The Fuorcla Mulix Bever: Piz Julier was peeping shyly over the billowing cloud — 166

Plate 69. Bergün: It was a case of "sip it, drink it, and drain it" — 167

Plate 70. Piz Kesch: the peak stood out like an islet in a fleecy sea — 168

Plate 71. Richard and I roped up and set off to climb the final peak — 170

Plate 72. The freezing cloud of the previous night had covered the snow with frost crystals — 172

Plate 73. Frost crystals — 173

Plate 74. The Grundlawine strips off the last vestige of snow — 176

Plate 75. The Tuoi Hut: the walls were blackened and the graffiti imaginative 177
Plate 76. The Zahnspitze: surrounded by jagged tooth-like rocks or "gendarmes" 179
Plate 77. Ramosch Church: it is worth making a détour if you are in the vicinity 184
Plate 78. The Weisskugel on the left; we looked back at the Hintereis Glacier leading up to it, and once more felt cheated that we had been unable to climb the mountain 186
Plate 79. A broken glacier falls away from the Wildspitz 189
Plate 80. The Amberger Hut 191
Plate 81. The Post Dog: a small rucksack lay between its shoulders carrying our letters and post-cards 196
Plate 82. The Schränkogel: at last the weather was clearing 198
Plate 83. The Daunjoch: once above the ice-fall a contour round the head of the valley would bring us to the pass 199
Plate 84. Avalanches were merciless everywhere 200
Plate 85. The avalanche squad were fixing sticks of dynamite on poles 202
Plate 86. The helicopter takes off from the Dresdener hut to plant the fuse 203
Plate 87. The dynamite stick is planted high up and three minutes later the avalanche comes down 204
Plate 88. The Seescharter lay to the right on the horizon 213
Plate 89. The route to the Bremer hut lay on the opposite side of the valley. 214
Plate 90. Practising getting out of a crevasse at the Nürnberger Hut 215
Plate 91. Descent from the Nürnberger Hut. Thick wads of snow bent branches half double against a grey ominous sky 216
Plate 92. The Riepensattel: our route for the next three days spread out before us 221
Plate 93. At the top of the picture is a hanging glacier which has overflowed down into the valley 222
Plate 94. The Waxeck Glacier: we descended four thousand feet on one of the finest ski runs in the Alps 225
Plate 95. The Schwarzenstein: the advantage of the early start is the climb in shadow when it is cool 227
Plate 96. The Kalser Tauern. We crossed between the two peaks in thick mist 235
Plate 97. The storm had broken trees and scattered moraine dust and twigs all over the snow, making it dirty 236
Plate 98. Fred in the Daber Gorge: the pathway was hollowed out of the mountain side and partly choked with snow 238
Plate 99. A snow wall blocked the path, and we would have to tunnel through it 239
Plate 100. The Gross Geiger from the Kürsinger Hut 248
Plate 101. The Gross Venediger seen from the Schlieferspitz. The Venediger can be seen from all the surrounding peaks 248
Plate 102. The knife-edge on the Schlieferspitz—mountains have no business to be so sharp! 250
Plate 103. The little chapel ingeniously created out of the rock 252
Plate 104. Above the Mööser lake and looking back to the Kapruner Torl in the centre 255
Plate 105. His Spirit lives in the mountains 257

Maps

Map 1. The Alpine Chain *facing page*1
Map 2. The Route taken 8
Map 3. La Minière to Césana Torinese 9
Map 4. Montgenèvre to Courmayeur 66
Map 5. Courmayeur to Saas Fee 97
Map 6. Saas Almagell to Andermatt 116
Map 7. Andermatt to Ischgl 140
Map 8. Ischgl to Sölden 180
Map 9. Sölden to St. Jodok 194
Map 10. St Jodok to Birnlücke Pass 218
Map 11. Kasern to Heiligenblut and Kaprun 244

Summary of the Traverse

Year 1:   Col de Tende to Césana Torinese: Distance*   about 118 miles

Peaks climbed:	Mont Clapier	9,987 feet
	Mont Ghilie	9,833 feet
Average height of passes		8,200 feet

Year 2:   Montgenèvre to Saas Fee: Distance*   about 325 miles

Peaks climbed:	Rutor	11,434 feet
	Rosa Blanche	10,942 feet
	Pigne d'Arolla	12,450 feet
Average height of passes to Courmayeur		9,184 feet
Average height of passes for *Haute Route*		10,824 feet

Year 3:   Saas Fee to Andermatt: Distance*   about 78 miles

Peaks climbed:	Jazzihorn	10,584 feet
	Breithorn	10,942 feet
	Blinnenhorn	11,040 feet
Average height of passes		8,823 feet

Year 4:   Andermatt to Ischgl: Distance*   about 138 miles

Peaks climbed:	Piz Medels	10,532 feet
	Rheinwaldhorn	11,158 feet
	Piz Calderas	11,129 feet
	Piz Kesch	11,207 feet
	Piz Grialetsch	10,269 feet
	Jamspitz	10,394 feet
Average height of passes		8,754 feet

Year 5:   Ischgl to Sölden: Distance*   about 90 miles

Peaks climbed:	Piz Tasna	10,440 feet
	Wildspitz	12,090 feet
	Inner Schwarze Schneide	11,050 feet
Average height of passes		10,282 feet

Year 6:   Längenfeld to the Dresdener Hut: Distance*   about 7 miles

Year 8:   Dresdener Hut to Ranalt and St. Jodok: Distance*   about 12 miles

Average height of passes	10,036 feet

Year 9:   Hintertux to Krimmler Valley: Distance*   about 92 miles

Peak climbed:	Felsköpfl	10,581 feet
Average height of passes		9,600 feet

Rudolfs Hut to Heiligenblut: Distance*   about 18 miles

Epilogue: Hinterbichl to Kaprun: Distance*   about 62 miles

Peaks climbed:	Grosser Geiger	11,020 feet
	Schlieferspitz	10,787 feet
Near misses:	Westliches Simony Spitz	11,283 feet
	Gross Venediger	12,050 feet
	Sillingkopf	9,377 feet
Average height of passes		9,426 feet

Distances are "as the crow flies" and do not include kick-turns etc.

AN   APPRECIATION

I have found that friendship has no limits. I am extremely grateful to the many people who read the first draft of this book and gave me their frank criticisms, and especially to Monica Dickerson. Strangely, Monica has never been near a mountain, but she knew both Peter and me. She helped me to construct this book in such a way that it will be of interest to the general public as well as skiers contemplating such a journey.

I am also grateful to the Alpine Ski Club for their financial grant to the little team on the last part of the journey.

Beryl Wilberforce Smith
Surlingham, May 1987

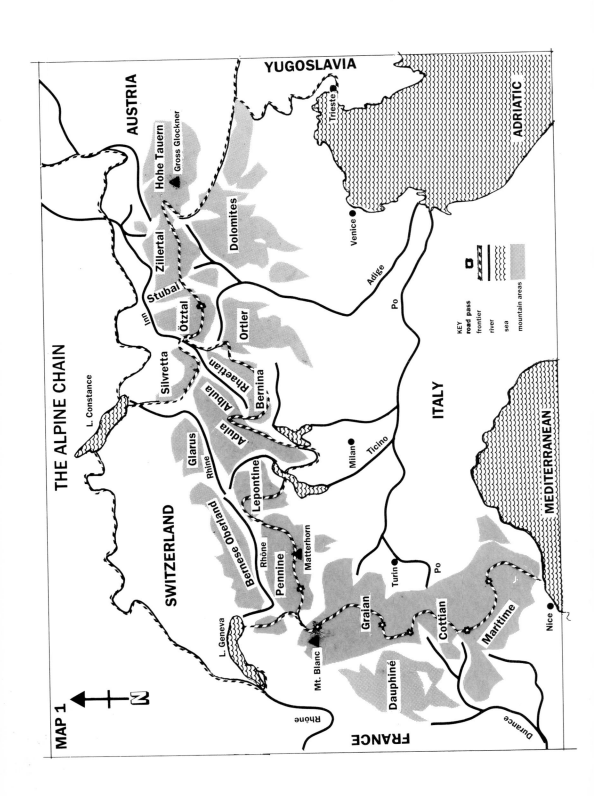

MAP 1

THE ALPINE CHAIN

KEY
road pass
frontier
river
sea
mountain areas

AUSTRIA

YUGOSLAVIA

ADRIATIC

Hohe Tauern
Gross Glockner

Zillertal

Stubal

Ötztal

Inn

Dolomites

Ortler

Silvretta

Rhaetian

Bernina

Albula

Adula

Glarus

Rhine

Lepontine

Bernese Oberland

Rhône

Pennine

Matterhorn

L. Constance

SWITZERLAND

L. Geneva

Mt. Blanc

Rhône

FRANCE

Dauphiné

Durance

Graian

Cottian

Maritime

Turin

Po

Nice

MEDITERRANEAN

ITALY

Milan

Ticino

Po

Adige

Venice

Trieste

N

Chapter I

The Idea

THE IDEA took root when Beryl and I were standing on the summit of the Dreiländerspitz—a mountain in the Silvretta Alps whose name conveys its position at the meeting of three countries. Surveying the surrounding mountains, I turned to her and said: "My God, wouldn't it be fun to do the Alps on skis!"

Or perhaps the idea was already there and it was merely the resolve which took root at that moment, and in that place. I have a feeling that the thought of a traverse of the Alps on skis first crossed my mind many years ago after reading Martin Conway's classic account of just such a journey on foot in summer.

Looking at a map of Europe, one can see at a glance that the Alps form a crescent-shaped chain of mountains across the top of Italy. Taking a rough measure of their length, the distance from one end to the other appears to be about six hundred and fifty miles. Maps, of course, are deceptive things (how often we proved this on our travels!) and convey nothing of the distances one toils up and down, or round the sides of mountains, to get from any one point to another. In all, the miles could stretch to four or five times as many as the map portrays.

There in Austria on the Dreiländerspitz, alone with Beryl, I voiced my thoughts and so took her whole-hearted support for granted that her reply did not register and I cannot now recall in detail her response! I had expressed my determination and from then on we had a common aim in this as in all else we did.

Some may think of ski-ing as a holiday pastime, of being borne by mechanical means to the top of a snowy slope and then skimming down the hill in a series of graceful curves and swoops. But skis were initially devised as a means of travelling over terrain covered by snow and otherwise impassable. Like every form of footwear, skis have been developed over the centuries and their material components have changed, yet very simple skis can be used effectively. The use of skis as a means of transport, however, has been overshadowed by the development of ski-ing as a sport. This original function of the ski has been steadfastly preserved by both ski-tourers and ski-mountaineers, and of later years it has been revived as the *langlauf* in Europe where skis are used as a means of taking a walk.

Many never have the good fortune to sample ski-ing and mountain climbing, so how did Beryl and I—two English doctors—start? My father, who had been a gynaecologist, was killed in the First World War when I was a small child, and my mother died when I was in my mid-teens, bequeathing me a sum sufficient to take me through Guy's Hospital Medical School but leaving me a lonely sixteen-year-old. I decided on a rock-climbing holiday in Switzerland, where a group of experienced, old-school gentlemen mountaineers, seeing me alone, befriended me; I could have desired no better inspiration or tuition than theirs on the subjects of mountains, rock-, snow- and ice-craft, and from then on my love of mountains could only grow.

I first met Beryl when she was a House Physician at the Brompton Hospital. She came over to the Cancer Hospital, where I was a Resident Surgical Officer, to see a friend on the staff, and we chanced to meet. Our friendship increased, as she was the only female Resident amongst fourteen males at the Brompton, and not wishing to spoil their stag parties she gravitated on these occasions to the Cancer Hospital. It was a hard winter in London that year, and two or three feet of uncleared snow lay on the roads—snow ploughs and gritting were unheard of in those days—and the patients were highly amused when they looked out of the windows and saw Beryl towing me on my skis behind her Austin Seven car around the hospital grounds and out on to the roads of Fulham. These were the days when young doctors had no hope of getting a hospital appointment if they were married, because they were expected to live in Mess quarters without impediments, and to be at the beck and call of the hospital at all hours except for one week-end in two or three when they were allowed off duty. No wonder young doctors who intended specialising never married until their late twenties.

With Christmas of that year over, we both cleared our heads and sat our higher degrees: Beryl took her M.R.C.P. and I my F.R.C.S., and within a week of each other we were on top of the world. Our resident appointments finished, and I went off to the Alps with some friends while Beryl and four of the Residents of the Brompton, with their girl-friends, had decided they wanted to learn to ski, and set out for Switzerland. There, Beryl was rapidly nicknamed "The Blue-bottomed Bomber", she sustained so many bruises in her determination to ski.

When we returned to England, Beryl had got an appointment at the Hospital for Sick Children in Great Ormond Street, and I departed to Sheffield to be Resident Surgical Officer at the Royal Infirmary. We were a long way apart, but I could not get Beryl out of my mind. She had a happy knack of entering into my many interests, of seeking the fun of adventure with the same enthusiasm. On my free week-ends I travelled to London to see her, and returned late Sunday night with an alarm clock in my pocket to waken me when the train was due at Sheffield. As I had no car, I had to walk the two miles back to the Infirmary. Occasionally Beryl came up to see me. Looking very nice in a skirt and jacket—women seldom wore trousers in those days—she must have spent a fortune replacing torn silk stockings each time after I had taken her rock-scrambling.

With the Autumn came the War. It changed all the authorities' ideas about married Residents—there was always the uncertainty of one or other of us disappearing into the Armed Forces, perhaps disappearing forever. Beryl and I got married six weeks after the outbreak of War and she joined me in Sheffield. There was snow in the Derbyshire hills and we took every opportunity to go out and ski. More often, however, on a free afternoon we skied on the snow-covered slag heaps of the coal mines nearby. Others sought to join us in the impromptu sport, and with our help fashioned some rudimentary skis from the staves of old beer barrels.

By the following summer the war was getting more intense and we moved to Hackney Hospital in the thick of the London Blitz and the Battle of Britain. When the worst of that was over I volunteered for the Army, but whilst at Hackney I must have contracted TB (as did some half-a-dozen others on the staff) because within six months I was invalided out of the Service with a spot on one lung. As there were no antibiotics in those days, and the standard treatment of rest was impossible for me, Beryl—herself by then a budding Chest Physician—persuaded me to see Geoffrey Marshall and have an artificial pneumo-thorax induced (this is splinting the lung by placing air between the lung and chest wall). Thus I was able to work, and we continued to practise in London hospitals until the end of the war.

With hostilities over, our first thought was mountains. We got ourselves fit by skipping, and climbing around the room across the mantlepiece and chairs without touching the floor—and then we set off for Switzerland. But there was one snag: my pneumo-thorax. The problem arose because the air in it would expand in the mountains because of the lower barometric pressure, collapsing my lung further and possibly making me breathless. So Beryl took with her an apparatus to remove some of the air from my lung when I went up the mountains, and put it in again when we came down to lower altitudes. Thus equipped, we arrived in Bivio, in Switzerland; there, Beryl spent two weeks in the ski school as a refresher, and then I took her on her first ski tour: it was the first of many ski tours which we were to make together.

When State Medicine was introduced, neither of us liked the prospect of being pushed around by civil servants, nor relished the idea of ourselves being Civil Servants with a Bedside Manner. The war was over, and although Beryl had established herself as a Harley Street Consultant, she only had one hospital appointment. For my part, surgeons were coming out of the Forces looking for jobs—they were two a penny; and, again, the TB haunted me, for when a short list came to the last two I was always rejected on my medical history. That settled it. We packed up and went to Iraq.

We ran a hospital in Mosul, well up in the north. They were exciting years, working under enormous difficulties to maintain the standards we were used to. An advantage, however, was the generous leave: six weeks a year, and six months at the end of a three-year term. What better way to spend those days than ski-ing and climbing in the mountains? We explored Kurdistan, and flew home to Europe—the Ortler Group, and Austria and Switzerland were our favourite hunting grounds. Later, we worked in Malaya and from there we flew to the Himalayas.

When we retired, we were still young—I was forty-eight—and it was then I thought that it would be fun to introduce others to the way in which mountains appealed to us, and to enjoy them—without mechanical aids—as part of an adventure and an experience with nature. So, becoming Chairman of the Touring Section of the Ski Club of Great Britain, I organized and ran Ski Tours with this in mind. Bivio was an ideal place, but we also took skiers to other parts of Switzerland and to Norway, in small parties of eight to ten people; and I am glad to say that to-day many of the members of those groups are making up their own parties and finding their own ways through the mountains without guides. It is an infectious and challenging pastime.

A true journey, from one point to another, has a great sense of purpose; even though hampered by vagaries of weather and snow—which in themselves are a challenge—a journey is a constant progress towards a distant goal from which there is no looking back. Rock-climbing, and ski-mountaineering and ski-touring, offer such a sense of purpose, but Beryl always preferred touring and over the years we did less rock-climbing and a great deal more of our spare time was devoted to touring together. All skiers who embark on the famous High Level Route between Chamonix and Zermatt at the western end of the Alps must experience not only the beauty of mountains under snow, but also the sense of achievement in conquering the peaks and passes. My idea was to tour from one end of the Alpine Chain to the other. From the outset I discarded the notion of a continuous journey for two reasons: such a journey, to be taken without undue haste, would take some three months, allowing for normal bad weather and for rest days during which any worthwhile peaks could be climbed. I also realized that a continuous journey would probably become a task to be completed rather than an amusing escapade. It seemed to me that by dividing it into sections which might be accomplished in three weeks, the main purpose would be fulfilled and the journey would then take four seasons—maybe five.

We decided that certain rules—of our own devising—would have to be observed. We must keep moving forwards, and no second attempt should be made on any peak which had eluded us, because such digressions would obscure the true object of the adventure. Clearly from time to time it might be necessary to use 'buses or taxis where large snow-free valleys had to be traversed—plodding many miles along valleys which offered neither snow nor ski-ing formed no part of our purpose—but the use of any such transport was to be kept to a minimum and the means had to be available locally. At the beginning of each season we should start where we had left off the season before. We would travel without guides, which I preferred to do, and this would mean we would be travelling alone. Two as a team would not be ideal, as it leaves no margin for error and would present difficulties whilst one went for help in the event of an accident to the other; so if any old ski-ing friends were available they were welcome to join us for parts of the way, and they would give us more security—particularly in the glacier regions.

Thus we established the basic plan; the next task was to decide the route. The choice here was enormous, for there are so many variations and lovely mountain groups which beckon almost irresistibly. Which end of the Alpine Chain to start was no problem: theoretically one could emerge dripping from the Mediterranean, shake off the water, and start climbing. It is probably not quite so clear-cut as that, because the true mountains—that is, over three thousand feet above sea level—start some little way north of Nice; but there was no real difficulty in deciding where the Alps began. The problem was, where to end? The Eastern Alps tail away sadly. Perhaps the last snow-capped mountain in summer, skiable in late spring, would be a reasonable yardstick—probably the Ankogel—and this would give as a finish at Mallnitz in western Austria.

Studying maps gave me a lot of fun as well as much bewilderment: the possibilities seemed endless. Alternatives would have to be noted, to allow for emergencies of various kinds. In the end I decided to use a ruler: a very flexible one because the Alpine Chain bends through nearly ninety degrees in its course. We would keep as far as practicable to the route outlined by the ruler. It seemed to follow the Italian frontier most of the way—for mountain chains are natural frontiers—but we would criss-cross this many times, sometimes even more than once in the course of a single day's journey.

Pondering on these problems, and mulling over the many aspects which were involved, I was suddenly conscious of a fact I had obviously ignored: that having been retired for some time I was already fifty-nine and Beryl fifty-seven—we had better not delay too long! We would make a start, and just see how far we could get in three weeks.

To resolve on a journey is one thing, to start it is another. Timing our departure was an important consideration in which we had little choice. As ski-tourers, we would walk up a mountain carrying not only our rucksacks but also, on occasions, our skis. Any down-gradients would generally be negotiated on skis, we hoped. We wanted snow, not slush on green valleys. The snow, ideally, had to be hard enough for ski-ing, but not frozen so solid that the surface was like a casually-iced Christmas cake and thus too rough for skis to slide over. In theory in the Alps the greatest amount of snow falls between October and February, and then the powder snow is compacted by the effects of the sun and winds, so that two feet of snow can be compressed to one foot in as little as three days. The weather—again in theory! begins to be more settled and daytime temperatures can reach +5°C or more in March, whereas earlier in the year the thermometer registers –10°C. Many of the valleys in the Alps are at sea level, and up to four thousand five hundred feet the snow, even on the mountains, would have melted or would be slushy by March or April, yet February would be too early for our venture because the days are short and we should sometimes need twelve hours of daylight for one day's journey. We had to leave in late March or early April.

Beryl and I had skied for so many years that we had inevitably acquired the equipment we would need, and like most people with long-standing interests, we had evolved systems and methods of storing our gear and keeping everything together. We had a very large drawer in a tall chest of drawers in which was stored all our ski clothing, and we kept a list of the items we would need—provisions and so on—as well as a note of the gear not stored in the drawer, so we had little fear of forgetting anything vital. We reduce as much as possible the equipment we take because it all has to be carried on our own backs, and we long ago assessed our own priorities—I preferred extra-long skis which increased my load, and Beryl always added her camera to her pack, even when this meant she had to smuggle it into her rucksack because I vetoed the item. For this journey we would have to carry provisions and emergency food rations, but clothing could be limited to the strictly functional and essential because we would not be staying in large or grand hotels. We tried to keep the weight of each of our packs below 30 lbs altogether, but mine with food was often much more, as the food had to last four days, plus emergency rations such as compressed dried meat which weighed six ounces. A compass, a monocular spy-glass, an altimeter which served also as a barometer, and basic First Aid equipment (which included such things as aspirins, morphia tablets for diarrhoea, penicillin for acute infections) were obviously essential, as well as a candle and matches, and an elementary repair kit. So determined was I to avoid any unnecessary weight, however, that I trimmed all the paper margins from the maps we needed, and as we sometimes walked off one map in a day we had to carry quite a few maps to cover the length of each projected trip. Our clothing was similarly severely scrutinized. We had the obvious things like anoraks, woolly caps, ankle cuffs, change of underwear, cotton shirt for me but T-shirt for Beryl, and changes of socks in addition to the two pairs we wore in our boots. We took pyjamas at first, but later Beryl was to substitute a thermosuit in preference to her pyjamas—it acted as pyjamas and also as a warmer if worn under the ski suit in colder weather, and in addition it reduced the weight of her pack by two ounces. It sounds very little, but these small amounts soon tot up. We preferred three light, 4-oz., pullovers each, as these gave greater flexibility through temperature changes and conditions, and were warmer than two heavier ones. We each had two pairs of gloves because a serious dose of frostbite can occur if one glove is blown away, although of course in an emergency a sock can be used. Two pairs of sunglasses were also necessary—again one pair as a reserve—to avoid sunblindness. Ice-axe, rope, light aluminium snow shovel, avalanche cord, crampons, and emergency cooker completed our equipment, but finally we each had the luxury of one paperback book. I did not carry a bivouac sack because of the extra weight, although we did have a foil blanket.

So, our skis cleaned, our rucksacks packed, our dogs handed over to the loving care of a friend, we were ready. Would my idea work? How far would we get in three weeks? I am certain now that the details of about a month of continuous mountain travel is near the limit for the brain to retain with any degree of clarity—but without memories, what purpose the journey?

Chapter II

1970: Year 1. A Little Walk on Skis

The Maritime Alps

WEARING mountaineering gear and carrying skis we must have attracted many covert glances as we travelled to France via Folkestone and the cross-Channel ferry on an English spring day, but I have little recollection now of this part of the journey. My memories begin with the excitement I felt on that Friday as the French train swayed along the winding track to Nice. In the far distance black fingers of rock thrust their way through the surrounding snowfields—the Maritime Alps. At that distance it was impossible to distinguish individual peaks or even districts, but all that interested me was that they were indeed the Alps and the starting point for our enterprise was almost at hand.

The air in Nice was balmy and the sky a welcoming blue; it was early April and spring had arrived. Our most urgent task was to get the hut keys from the local branch of the French Alpine Club—the *C.A.F.* There are many huts in the Alps—some literally primitive shelters for emergency use only, but others more like simple hotels, with paid hutkeepers; some are practically inaccessible at certain times of the year. A few huts are run by private enterprise, others are built and maintained by interested groups such as the Alpine Club of the country, and this last group of huts is open to all members provided they obtain keys in advance. The keys were vital to us but when we located the *Club Alpin Français* office in a large and gloomy building we were dismayed to find it shut—though it was still early in the morning. We wandered disconsolately through deserted corridors, and on the spur of the moment I entered another office. A girl behind the counter assured me that the *C.A.F.* office would indeed be open later on—much to my relief as I had had visions of us having to kick our heels till the Monday.

Beryl and I filled the time prowling round the small shops and buying provisions for the next few days. We needed some food supplies which had not been worth carrying from England. We always avoided tinned foods because they were heavy, though we did have packet soups. We preferred to buy fresh meat to provide muscle protein and, because it saved the weight of carrying bones, we usually chose steak. Fresh bread was bought and we used to find brown bread more satisfying—and it kept fresh much longer—than white. Butter and cheese were commodities always to be obtained locally as were regional sausages, ham and salami and oh! the delightful patés, some of which

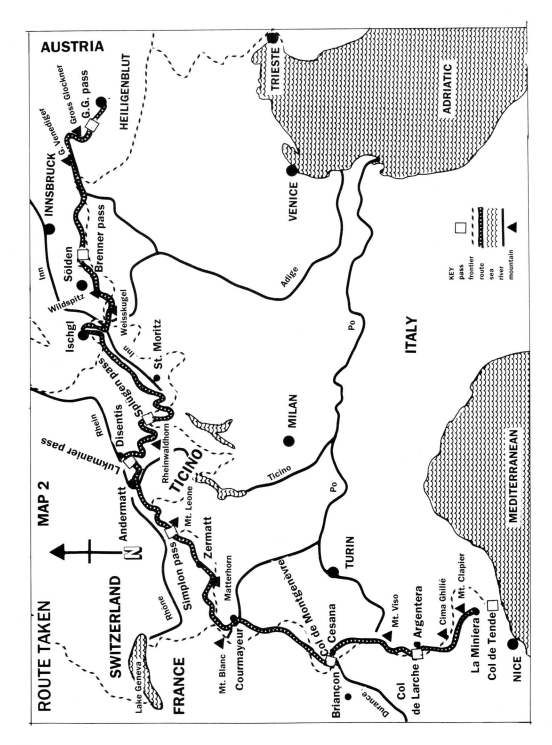

alone made the trip worthwhile. We also bought honey, tea and Nescafé. We debated the question of eggs—obviously broken eggs in a rucksack were hazard enough to give one nightmares, but we sometimes took the risk, a risk assessed on how much downhill running was involved, because a fall would be extremely hazardous! At such times we might hard-boil the eggs first. The appetite can be capricious at higher altitudes and we tried to vary the provisions to allow for this. We took sugar in lump form in case we needed a quick rise in blood sugar levels and we chose to carry vitamin tablets rather than oranges or other fresh fruits. We each carried a pint water bottle, useful for a quick cup of tea or Nescafé if there was no water immediately available at a night hut. We took salt and, to add further flavour to our rice and spaghetti, garlic and tomato paste. Finally, again for rapid restoration of blood sugar levels, Beryl preferred boiled sweets but I indulged in chocolate.

Having made our purchases, we returned to the *C.A.F.* office and I tentatively tried the door handle, fully expecting it to be locked. To my delight it responded to my touch and the girl in charge inside the room gave me three enormous keys, surrendering them with the strict instructions that I should return them before leaving France. She need have had no fear that I would forget them: they must have weighed about a pound, and I felt like St. Peter with the keys of heaven as I joyfully made my way downstairs once more.

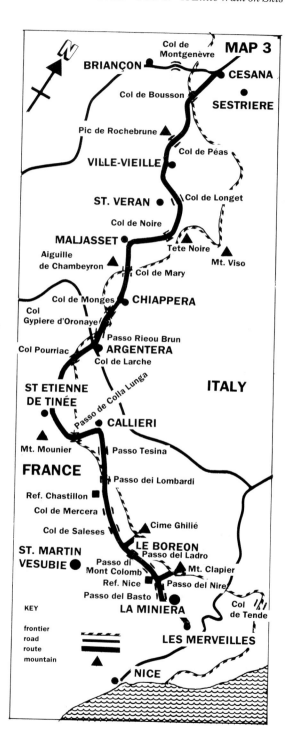

There was still some time to wait before the local train would carry us into the mountains and so we lazed in the warm sunshine outside a little café. The sky was almost clear, but a band of diaphanous clouds swayed back and forth practically above our heads, forming and re-forming as a light northerly wind conflicted with the sea breeze, first one and then the other having the upper hand. I felt that we had good weather in store for us.

At last we boarded the train and we settled in a compartment aware then that we were eyed with some curiosity by our fellow-passengers, because down in Nice skis seemed out of place. An American who got into conversation with us showed interest when we said we were tourers and he asked what car we would be using. When we explained we were to tour not by car but on skis, he exclaimed: "Say, that's great! Personally, I've never exposed myself to skis." Oh, the pitfalls of language! His phraseology enlivened for me the journey in the gathering darkness which had prevented us from seeing anything of the surrounding countryside. We had to reach St. Dalmas, our goal for the night, but had to travel the last stretch by 'bus as the railway did not go beyond Breil. The 'bus was waiting at the station, and before long we had reached a village which even in the dark was obviously rather characterless and almost empty. Of the two hotels we chose the less ostentatious one, feeling that the alternative was too "grand" for us. There were no other guests, and the miserable girl who was the entire hotel staff informed us that it was impossible to give us dinner. We had no option, therefore, but to take dinner at the "grand" hotel after all—which was not as pretentious as we had suspected and the friendly owner even helped me to fix a taxi for the following morning to take us to our real starting point at La Minière, a short distance up the valley, close to the Col de Tende.

We were up soon after dawn on a perfect morning. To my astonishment the daylight revealed that we were facing a most impressive railway station of the Victorian era; it was quite dead and there was no longer sufficient traffic to warrant its continuing existence. In 1945 the Germans destroyed most of the bridges above Breil and repairs to the railway had never been put in hand.

Having paid the bill the night before, we crept out of the hotel and carefully closed the door; and with the click of the lock I realized that we lacked one essential article of equipment. We had no newspaper. Old newspapers are invaluable for lighting fires in the huts, for insulation against cold and for many other purposes as past experience had taught us. Unable to go back inside the hotel, which would have meant arousing a sleeping establishment, I remembered a little bucket near the 'bus stop. I trotted off and yes! there were some discarded newspapers, tatty and unwanted, yet I looked round furtively and felt decidedly embarrassed as I seized one and hurried off with it to the taxi now waiting at the hotel.

My French is halting, to say the least, but I soon discovered that the middle-aged taxi driver was an Italian and our conversation became more animated. He told me that the frontier here had been re-drawn twice in his lifetime, but he was content to live and work on what is now the French side of the border; in 1860 parts of the southern slopes of the Maritime Alps were left to Italy in order to preserve the hunting rights of King Victor Emmanuel. Our taxi driver was a fount of information about the region, going on to tell me that tin, lead and silver mines had existed in the neighbourhood since Saracen times and had been worked until quite recently; then the lower import prices of these metals made the local mines uneconomic and they were now defunct. Many place-names in the district related to mining activities, La Minière, the village where we were starting from, being an example.

The road was clear of snow and we soon reached the village, but all further progress by car was halted by a large stretch of ice. As the driver said goodbye, he warned us to take great care: even the path was as slippery as a skating rink. The village consisted of two small hotels, which were being re-built, and no other habitation, so we started walking on our skis.

We had not gone far along a track when we came to a farmhouse-inn. We had left St. Dalmas soon after dawn without breakfast and we were glad when bowls of hot coffee and loaves of home-made bread very quickly appeared. Whilst we ate and drank, the owner, an enthusiastic archaeologist, told us of the ancient rock carvings nearby which gave the name, *Les Merveilles,* to the valley. Thousands of photographs had been taken and he showed us a few of them, some with such excellent technical quality that the actual chisel marks in the rock were clearly visible. One particularly interesting scene cut in rock was of a man, who must have been the tribal chief, holding an arrowhead against another man's head, thus indicating that he had the power of life or death. The innkeeper added further corroborative information about the disused mine workings and just behind the inn was one of the shaft entrances. The stones, once carefully built up to form the entrance, had been displaced by time and weather and any exploration would have been an adventure on its own, if not fatally hazardous.

As we lingered a while talking to our host, a friend of his came in and joined us. Somewhat condescendingly he asked us if we were going to make *"une petite promenade avec les skis"* and without thought I replied casually: "Yes, to Briançon." His startled expression swiftly changed to one of comprehension: of course! we were mad—were we not English? A little walk on skis indeed: perhaps a hundred and fifty miles!

La Minière to Refuge Nice

Our conversation could have gone on longer, but we had to get on. Our friendly host was most reluctant to accept any payment, and we were to experience many more such instances of generosity later.

We started walking up the valley shortly after nine o'clock. It was warm in the morning sun and a lake, still frozen, sparkled like a sea of diamonds as we passed. The valley narrowed and soon we were on a rather uncomfortable wooded path which took us above the tree line, where the valley opened out again. Ahead of us was a large hut, with open door, but no sign that it had been recently occupied. I was not too certain of the exact whereabouts of the ski hut we wanted, as it was not marked on our map, but this was clearly for farm use and was not the Club hut. We scouted around, and a short distance further on were two more snow-covered lakes with the Refuge des Merveilles on the far side.

Plate 1. Valley of *Les Merveilles* from outside the hut

Beryl had been having to stop periodically to adjust one ski, which kept falling off, and although I urged her on she continued to lag behind. Reaching the hut together, we unshouldered our heavy rucksacks with relief, the thought of a welcome mug of tea foremost in our minds. It was not to be. When Beryl removed her skis she found a vital piece of her safety binding was missing and this was why her ski kept coming off. The binding tethers the boot to the ski and it was a safety device by which the boot is released from the ski if the skier has a bad fall, or the legs and skis get into impossible positions. The skis were new and the part must have dropped off somewhere on the way. We could fix it so that the boot would hold firm to ski, but the safety device would no longer open. Only recently had I been converted to the value of the safety device since I had fallen and torn my achilles tendon. It was just pssible that the part had fallen off when we removed our skis to peer inside the farm hut on the far side of the lake, so we left our rucksacks and set off to look for it, but our search proved fruitless.

This was very disturbing. There were only the two of us, we would be travelling through areas which were very remote, and we should be far from help. To return to Nice for a new part was unthinkable. It was unlikely in any case that we could obtain a replacement binding in Nice—it is not a ski-ing centre. Moreover, we were in France and the binding was Austrian. Yet if Beryl had an accident it would take time to dig a snowhole or shelter around her, and I would have to leave her in order to go for help. There were no quick or easy ways down to any habitation at all in these isolated valleys. It could be twelve hours—even longer—before a rescue party could reach her and this was assuming the weather was good. We had both known of these risks when we embarked on the journey: they were part of the challenge.

"I'll just have to ski more carefully," said Beryl. "The writing isn't on the wall yet."

We both knew what she meant. Six years before, 250 volts had passed across her heart by accident when she had had both hands in water—since when, she has been convinced that her life-span is pre-destined.

We therefore abandoned the search for the missing ski part and as it was close to two o'clock we decided to climb a little higher up the valley. This would serve the two-fold purpose of giving us a better view of our route for the following day and of finding our ski legs. Although we had been wearing our skis, we had so far only walked upwards; now we had the chance to ski downhill. The route appeared to present no problems for the morrow, though the final slopes below the Baisse de Valmasque, which was our first pass, were rather steep. Having assessed the situation, we had a pleasant run back to the hut, unencumbered by our rucksacks.

The snow and ice were very deep in front of the hut and although we set to to clear them with our ice-axes and a light avalanche shovel, the task was obviously going to take an inordinate amount of time and energy. Like all French Club huts, the doors and windows were closely barred by steel shutters—pilfering and vandalism are common even in the mountains. However, I spotted a keyhole in one of the upper windows which had an iron ladder leading to it, so that was clearly the normal winter route of entry. One of the keys fitted the hole and within a few minutes we were inside.

It was not very cold, in spite of not having been used for ten days, as we later learned from the hut book. There was plenty of wood and to our surprise—as we were not used to French huts—there was a Calor gas cooker which actually worked! This would save time in the morning, but for now a wood fire would warm the place as well as serve for cooking an evening meal. There was a shortage of cooking utensils, unfortunately, and as we carried none we were forced to cook our meat in the ashpan—which certainly seemed to give it a new taste. We leafed through the pages of the hut book, as we rested. These books are provided to enable users to enter in them their names and their next destination. Inevitably travellers often add comments of their own and some passages provide amusing reading.

There were a number of bunks in the kitchen, for it was also the Winter Room. These Winter Rooms are usually sealed off from the main building, to be used when a guardian is not there. In summer, except in very remote areas, there is generally a resident guardian or hutkeeper. We were at this time the only occupants and as soon as we were comfortably warm we turned in. Our adventure had really begun.

The next morning was perfect, with a gentle breeze blowing from the north. We were off walking again before eight o'clock and we passed a frozen and silent torrent which widened from time to time forming lakes along its way. The wild and narrow valley was leading us to the Passo del Basto, which we had to cross. Both *passo* and *col* mean a pass, or passage-way between mountains, but in this region we also meet the local word *Baisse*—probably a dialect version of *passo*. Many names of mountains, passes and valleys convey the atmosphere, appearance or use and in this instance *"basto"* is Italian for pack-saddle. It was in this valley leading to the pass that many of the gigantic stone carvings had been found, and I wondered what attraction had so overcome the wildness of the place for even primitive man to inhabit it. There are said to be about forty thousand carvings from a Ligurian cult that survived from Palaeolithic times to the Iron Age.

We had been carrying our skis, for walking on the hard spring crust was easy, but when the slope steepened considerably on the last stretch to the pass we had to cut a few steps with an ice-axe. From the top we saw a lake below us and the run down to it was so pleasant that it was with regret that we had to bear off to the left and climb up once more. We were beginning to feel a little tired, as it was our first full day on skis, but the slope was easy and soon we were peering over the Col de Nire, where the rocky peaks were steeply bunched upwards.

Plate 2. Passo del Nire. We cut the last few steps with an ice-axe. It was here that I had my first experience of the inadequacy of the 1:50,000 French maps. The picture shows the typical bunched-up peaks in the area

Yet as I peered over the col a feeling of panic came over me. Three ridges met at this point and I experienced for the first time the inadequacies of the French 1:50,000 maps. The cartographer frequently submerges his ignorance in a confusion of cross-hachuring. I had anticipated a valley descent, but in fact there were two valleys which led down and I had no means of knowing for certain which one to choose. The wrong decision would take us not only off course but also off the maps we carried. We would not know where we were, nor would we have any means of knowing where there might be a hut—assuming there was a hut. These regions are very remote and huts do not appear at regular distances; their location cannot be guessed at, or counted on, in the way one arrives sooner or later at a café along a main road. We would not meet any other travellers of whom we could ask directions. Even to take a chance and then perhaps retrace our steps, would be no simple matter: the descent might be accomplished safely, but climbing back up to the col if we were forced to return could be difficult, and we might be defeated by the onset of darkness. Recollections of stories of climbers lost in such alien areas suddenly became too vivid for comfort. We would not be the first to go astray in the mountains, nor the last; I hoped we would not be part of the statistics in between.

After a pause for consultation over map and compass, I took the plunge and led the way down. We descended a short couloir, or gully, and then put on our skis and set off. The snow was light and powdery, but even so we fell from time to time, partly through not yet having got accustomed to our heavy rucksacks. I prayed that Beryl's ski bindings would not break under the strain and turned round frequently to look back towards her. Once when she fell the weight of her pack made it difficult for her to get up again and I had to help her up. As we travelled, streaks of cirrus were collecting on our left and I wondered if the weather would hold for the next day. I was keen that it should as all being well we hoped to reach the top of Mont Clapier. Always assuming, of course, we were not lost.

We continued down a series of broad terraces to the bed of the valley and saw—ski tracks. Usually I recoil at such signs: so often they betoken crowded slopes and packed huts. In this instance, however, the ski tracks were welcome: we could not be too far from human contact, even if we were off course. We rounded a rocky promontory and the Refuge Nice was just below us, with a single pair of skis standing outside. Yes, I had made the right choice of valley.

In the living-room three Frenchmen were preparing a meal. They made us welcome as we settled in. Two of them, we learned, were without skis for they preferred climbing mountains on foot—clearly adherents of nineteenth-century tradition! They had just returned from Mont Clapier, and the youngest took me outside to show me the start of the climb, because the summit itself was out of sight from the hut. They endorsed our plan to climb the mountain the next day and were enthusiastic about the panorama visible from the top. It is a renowned viewpoint: on a clear day, from its peak nearly ten thousand feet up, can be seen to the north the Matterhorn in the Pennine Alps and Mont Blanc some hundred and twenty-five miles away, and to the south possibly as far over the Mediterranean as Corsica.

After their lunch, the other party set off for the valley, as their short holiday was at an end. Before leaving, they gave us the remains of a large loaf of bread—a most acceptable gift, because of course we had kept our loads as light as possible and reduced bulky items to the minimum. We watched their progress down the valley, then returned to our meal. It was cosy in the little kitchen, which was furnished with Calor gas cooker and wood stove and which served also as our sleeping quarters.

It was nine o'clock by the time we were under way next morning, later than I had actually intended although I had reckoned that the climb of Mont Clapier would only take about three hours. We could leave most of our gear in the hut and thus carry lightened rucksacks for a spell. We both found the climb dull and laborious; the word *clapier* means stony and boulder-strewn, as indeed the terrain was at the top. The cold freshening wind seemed to sap our energy and we could never get a sight of the summit: it always lay behind the next shoulder. At length we had to plant our skis firmly in the snow and set off on foot, as the last slopes were quite steep. The sky had been steadily clouding over, and distant visibility decreasing, while away to the south-west large whale-backed clouds had built up with all the evil prognosis which they possess. In the flat light, all we had for a view from the summit were the nearer mountains—so much for seeing the Matterhorn and Corsica! How often this happens in the mountains. Although it was not snowing, the cold wind made me reluctant to bring out the map and study the route for the next day from this vantage point, yet such a practice is always repaid in strange country. I was later to regret my laxity, but meanwhile we hastened back to our skis and ran some way down into the valley before we could find a spot sufficiently sheltered to pause for a bite of food. The fine, powder snow of yesterday had been badly crusted by strong wind and we had to run with care, fearing that we might break through the surface. We did occasionally find patches of powder snow which were light and feathery, lying under the lee of shoulders, but all in all it had been a disappointing day—we had looked forward to a carefree descent without our heavy rucksacks.

A party of skiers had arrived at the hut in our absence and were gathered outside the door on our return. Before even greeting us, one solemnly announced: "We have a dog." Whether this was a warning or merely a statement was not clear from his tone.

We entered the hut and there was the prototype of the shaggy dog: large, curly, unkempt and dirty. He was eating spaghetti and knowing it is the height of bad manners to interrupt a dog while he is eating, we refrained from immediately introducing ourselves to him. This was just as well, because having dogs of our own we would normally have been delighted to enjoy canine company again, but the brief interlude while the dog finished his meal gave us time for reflection.

"Do you always take him with you on your tours?" I asked the solemn Frenchman.

"He's not ours," was the reply. "He just attached himself to us."

"Mind he doesn't attach himself to you, then," Beryl murmured quietly to me. I saw her point; we resolved that the animal should not transfer his allegiance to us. When he finally lifted his shaggy head from the dish he looked so funny that it was difficult not to pay attention to a dog whose long-pile hair and whiskers were intermingled with the strings of spaghetti dangling from his mouth.

The French group obviously intended to enjoy a fine repast. They had a young woman in their party of five and with four stalwart men to help carry provisions for only a short time away, they had been able to include vegetables, tinned food, fruit and wine in their packs. The cook was officiating with both Calor gas and wood stoves at full blast. No effort was being made to husband the wood, which is the normal custom, but there was plenty of it and the hut was cosy and warm after the chill wind outside. Young and very pleasant, the other skiers seemed worried about their choice of route for the following day. Like us, they were bound for the little village of Le Boreon. They were debating whether or not to take a route longer than the usual one, doubtful because the young woman in their party might find it too arduous. As we were planning to take the shorter way, I suggested that their less-experienced member could accompany us. They finally decided that we would all take the same route which, though easier, still involved crossing two passes.

Refuge Nice to Le Boreon

We decided that the next day we would let the others get clear first, as the little living-room was cramped with seven of us moving about. As it happened, we would not have had much choice, because during the night Beryl was attacked by a mischievous dose of diarrhoea, most probably the result of eating meat out of the ashpan at the Refuge des Merveilles on our first night. She had to get up several times from her bunk and go outside into the snow, because there is no form of sanitation available in the Winter Rooms. When any is provided at huts, for use in the summer months, it tends to be a "thunder box" of the type so well described in that classic book *"The Specialist";* at other times of the year a hole is dug in the snow.

It was therefore a relief to both of us that the French skiers were up before dawn and away by first light, while we were still having breakfast. Then a contented sigh came from under the table. The dog: the Frenchmen had cunningly abandoned him and he was still with us. Fortunately they had not got beyond hailing distance and reminding them of their responsibility I sent the dog away to rejoin them. The diversion was, in fact, to their advantage: they yelled across the valley "We've forgotten our *Bundnerfleisch*," and we were able to assure them that we would take their dried meat to Le Boreon for them.

By the time we started off, it was nearly eight o'clock and the narrow valley lay in deep shadow. We ran down, then had to climb into a subsidiary valley to our right. But which valley? Although the best we could buy in England at the time was the 1:50,000 map, it was once again woefully inadequate. There were several valleys to choose from and they all looked steep, narrow and uninviting.

We cast up and down and finally chose the least repulsive—its upper slopes were in sunshine with a red spire of rock at its head silhouetted against a deep blue sky. Then to our delight we saw the faint tracks of the French party—unmistakably theirs as they were accompanied by the prints of a dog. We now knew that we were in the correct valley, because the others were using the more detailed 1:25,000 map.

The valley opened out into a pleasant combe—a depression or small valley—and the narrow couloir at its head led straight up to the pass. Snow slides had come off the rocks at each side and fallen into the couloir, but it was safe enough as long as we kept to the middle. Here, the snow was still firm, though it was beginning to soften in the morning sun. And was it hot in that couloir! There was no breath of wind and despite the early hour the heat from the sun was reflected by the snow. We were both sweating hard and welcomed the refreshing light breeze which met us at the top. Il passo di Mont

Plate 3. Passo di Mont Colomb: our first wild little pass lay golden in the early morning sun

Colomb—why "the dove's mountain"? How long ago did it get its name? Did some imaginative person see a semblance of a bird's shape in the outline of the mountain? or did a stray dove fly into folk-lore as in the story of Noah and the Flood? Far across the head of the valley stretched our second col, Passo del Ladro—who was the robber and why should his memory be immortalized by this pass? Sometimes we might get the answer to these speculations when we talked to local people in the villages on our route; other times the mysteries remained, subjects for conjecture as we made a tedious ascent.

Over the pass, we ran down on crusted snow which improved and softened as we went; the slope led to a wide bowl at the head of the valley. We reached the spot where we had to start climbing again. It was nearly ten o'clock and we were ready for our second breakfast. This is a hallowed ritual for mountaineers. Dawn comes about four o'clock in the mountains in spring; without stopping to eat a large breakfast first, a start is made with the emergence of daylight. Thus the second breakfast is welcome as a brief rest, a pause and a light meal—perhaps a hard-boiled egg and a piece of bread.

The gurgling of a stream encouraged us to stop—it would conserve our water supply and slake our thirst. The air was still and we lay and basked in the sun filling lungs with the clean atmosphere and eyes with the beauty around us.

We could have stayed there gladly for hours, but the slopes to our next pass were steep and in full sunshine. Almost reluctantly we got to our feet and started off once more. It certainly was steep, the snow reflected the heat of the sun like the back of an electric fire and we sweated. How we sweated! One of the vivid memories of this holiday was the smell of scorching flesh, recurring again and again as the variations in weather brought more periods of such conditions. On and up the slope—easy, then steep; avalanches had come down and several days had passed since the last snowfall so the slopes had had time to rid themselves of excess snow; on and up ... we were at the Passo del Ladro, but the robber was not at home.

A lovely valley opened on the far side, with a splendid cirque of mountains whose rock ribs and snow-filled gullies plunged down to the pleasant woods far below. Slope after slope of perfect powder snow carried us in a series of joyous swoops through the trees. The sight of a little pool sparkling in the warm sunshine was irresistible—what better place to stop for lunch? We unshouldered our packs, our eyes on the clear water and then, looking at each other, we shared the same thought. We stripped naked and it was an indescribable sense of luxury as our skins tingled with the cool water. We splashed around, washing off the sweat of the journey and although we still had some way to go to Le Boreon we set off re-invigorated.

At Le Boreon we found an inn, friendly and truly delightful, in a dream-like setting. It was situated beside a lake of deepest green, encircled by sparkling diamonds of snow and nothing more lovely or more perfect could be imagined to end a day in which we had experienced such extremes of emotion.

The party of French skiers was about to leave, but they were glad we had arrived in time to hand over their *Bundnerfleisch* as it was part of their luxury rations. They intended to stay the night in a hut a couple of hours' walk up the valley, but it was so enchanting by the lake that they found it hard to tear themselves away, and I wondered if they would be overtaken by nightfall before they reached the hut. However, they set off at last, with the dog.

Our plan had included a two-night stay at Le Boreon, so we were able to enjoy the rest of the day without sense of urgency. The lake by the inn was already half melted and a number of fishermen were trying their luck from the shore, while we ourselves had been promised a lake trout for our dinner. We lazed in the sun, quenching our thirst with excellent beer and allowing our thoughts to roam more freely over the pleasures of food. It is an ever-present concern with cross-country tourers to reduce to a minimum articles carried in the rucksack because the weight adds hazards of its own. Beryl had already fallen over and been too hampered by her heavy rucksack to get up again unassisted. We never carried more than we needed and anyway both of us often acquired almost an antipathy to food, if not a positive distaste for cheese and sausage which become squashed or covered in crumbs and sundry other foreign bodies while stowed in a rucksack. Down in the valleys, therefore, the process of satisfying re-awakened taste buds became another of the contrasts experienced in ski-touring.

Our trout was delicious, washed down by long, long draughts of exceedingly good Provençal wine and it was not long before we retired to bed.

We were to set off next morning soon after dawn, before the snow was spoilt by sun. I have spoken of powder snow, crust, spring crust and avalanche dangers, all of which may be confusing because to most skiers snow is just snow; and unless they stray away from the piste they probably regard snow as being something firm and safe to ski on.

However, it is important for the ski-mountaineer to have a deeper knowledge of how snow behaves and the changes which it undergoes in the process of settling. In the course of his journey across the mountains there is an ever-changing terrain; it may have snowed on one side of the mountain but not on the other. There are many factors which change the quality of snow, such as the depth of snowfall, whether the snow lies in sun or shadow, whether there has been wind and if so from which direction and, above all, what was the moisture content of the surrounding air? Upon the use of this knowledge depends the ski-mountaineer's survival and safety, and his ability to avoid conditions which are dangerous.

In order to make it more interesting—as indeed it is a very fascinating subject—it is worth considering in simple terms how snow is formed, for that is all that is necessary for practical purposes. One has to think in terms of water vapour in the atmosphere—humidity—and the surrounding temperature. If the water vapour in the air becomes saturated at temperatures above freezing, it turns to rain; and if it becomes saturated at temperatures below freezing, it turns to snow (which is crystals of ice). During calm, clear nights the ground cools and the water vapour is deposited on the ground, as dew if the temperature is above freezing, or as surface hoar frost if the temperature is below freezing.

We are all familiar with the "logo" snowflake, with its central core and radiating plumes, but no two snowflakes are alike either in size or in shape; some may be flat hexagonal plates, but whatever shape they are, the moment they fall they start to undergo a progressive change. When the snow falls it is light and fluffy and the flakes hook together by their plumes with a good deal of air circulating around them. At this stage it is perfectly safe to walk on, except on steep slopes if the snowfall has been excessive. After a heavy fall the snow can be calf-deep, yet in a matter of a few days it will settle to a depth of six or eight inches. Why? What happens to the snowflakes as they compact down to this depth? Why is it that during this process of settling, the snow becomes unstable and dangerous and liable to avalanche, and the skier is advised not to venture forth until the snow has settled into powder snow, having lost its feathery quality and become granular and crystalline? The settling process is affected by sun, wind and moisture, which cause the "plumes" of the snowflakes to disintegrate so that they unhook, just leaving the central core surrounded by water vapour: it is now very unstable and liable to avalanche and the most dangerous time is one hour after the reappearance of the sun, or the day after a snowfall. What happens next? The cores crowd together, the smaller ones freeze on to the larger ones as the water vapour freezes into ice and cements them together as crystals. This is now powder snow and it is safe and stable. It can be recognized by all as plumes of snow spray seen in photographs of skiers descending a slope. This change from new snow to powder snow may take place in as little as four days, or even faster during spring, and this is one reason—apart from the longer hours of daylight—why we chose to make our journey in spring.

But powder snow is not the final stage. Once it has lain in the wind or sun, the

Plate 4. The disintegration of a snowflake
A. The newly-fallen snowflake has
plumes which interlock with adjacent
flakes and the snow is reasonably
stable
B. The plumes soon evaporate and un-
lock, and the snow becomes unstable
and liable to avalanche
C. The plumes have gone but the cores
remain and freeze together forming
stable, powder snow

surface becomes crusted due to melting in the day and re-freezing at night. This crust is particularly troublesome to the skier, as it will not bear his weight: the surface breaks and the skis wedge in channels making it difficult to swing round in turns. It is especially dangerous if one ski tip drives under the crust, bringing it to a sudden halt, because that may cause a twisted knee or broken leg. Fortunately surface crust does not last for long, as the melting and re-freezing continue to operate down through the whole thickness of the new snow, and it bonds together to the underlying layer, to form spring snow, known in the Alps as Firn snow (which means old snow). Once it has reached this stage it is hard, stable and smooth like a piste. Only an inch of it will melt in the sun to form a feathery powdery surface in the morning which will gradually soften in the sun, but the wind can no longer affect it—it becomes a skier's dream.

For the ski-tourer several of these transitional changes may be present on the mountains in the same valley, or even differ from one side of a knoll to the other. In general, north-facing slopes which never see the sun are covered with powder snow, whereas south-facing slopes which lie in the sun in spring for long enough, provide the perfect Firn—it is possible to distinguish them by their appearance, as the former looks granular whereas the latter has a dull, lustreless character. Where both types of snow exist in the same valley, the skier must be ever vigilant to look out for the dangerous breakable crust which may lie in between.

Plate 5a. Powder Snow

So, from Le Boreon we wanted to set off soon after dawn, but it was with difficulty that we persuaded our hospitable hosts to leave us a thermos of coffee for our breakfast. We did not wish to disturb them just because we chose to make an early start. Our aim was to climb Cime Ghilie and our eagerness was the greater for the pleasure of climbing with only light rucksacks.

The morning was as perfect as one could wish for and we were off just after six o'clock. The wind had been blowing hard all night, but we carried our skis up the wood path with only the sound of the dawn chorus from the birds. As we walked through the trees, we could see the deep emerald of the lake below us. From time to time we came close to groups of grave-faced moufflons, which are wild Corsican sheep. Their woolly chestnut coloured coats blended as perfect camouflage amongst the tree trunks and bushes, while patches of sun splashed on their coiled, ribbed horns giving them the appearance of a bewigged judge. I always thought that sheep ate grass, but I was surprised to see them chewing acorns and plucking pieces of spruce off the trees. They just stared at us and slowly ambled off. Under any other circumstances they would be difficult to stalk, for they rely on their keen eyesight as well as scent, but this was a National Park and they had no fear of hunters.

The trees thinned out at the end of the narrow and tortuous path and we were soon climbing the steepening slope above us. Far up, the broken rocks bounded the valley, glowing golden in the sun. The snow was very hard after the night's frost and we were constantly slipping, but as the steep slope would only take about twenty minutes to negotiate I did not feel that it was worth the effort to put on crampons. Nevertheless,

Plate 5b (top). Firn snow: compacted by sun and wind. It has a dull sheen. The animal track which initially compressed the snow in the powder stage remains proud

Plate 5c (bottom). Spring crust: it is frozen hard and only the surface will soften in the sun

there was mutinous muttering from below me and I heard the clanking of metal as Beryl put down her sack and pulled out her crampons. I turned and watched as she slid the metal spikes on to the soles of her boots and fastened the straps round her ankles. As she stood up, a smile came over her face. She slung her rucksack on to her back and shouldered her skis—it was now easy, for the metal spikes bit into the ice and she walked straight up without slipping to the top of the slope, and arrived there before I did.

As the valley opened out, we could see ahead of us the rocky face of Cime de Mercantour, though our goal, Cime Ghilie, lay out of sight behind. However, we put on our skis again and the climb was enjoyable because the valley floor was broken by little hills and dales which promised pleasurable running on the way back. Soon in scorching sun, off came our spare clothing and the smell of grilling flesh returned. We paused for breath at the top of the next valley and lying in the sun we could see the route we had taken the day before. It looked as though we were covering the ground on our journey fairly fast, but in reality we had scarcely begun and scale is deceptive in mountain country.

At last, round a shoulder, we saw our mountain: a little sugar loaf at the very head of the valley. The rest of the way was clear and we were able to relax and have our

Plate 6. *Skavla:* windswept snow. The "step" is on the windward side, and provides useful information about the direction of the prevailing wind.

lunch before tackling the final stretch. As we lazed, we watched in fascination the chamois on the far slopes of the valley, leisurely browsing off the exposed stones oblivious of our presence. We did not linger long and to save losing height we made our track along a narrow shelf beneath some rocks. The wind had gusted and gained speed round this corner, because the snow was wind-blown with ripples and waves called *Skavla*—the Norwegian for waves at sea—or *sastrugi* which is the Russian for grooves of a plane. They were frozen icy hard and we negotiated them with care, for one false step would cascade us into the valley; although this was not far below, we had no mind to suffer from scored bottoms and thighs even allowing for some protection from our ski trousers!

Plate 7. Mont Ghilie: a slippery traverse on wind-blown ripples of *Skavla*

We left our skis below the summit and walked up an easy slope to a narrow corniced snow crest, which accommodated the two of us nicely. We had expected it to be corniced because the prevailing wind had come from the south-west and if the windward slope lies between 30° and 42° the snow blows across it and settles as an overhanging canopy or cornice on the leeward side. Cornices may break off and we took good care not to go too near the edge.

Basking in the sun with scarcely a breath of wind, we luxuriated in the superb conditions not encountered all that often at the top. To the north ridge after ridge stretched almost endlessly like waves of the sea, to lap around the tooth of Monte Viso just discernible in the extreme distance. Though we could not climb it at this time of year, as it is a summer rock climb, it was a landmark to me as the most southerly really high peak I had seen till then and when I had viewed it previously it had been from the Matterhorn. Here I was, looking at it from much closer and from the other side. The frequent change in orientation is one of the great thrills of mountain travel. Now to our south a violet haze showed where the last ridges fell towards the sea.

Plate 8. A Cornice: the prevailing wind had come from the south-west and the snow had settled as an overhanging canopy on the leeward side.

Almost overpowered by the view, we made our way back to our skis. The snow was in transition between powder snow and the thick hard crust of full spring, and the breakable crust had to be treated with respect. It was not until we reached the steep slopes above the trees that we could let ourselves go with abandon on the firn or spring snow.

Returning through the trees, we saw large green lizards sunbathing on the rocks. They lay at their ease and only moved when we approached too close. Back at the lakeside a few fishermen were still casting their lines and from the inn a small white dog came out to greet us. He too loved the mountains and would go off sometimes on his own for days and would just as suddenly reappear.

Le Boreon to St. Etienne de Tinée

After our two nights at Le Boreon we were off again. The break in the journey was not only refreshing, it was also useful as a means of catching up on our laundry. Many of our ski-ing friends—like the French party in the Refuge Nice—were content to sleep in their clothes, finding it warmer. They also came with no change of underwear and shortage of water made it an excuse to abandon washing altogether. Both of us were more fastidious. Beryl in particular disliked the discomfort in the huts, the rough dusty blankets and shortage of water—at times only sufficient to clean the teeth—the sticky feeling on the skin grating against sweat-encrusted clothes and, above all, people handling food with unwashed hands was enough to destroy her already capricious appetite. There was no greater joy for us—apart from food and wine!—than to return to the valley and soak in a hot bath, put on clean shirt and pants and find our appetites restored. At the first opportunity we then rinsed our clothes through, to start afresh on the next stage. The little inns and hotels were most co-operative, willingly making linen lines available and the washing dries very quickly in the sun.

We were away soon after six o'clock, with three days' travel across the mountains to St. Etienne ahead of us. Our first break would be at the Refuge Chastillon, at about 6,675 feet, but even that was a fairly long day's journey across two passes. The clear and cool morning gave us an excellent start and once again we had the dawn chorus to accompany us along the primitive road winding through the trees towards the first pass, the Col de Saleses. Part of the road was still being constructed to give access on the far side to the village of Margheria Calé. The village is uninhabited in winter and we wondered if it would survive or be ruined by organized winter sports. In these remote areas we developed a sense of guarding our privacy, believing it to be a privilege to see the landscape and nature in its true state.

On the way up through the woods we passed close by a chamois, intently watching us but apparently without fear—an achievement for which the National Park could undoubtedly take credit. Further on, in a clearing, we came to the chalet built of stone which belongs to the Ski Club of Nice. It was open and the chimney was smoking, though we saw nobody about. Possibly our French friends had passed the night there—more than likely, as we saw no other tracks all day—but we did not stop to investigate. The remoteness of the woods conjured up pictures of the Russian Steppes and we would not have been surprised by the appearance of a horse-drawn sledge, with fur-capped coachman driving to the accompaniment of clanging bells. But no! Our only encounter was with a French frontier guard. As the snow was hard and there were no tracks to make, Beryl and I had become separated, a short distance apart, in the woods. The guard was disturbed to meet Beryl alone, but when he learned that she was not travelling on her own and that I must have passed close to him without his being aware of it, he was quite upset.

The pass was soon reached and it was somewhat flat compared with all the others we had recently crossed. It ran through the woods and in summer was undoubtedly a track, although it would soon be a road. We set off down a glade on the far side, ski-ing on the most perfect spring snow. The temptation to continue was almost irresistible, but I knew that if we did it would take us into the main valley and to the village of

Margheria Calé, and there would be a long climb to gain height again. We felt that it was better to contour round on the path, which seemed to wind interminably, cutting deeply into side valleys, but at least we knew that this would greatly shorten our uphill climb to reach the Col de Mercera. Far below us, tiny and deserted, was Margheria Calé, and except for the noise of our skis on the snow all was silent. Rounding a shoulder we could see the col ahead, very close—so near and yet so far, for in between us lay a steep gorge descending nearly a thousand feet to a snow-covered river. The sides were lined with trees and precipitous rocks; to descend it here was unthinkable as it was far too steep, so we struck further uphill towards the river's source, but I was a little worried lest we might have to turn back and try another route. However, the snow was in excellent condition and quite safe and we crossed at the head of the gorge with minimal loss of height. We could hear the gurgling of the stream beneath our feet,

Plate 9. Col de Mercera. In between us lay a steep gorge

but it was hidden by snow—tantalisingly hidden, for we were very thirsty—but to our joy we found a rivulet lapping around the base of an exposed rock and there we took a rest before our last climb to the pass. Far below us we could see the village of Mollières, framed between the steep sides of the gorge; viewed through my spy-glass, it too was clearly uninhabited in winter and a lonely place.

The final climb took us an hour and a half, as by this time we were tired and going very slowly—we had been over nine hours on the climb except for that brief run down. The pass was guarded by a number of stone-built fortresses and military huts, most of which were in ruins; they stood as a stark reminder that the frontier was near at hand. Which did they perpetually signify—man's greed for territory or his need to defend it? On the far side of the pass the valley was broad and gentle slopes led down. We could see the Passo dei Lombardi—which we would be crossing next day—beyond which a long row of black spires soared upwards. The whole character of the mountains was changing, a fact which never ceased to surprise us on this part of the journey. When we had left Les Merveilles in the south and travelled as far as Le Boreon the mountains appeared bunched up, the deep valleys sweeping up to sharp rocky peaks *(Plate 2)*. But here, on one side of the pass the mountains were wild and craggy in the extreme whereas on the other side the slopes were broad and gentle.

We had a poor run down, as the snow was damp and sticky. It was late in the afternoon and it had had every chance to thaw in the sun for a very long time. We found that Barrache was a summer grazing alp with a little chapel but uninhabited at this time of year. We knew that the ski hut must be somewhere amongst the farm chalets and hay huts, but the problem was, Where? Plenty of old ski tracks wandered in and out amongst the buildings and obviously we were not the only ones to have difficulty in finding it. Some of the tracks were recent and there was an eerie silence about the whole place. For a moment I tried to imagine what it was like in summer, with the tinkle of cowbells as the cows wandered and fed on the green pastures, the chatter of the shepherds and their wives who move up from the valley as the snow recedes, the smell of sheep, hay and mountain flowers.

Plate 10. The Chastillon Hut: its attractive appearance contrasted with the squalor within

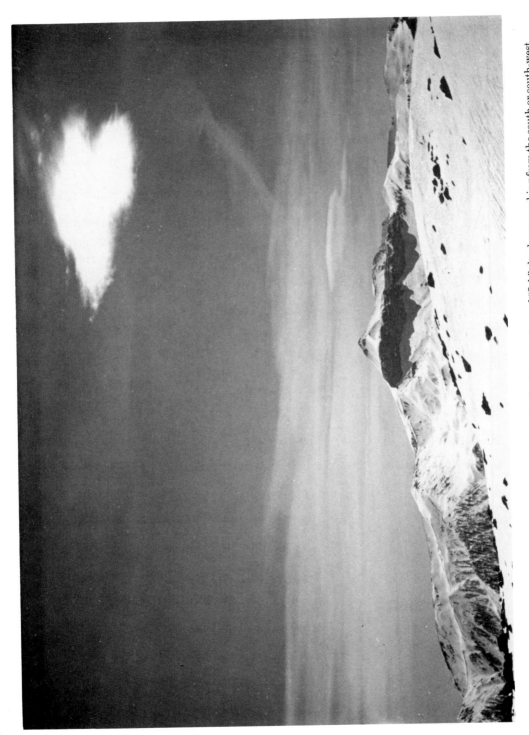

Plate 11. Mont Mounier. The first signs of bad weather—bands of cirrostratus and "fish" clouds approaching from the south or south-west

Plate 12. Lower ominous clouds of altostratus begin to cover the whole sky and surrounding peaks bringing snow with them

Eventually we found the hut—the highest building on that particular alp, but it was tucked in a hollow and we had passed it on our way down. Inside we were confronted by a state of absolute squalor. There was only the one room, which had a cracked, stone floor. Grubby and tattered blankets hung from a line, and we felt that dirty though they may be they would at least be aired. As we viewed the dis-array, we realized another advantage of the line—it had held the blankets aloft while mice had been using the mattresses for their own purposes, scattering little piles of foam stuffing all over the sordid floor. We were hardly surprised to find a wry comment in the hut book suggesting the immediate appointment of a resident cat. There was an unpromising-looking stove in a corner and in a spirit of resigned futility I chopped wood, retrieving at regular intervals the loose head of the axe as it kept flying off in all directions and I was appropriately mocked by a cuckoo calling from the valley. However, to my delight there was at least no difficulty in lighting the stove and after numerous cups of tea and plates of bacon and eggs, our morale was restored.

Before turning in I looked anxiously at the sky. The weather again appeared to be threatening with great streaks and banners of cirrus. In winter and spring I have noticed that bad weather in the Alps is often due to a warm or occluded front. The whole development usually takes eight hours, so that there is normally plenty of time to turn back or alter plans when touring from a mountain hut. The first sign is cirrus coming in from the west or south-west accompanied by low "fish clouds". The cirrus steadily develops to cover the whole sky and as it becomes denser it banks up into bands of cirro-stratus. As the front builds up lower ominous clouds of alto-stratus and cirrus begin to cover the whole sky and surrounding peaks, bringing snow with them *(cf Plates 11 & 12)*. However, I have found that a forecast cannot be made on a single observation of cloud formation, as it is necessary to watch its development. It is this development which provides the clue as to what is to come. Sometimes the portents of bad weather may take several days to develop fully, the clouds each day collecting with increasing thickness then dissolving, but only to return once again even more ominously. I thought that conditions were spanning just this phase and if I was right the weather would turn bad. At this point of our journey this was extremely disconcerting, for at best it would take two days to reach civilisation. Our next night would be passed in an isolated grazing village, unlikely to be inhabited until later in the year, and we would have to attempt to find a barn in which to sleep.

There were no ski huts in the vicinity, and I had at the outset noted possible alternatives and lines of retreat, but they would add considerably to our mileage and were not the most desirable of routes. I did not wish to be forced to use them. Luckily there were two good signs: the barometer was steady and, although the upper wind was in the south, the lower wind was in the north and I hoped that this north wind would win and drive away the bad weather. I decided to keep to my original plan.

Travelling alone in these isolated regions, as we were, all our decisions had to be made without reference to other sources of guidance, such as weather forecasts on the radio which are extremely useful in the Alps. Here we were not carrying a radio, and we were entirely dependant on our observations and previous experience, in the same way that peasants know their own local weather conditions. It was part of the challenge: it was our own decisions which affected our success, or even our survival.

Next day's journey to the alp huts of Callieri meant crossing two passes again—the

Passo dei Lombardi and the Passo Tesina. We were away by half-past-six, half-an-hour later than we intended. It is surprising how much difference those thirty minutes make. The necessity to catch up time is always there and it is most fatiguing trying to quicken the pace, whilst the possibility of lengthy halts to restore energy no longer exists. On the route I had planned is a small village alp called Sta. Anna, perched up on a shelf. A shrine there I understood was tended by a hermit who, possibly because of his otherwise solitary existence throughout the year, had a reputation for giving hospitable welcome to any travellers. We intended paying him a visit and seeing the shrine. After a steep slope of frozen snow just below our first pass, our start was an easy one and on the other side of the splendid, wide valley at our feet we saw Sta. Anna in the far distance. We had a fast run down the valley because, being still early, the snow was hard. This was lucky since the lower part of the valley is comparatively flat and under other conditions of deep or wet snow our momentum would have been insufficient to propel us forward without the aid of our ski sticks. Just above the alp of La Margheria we started to climb once more. It was a steep slope and had been crossed by recent avalanches and lay in full sun. There was an unnatural warmth in the air and the softened snow made track-making laborious. It was an unpleasant kind of place and we were racing against time: minute by minute it was getting warmer and the snow was getting softer, with the attendant risk of avalanche. It was far safer to climb directly upwards on foot, instead of zig-zagging up the slope on skis. Once above the steep part we looked back at Sta. Anna, which was now below us. We reluctantly admitted that we had neither the time nor the energy to go down, with the prospect of an additional half-hour's climb back, so we continued on to our next pass, the Passo Tesina. This was just as well—I have since learned that the hermit is no longer there in winter.

The pass was concealed by the lower hills but over two hours' distance away. Distances in the mountains are often judged by time rather than linear measurements: one might be fit enough to cover five miles in an hour on a walk along country lanes, but three miles, or a climb of a thousand feet, in an hour are averages to work on when calculating routes and resting points in mountains. The lie of the land kept constantly turning us away from a direct line to the Passo Tesina, but we did finally surmount the last shoulder and see the pass reasonably close. We had climbed higher than was necessary and had been on the move for four hours, without much pause, so were glad of the opportunity to run down to a lake and halt a while for some food and a brief rest in the warm sunshine—warmth that was pleasant while we rested but which reminded us of the need to continue our journey as quickly as we could. The narrow valley leading to the pass looked relatively easy to negotiate and my worry was whether or not the snow on the far side would remain in reasonable condition. I pinned my hopes on the fact that the slopes were facing north and therefore less affected by the sun.

We resumed our journey and met ski tracks, clearly several days old as they had melted and re-frozen. There obviously had been several skiers in the party, including one member whose skins had failed him, for he had climbed the better part of a thousand feet half side-stepping. Skins are put on the soles of the skis for climbing uphill. They are tailored strips of plush-like fabric, either buckled on to or stuck on to the ski. The hairs of the fabric are laid in one direction, like the scales of a fish. This enables the ski to glide forward but the laid hairs grip the snow and prevent the ski from sliding backwards when walking upwards. As I climbed I thought of that poor fellow, feeling the weight of his pack dragging at his shoulders, as he side-stepped upwards: and I tried to calculate the amount of sweat which must have poured from him. Perhaps he was lagging behind and getting pitying glances from his companions as they clambered up easily with their skins; did they shout encouragement once they had reached the col? Did they have to wait long for this involuntary slimmer, losing weight by the gallon as the sweat continued to pour?

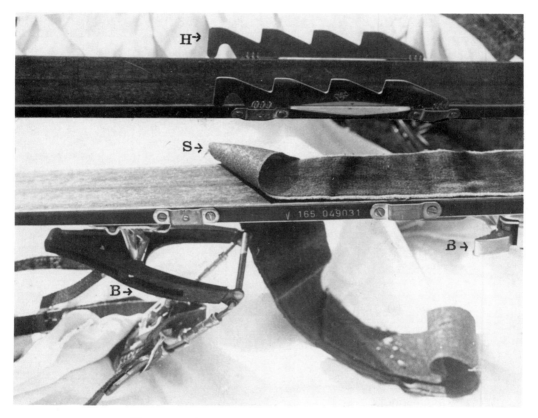

Plate 13. Underside of Skis showing: (S) skin rolled back;
(H) Harscheisen (ski crampon);
and (B) binding to tether ski to boot

The col was guarded by a corniced ridge, where the wind had carved out a hollow beneath an overhanging crest. We sought along it for a place to cross where the cornice was barely overhanging. A welcome breeze met us. I had looked forward to this wind for the past hour: it was refreshing after the sultry climb. We lay on a convenient rock and glanced back on our previous day's journey. But no time for more than a brief rest: shortly below the col we replaced our skis and our respite was over. The sun beat down remorselessly and only the breeze caused by our own movement gave any relief. There was just no escaping the heat: it penetrated right through us.

Still we raced against time. It was two o'clock. If we had been ski-touring from a mountain hut in the more usual way we would return to it normally by noon to avoid the attendant dangers of snow which had lain in the sun for too long and softened right through. Here, though, the distances between our starting point and our abode for the night, on a traverse such as we were making, must inevitably be longer than usual, and we were now ski-ing on snow which was melting and very wet. Our skis were sticking and sinking in and it was not only very difficult to turn but it was also becoming dangerous. Despite a lovely valley full of humps and hillocks, which would have provided us with very amusing ski-ing, we ran down in long traverses, stopping at the end of each to make unashamed kick turns—first, one leg and ski were swung over and planted in the snow in the opposite direction and then the other. Although a tiring process, it was a safe way of turning round, especially when the snow conditions were treacherous. Here we could take no chances of falls—not only because we did not have the energy to pick ourselves up again, but also because we could not chance an accident in this remote district. We passed little pools in the bed of a stream and they tempted us to bathe, but I felt it wiser to push on down because we still had to find quarters for the night.

The valley was unbelievably lovely and as we approached, the finely sculptured mountains bounding it continued in graceful curves of snow before merging with the valley floor. Over everything hung a heat haze such as I had rarely met in the mountains and certainly not at this time of the year. The towering peaks ahead of us shimmered with an ethereal splendour.

The chalets of Callieri lay some hundred yards off and seemed to be deserted, although I had hoped there might by this time have been perhaps a few inhabitants already moved in for the summer grazing. We found a little stream by a bridge and washed off the sweat of our travel. Then, leaving Beryl on a grassy bank, I set off to find suitable accommodation for the night. The untracked snow on the road showed how unlikely it was that there would be anyone in the village, yet I prowled around with the most extraordinarily uncanny feeling that I was being watched—but it could only have been by the invisible spirits of the place. I found three barns which might provide shelter, though there was little to choose between them for they were all dank and gloomy after a winter without use. Of the two better huts, one had wood chips on the floor and the other a trough outside into which water was pouring through a pipe from the hillside—and, what was more, there was straw on the barn floor. I returned to Beryl with the news that there were three hotels open and one of them had running water in the bedroom. For a fleeting moment she looked at me with stunned delight; but one cannot share a life so closely with another, for as many years as we had, and still expect deception to be possible. She soon read my thoughts and said: "Tell me the worst: let's look at the hotel with the running water."

In retrospect even the mice-ridden Refuge Chastillon had had advantages. We viewed the scene with almost masochistic fascination. We ate our evening meal, of bread and ham, by the trough, watching the sky. Our exercise had given us good appetites, and with only one more day to go before we could replenish some of our stores, we thought we could justifiably break into our emergency rations. Part of our ski-ing equipment included a small meta stove, and I selected a block of compressed dried meat stew. Trying to shred it into the pot was rather like cutting shag, but I had had some experience of these weight-savers in Spitzbergen, and before adding oatmeal to it—to give it "body"—I tasted the concoction. It was sweet! Oh well, we had had bread and ham; this would do for the dessert course.

We sat in the last rays of the sinking sun and watched little pink puffs of alto cumulus coming and going with a glow in the evening light. So far the weather had been kind and I felt it could last for at least one more day, but the crucial test would be to see if these clouds had increased by morning.

Plate 14. So *this* is the hotel "with running water"

There was still some light when we turned in. Our "bedroom", on the first floor, was entered through an upper window. It was airy, as there were large spaces between the roof and walls and no covering at the apertures—except one: a window blocked by a menacing bulge of snow pushed in from the hillside. Window sections and tools were propped against a wall, so clearly some reconstruction was in mind. The wooden floor was covered with straw and this would have to serve as a covering, but unfortunately it was short straw and contained a high proportion of dry cow dung. For once we slept in all our clothes, covered ourselves in our newspapers and tried to rake up mounds of straw on either side, but it was all too short and thin to give us much cover or warmth. The evening breeze wafted gently down the mountain into our quarters and we snuggled closer together, but could not prevent the exposed side from getting colder and colder. The steady trickle of water from the bulge of snow became a drip and then ceased altogether as it froze. The cow dung was very lumpy and uncomfortable and in wakeful moments I thought of the fairy-tale of the Princess and the Pea. Sleep was fitful, and as usual in such circumstances my dreams were vivid. At one time I thought that cows had arrived in the barn and their noise woke me, but it was only Beryl snoring.

At first light we emerged from our nest with straw lodged in our hair and sticking to our clothes. We had stuffed our boots with newspaper and straw and they had dried off reasonably well. My first anxiety was to look at the sky: what had happened to those warning pink puffs with streaks and banners of cirrus I had seen last night? Had they dissolved? It was very warm and I looked at the barometer—it had fallen for the first time in a week. I went outside with some misgivings. Looking up, I saw the worst—the clouds were becoming denser: bad weather was on its way, though we still had a few hours to spare. We would have to race ahead now or be trapped on this side of the pass. Neither of us relished the idea of spending another night in the barn, nor the probability of being snowbound in Callieri without much food, with no proper shelter, and no heat, for several days.

There was no time for breakfast. We had a quick cup of coffee and set off towards San Bernolfo through the woods, but even as we climbed, threatening banks of cirro-stratus began to build up and the glare of the sun was obscured. We passed the village and re-entered the woods, climbed over an old avalanche in a glade and pressed on as the track doubled and re-doubled while we climbed. Now and then ominous puffs of warm air engulfed us, emphasizing the urgency, and when we reached the tree line the sun was completely covered and the clouds still dense. I began to wonder for the first time whether we would have to retreat before the end of the day, but we pushed on without pausing for a moment. We passed a little Club hut completely snowed up except for a chimney thrusting through its white blanket. From the upper bowl of the valley the Passo di Collo Lungo was still a long way off and many old avalanche tracks scored the slopes to our right.

The valley was broad and we found a safe route up its centre. As if to encourage us forward, the sky began to clear and even the pale disc of the sun gleamed through from time to time. Avalanches began to fall, starting in rocky gullies high up and gathering size and momentum: we could safely watch their progress as they rumbled down the slopes to our right and then fanned out across the valley floor. They were wet-snow avalanches and the conditions were just right for them. It had been cloudy and far too warm, the snow had started to thaw but the water had not had a chance to evaporate as the air was too humid. We stood and watched them for a moment, for they flowed just like the rivers I sailed on in Norfolk. The advancing middle and top layer were cascading down much more rapidly than the sides were travelling, in the same way as river banks delay the speed of a stream due to friction. An avalanche behaves in this way, for after all, snow is frozen water. But it was easy to see why a skier caught in the middle of this fast advancing centre could be bowled over and submerged by the snow rolling over him just like a tidal wave. The greatest danger would be when the avalanche came to rest, as it would instantly re-freeze and compress the skier's chest so that he would be unable to breathe. Yes, it was a warning: we must take care, although these were far enough away not to matter for the moment,

We reached the frontier guards' hut below the col, but it was shut and no-one emerged to ask us if we had anything dutiable to declare. We were back in France once more.

The last stretch was somewhat complicated and I think I made the mistake of taking the steep summer path straight ahead, possibly encouraged by some old ski tracks. It was laborious and tedious and we would probably have done better to have made a slight détour over easier ground. However, we gained a small plateau, which was the pass, and could see down into the Tinée valley. It was void of snow and appeared as a dark green gash in a bed of white. I looked around us at the mountains and sky; I was glad we were so near the fleshpots of St. Etienne: on the far side the snow-covered sugarloaf of Mont Mounier thrust its head aloofly above its neighbours, but it was the clouds which absorbed my attention. Once more they were collecting densely in the distance and were making steady progress towards us, the whole sky becoming opalescent. Tiny lens-shaped clouds were congregating round the peaks of Mont Mounier opposite, and I was sure that this time the weather really meant business: strange that such harbingers of bad weather could look so beautiful *(Plate 11)*. A slow build-up such as this to bad weather is usually a fore-runner of a prolonged snowfall, but we were now reasonably certain of reaching shelter before the weather broke.

It was mid-day, and the slopes on which we had to descend faced full south; they had been in the sun for too long for safety and after the warning of the avalanches on the way up I studied the snow carefully. The ski-mountaineer may well ask why firn snow is safe and stable in the daytime when the surrounding temperatures are well above freezing—even up to 10°C and yet on this day the firn snow was wet, soggy and highly dangerous.

In spring and late spring, firn snow does not melt, it dissipates by turning into water vapour which evaporates in the sun if the atmosphere is dry. Just watching a small patch of snow lying in the sun on a warm rock demonstrates this: the patch gets smaller and leaves no water behind. The snow crystals sink down closer together and any water vapour between them freezes at night and consolidates them, making a stable and hard snow. Under the conditions we had had, however, the atmosphere was not dry—it was humid, sodden with water vapour, and so the firn snow could not evaporate and the vapour had no alternative but to turn to water. Water lying between snow crystals is dangerous because it separates them and lubricates them—producing all the necessary conditions for a wet-snow avalanche.

There was a single track leading down, which must have been made by a frontier guard. The slope was not steep so we followed the track, but on rounding a corner we came to a broad gully. We stopped. The ski tracks crossed the slope, but they must have been made when the snow was freezing and it would be suicidal for us to cross it now. Gullies are the very places in which avalanches choose to start, and the chute makes an ideal groove for their fall. We looked around us for an alternative way. The slope steepened and the snow was very soft. I caught sight of a rift with grass showing through. The grass was wet, it was well lubricated ... just right for this lot of snow to slide off like a blanket. No! this would not do. Perhaps we ought to wait until evening for the snow to re-freeze? It would be safe enough then—but we still had a long way to go. Then I spied a rock ridge just below us. We took off our skis, tied them together and walked down to the ridge. It made an amusing scramble, but it was steep in places. First one of us would climb down and take the skis from the other. Occasionally this was extremely difficult and Beryl, in twisting round to take my skis, ricked her back. This was no place to linger, and despite being in acute pain she carried on. Before long we were able to put on our skis when the slope eased and we resumed our run down to the edge of the last tongue of snow. Here we found a small stream and after splashing about in it we had a late but unhurried meal basking in the sun. On a nearby rock I had spread out my sweat-soaked shirt to dry and when, more relaxed, we were ready to move once again, what a luxury it was to don a shirt straight from the celestial laundry! Already a sense of achievement stirred inside us although we had more ground to cover to reach our destination for the day, let alone our further goals of Briançon and—who knows—would we reach the further end of the Alpine Chain? Here we were at the edge of the snow line but we still had to walk down to the valley and up the road to St. Etienne, now within sight. We took an easy pace and could hear voices from below. Then a dog barked. Clearly there were inhabitants in this village and we thought of refreshing draughts of milk. The dog must have seen us from afar and he came galloping towards us, the bell round his neck tinkling as he ran. However, the sight of us, with Beryl walking in discomfort, must have given him second thoughts, because he was too timid to approach closely.

Our path wandered through a grove of silver birches, the fallen leaves making a thick brown carpet under our feet, dotted here and there with Christmas roses, then giving way to a pattern of spring flowers as we got nearer to the valley floor by the village of Dounse. We passed a rosy-faced woman in the doorway of one of the summer huts and I enquired about some milk.

"We only have sheep's milk," she said, "and I doubt if you would like that."

Reluctantly we had to agree—sheep's milk and butter were the staple diet when we were in Iraq and we found it tasteless.

St. Etienne was some five miles further and I asked a farmer if it was possible to hire a car. He answered me, in a wonderful dialect which was a cross between French and Italian, "there was no taxi available, but he would be happy to convey our skis and rucksacks to St. Etienne that evening". This was a kindly gesture, but we were even more in luck: a man who had been listening to our conversation offered to take us in his van. He insisted it would only be a slight deviation from his own route. He was Italian, an agent for a farm machinery firm and over the short distance he chatted and entertained us, so that it seemed in no time at all we were clambering out of the van in a little square by the church. We had stopped near a bar-cum-shop, and we went in with our Good Samaritan. It was small and rather dark inside, but the reception we got soon dispelled the gloom and our driver was greeted with chaff and banter in French, Italian and dialect—the cheerful hostess insisting he had devil's horns. Our own arrival aroused the curiosity of a knot of men drinking nearby, and they were intrigued to hear about our "little walk on skis". We drank excellent beer as we talked and soon had both a comfortable glow in our bodies and something of a haze in our minds. We were tired, we were relieved, and in the friendly atmosphere time passed quickly and it did not seem long before the farmer arrived with our belongings. It transpired that he owned the shop and he and the others around us seemed to have assumed a patriarchal, almost a tribal, responsibility for our welfare and they decided amongst themselves where we should stay, even detailing the farmer's young daughter to act as guide. Our chauffeur friend firmly refused to accept anything for his fare, and we thanked him warmly for his help as we bade him adieu. Our hotel was only a short step away and again we received a hospitable welcome which was followed by an excellent meal. Contrasting it with our cold ham and compressed stew dessert, it was hard to believe the change in our circumstances in less than twenty-four hours.

After dinner I went outside to scrutinize the sky as usual. It was still very warm and the heavens were uniformly overcast—the weather had certainly broken at last. It was a delightful place where we were at St. Etienne and I was thankful that we had reached it safely—like a ship entering port ahead of a storm. We were ready for a rest and it looked as though we would be having a couple of days here.

I went to the chemist's to get something for Beryl's back. The pharmacist gave me some minute tablets of streptokinase, which he strongly recommended for sprains. Sadly we have not been able to buy them in England, but they had a miraculous effect on Beryl. The nearest I have been able to buy in this country is Chymoral; it is used by footballers for sprains and is nearly as effective. For the rest of the Alpine trek we carried them with us. I had been particularly worried about Beryl's back because some years before she had slipped a disc and been told by a neurologist not to ski again! However, as he was not himself a skier she decided that he did not really know what he was talking about;   had he been a skier she might have paid more attention to his advice.

During the night we could hear the rain and when we arrived for breakfast it was still drizzling steadily. One of the joys of ski-touring is taking a rest in the valley and making the most of bad weather. Beryl and I were happy to wander round St. Etienne, exploring the little village and taking photographs. The houses were built of stone, huddling together as though for protection. They had a mediaeval air, with narrow alleys that seldom saw the sun and an arcaded square dominated by the old church. Beryl had a strong creative instinct and was a reasonably competent oil painter, until the day she bought a camera. This she did to teach herself micro-photography for a book she was writing. The book related to some research work she had done in Malaya and which won her the British Tuberculosis Association's research prize. Probably this success spurred her interest in photography and spread to cinematography, and made her keen enough to enter international competitions after she retired from medicine. Her "still" photographs were always taken in black and white, which suited me since I preferred to work in colour. For my own part, my interest in photography must have started after my father's death, when my mother married the maker of the Ensign camera (which was later known as Ensign-Kodak) and my first camera must have been one of the earliest folding pocket cameras—the Ensignette.

In order to cut down the weight in our rucksacks I had forbidden Beryl to take a camera, as I felt that my Leica would be adequate; but I might as well have told her not to breathe, for without telling me until we arrived in Nice, she had brought with her a Cosmos 35—a plastic Russian camera which was very light but had a very good lens despite its price of £5! I was glad that she had brought it, because we were able to make a complete set of both colour and black and white photographs of the whole Alpine Chain, which I found to be invaluable later for writing articles and lecturing. Wherever we went in St. Etienne either looking for subjects to record or just looking at the quaint and unusual, we were met by a host of friendly dogs who had none of the cringing timidity usually displayed by dogs in France.

Sunday lunch in St. Etienne seemed to be a special occasion, for our little restaurant was packed with family parties and a happy atmosphere pervaded the place. By contrast, when we entered the restaurant in the evening a fierce dispute was being waged between the proprietor and a hard-faced little man, the latter protesting against the incompetence of the road-mender who, it was vehemently asserted, did nothing about removing boulders from the mountain road above. Some of these boulders had damaged the irate little man's car and he held the hotel proprietor partly to blame by virtue of his holding a position on the local council. The verbal battle was conducted in a patois and was not easy to follow in detail, but it was clearly the kind of heated exchange liable to occur in any compact community. Every now and then the belligerent protagonist turned to me for support—though he hardly seemed to need it. I answered as diplomatically as I could, for it would not do to get mixed up in a partisan argument. The contentious individual left at last, still raging against the back-sliding of the road-mender. The proprietor glanced at me and smiled sadly, as though to convey: "How does anyone reason with such a person?"

The following morning was much clearer, though the barometer was still low and I was not convinced that the improvement would last. I need not waste the time entirely, I thought, as there was a mountain hut further on our route which I could enquire about. I was not sure of whether or not it would be open at this time of year and decided to talk to the local representative of the *C.A.F.* He was in another village and not accessible by telephone and this gave me an excuse to set off on foot across the mountains. The walk, uphill, was a pleasure unencumbered as I was by the weight of a rucksack and skis. Beryl's back was almost better, but she always liked to make the most of her respite in the valleys and saw no point in working when she had a chance to take a good rest and enjoy herself, as a change from stretching herself to the limits.

The path took me through small grazing alps, the huts untenanted as yet, and round a corner I startled a huge lizard—a splash of bright green against the rock where he had been resting. Behind me down in the valley the clouds hung sombre and grey and when I reached the pass the snow on the far side lay fairly deeply. Without skis the snow was difficult to walk on and I began to realize what winter must have meant to the inhabitants in the old days when they had no skis or snowploughs. At the head of the valley which I was struggling to reach lay the frontier village—another St. Dalmas, St. Dalmas le Selvage—strategically placed, grey and forbidding. I could see the road—kept open by a snowplough—but between me and the road was a river in full spring spate. I had not reckoned on this obstacle—and obstacle it was, as there were no bridges nearer than St. Dalmas, which could mean a fatiguing and wet plod through the deep snow. I explored to right and left and found a tree had conveniently fallen across the torrent and might make a natural bridge. I climbed on to the precariously-balanced trunk, glad of the surefootedness and experience of negotiating narrow ledges in my rock-climbing days. I had one nasty moment when I reached the middle and the tree bent alarmingly, down to within six inches of the raging torrent beneath me. Once on the other bank I could allow my imagination to wander over the vision I must have presented, doing my impromptu impersonation of a comic circus act on a tightrope in boots.

Before long I reached St. Dalmas. The *C.A.F.* representative was away, so my journey had been fruitless. In order that it need not be totally wasted, I decided to sample the beer in the one and only tavern which the village supported, and I decided to have lunch as well. To my astonishment, Beryl appeared, with two men escorting her. One was the Customs Officer—with the improbable name of Chopin—and the other was the local taxi-driver for St. Etienne. They had met and got into conversation with Beryl at the hotel and decided to take the day off! Their arrival naturally justified a call for more beer and by the time we had lunched together we were all in very cheerful mood. We returned to St. Etienne in the taxi, in a most amiable frame of mind.

Once back at St. Etienne we were to make further acquaintances: this time the Police Mountain Rescue team, who were on a two-day training exercise together with a rather poor-looking avalanche dog. The team leader clearly did not relish the possibility of their practice exercise becoming a real one, and he earnestly pointed out to me the dangers of our resuming our tour before we had had a cold clear night. In this I agreed with him: in any case it was no good making plans for the next day, as the drizzle had started once more and part of our way over to Argentera in the next valley lay across some very steep slopes—it was essential to negotiate them on firm snow.

In fact, the next day was lovely and fresh with a cloudless, deep blue sky: the snow would pack and freeze. Beryl's back was better and I felt it was reasonable to resume our adventure the following day. We took the opportunity to check and repair where necessary our equipement. Our next objectives were Grangie for lunch and Argentera for the night, only a day's distance, but we bought a few provisions and encountered cheerful banter wherever we went: the promised improvement in the weather affected the villagers, too. If all went as I planned, we would be able to spend the next few nights in villages, which could afford us accommodation, and I would no longer require the keys of the *C.A.F.* huts. I strolled over towards the local post office, to despatch the enormous jangling bunch back to the *C.A.F.* office in Nice, and I had half a mind to address them to St. Peter—the light-heartedness of the villagers was affecting me! I passed our taxi-driver friend sitting in his taxi waiting for a fare. A villager approached, got in the taxi, and asked to be driven to the Post Office—a matter of fifty yards only! Such was the good humour and mood of cheerfulness brought about by a simple thing—the change in the weather. After the harsh conditions of winter it was not difficult to understand the mood.

Having sent off the Club keys, I arranged with the taxi-driver to take us up to the snow line the following morning. Strolling back, I looked around me. In the intensely clear morning light the contrasting greens down the valley shone vividly, ranging from brightest emerald to a deep olive where billowing heaps of cloud cast a shade which drifted slowly down the valley transforming and highlighting the scene beneath.

The Cottian Alps

St. Etienne to Saretto

We had arranged to be up well before dawn and our taxi-driver was on time. It was important for us to make this early start in order to get above the steep and narrow lower slopes of Salsa Marouemma valley before the snow was softened by the first rays of the sun. In taking us as far as possible up the road, the taxi-driver had more than once to edge his vehicle round and over old avalanche falls until eventually the road was completely blocked by a large avalanche and he could take us no further. Saying goodbye, as to a friend, we shouldered our rucksacks and skis and started walking at a leisurely pace to get our circulation going. We were still half asleep, really, from the misery of crawling out of the nice warm bed and the walk warmed us up—and what a sense of re-vitalization invaded us as the dawn broke and lightened the sky. We continued walking, clambering over the many old avalanche tracks which completely isolate the tiny village of Le Pra during the winter months; and it was no surprise to us that it was still uninhabited when we reached it. Once beyond, our path to the Salsa Marouemma valley lay to the right. Dawn was just breaking as we entered the gorge and the steep cliffs forced us into the stream bed now covered with frozen snow. The sides got steeper and steeper, giving an uncanny sensation of hemming us in. One of the delights of ski-touring as opposed to piste ski-ing is the variety of scenery: at one moment seeing a lush green valley all round with the peaks towering oppressively above, and within a matter of hours seeing the valley from those very peaks but with a sensation of freedom and space. In between, there is a feeling perhaps of near claustrophobia in a ravine or gorge. Perhaps best of all is the speculation on what the next unknown will be, lying round the corner.

I looked up, and the newly-fallen snow sparkled in the slanting sunshine framed by the sides of the gorge. This really was worth recording, and I stopped, carefully took a photograph and then, just as I had put my camera away, I heard a clatter from above. Out of the corner of my eye I saw what appeared to be a huge boulder bounding down the side of the gorge directly towards me. I straightened quickly, ready to jump, poised—which way to go? It was no boulder—it was a fine chamois and it paused on the rocks a mere twenty yards above me. I longed to retrieve my camera without frightening him. Both he and I froze, eyeing each other, he no doubt wondering warily what strange creature had invaded his privacy. After what seemed an eternity, he bounded off, then stopped once more and looked back to eye me yet again before making off in great leaps which scattered a hail of little stones at every thrust of his powerful and nimble limbs. As a photograph, this was certainly the one that got away!

Working through a cleft in the rocks we climbed on crampons and were soon in the sunshine ourselves. Visible above the mound of a hill ahead of us appeared the rocky tooth of Cima di Mal, not unlike the Matterhorn from this angle. We were well above six-and-a-half thousand feet, yet there were still a few trees scattered above and the gorge opened out into a splendid amphitheatre surrounded by a fine cirque of mountains, the Pic des Très Evéchès. To their right was the Col Pourriac, which we had

Plate 15. Pic des Très Evéchès on the way to the Col Pourriac; the gorge opened
into a wide bowl bounded by a fine cirque of mountains

to cross and what better place could we find in which to enjoy our second breakfast. It
had been a cold, clear night and plates of surface hoar frost covered the snow, reflecting
the sun like a mirror, giving it a blinding silvery sheen. The air was absolutely still and
the sun soaked right through us as we sat contentedly looking at the view on the other
side of the valley. The whole character of the mountains had changed once again. Here
wide valleys of open snowfields led up to mountains far less severe in appearance. What
a wonderful ski-ing area it could be, though the difficulty would be to find somewhere to
stay, as the nearest village was miles away. The lower slopes were covered with larches, which are the common trees of these parts and presumably give their name to
the French village of Larche on the Col de Larche which joins Cuneo in Italy with Gap
in France.

Once again refreshed, we had plenty of time in hand for the good lunch we had
promised ourselves at an inn in Grangie, a village on the far side of the pass. To our
right the nearer slopes still shone like beaten silver and as we climbed, Mont Aiga's
rocky spine crept into view. We were travelling reasonably high up and to reach the Col
Pourriac I wanted to maintain the altitude. In order to avoid going down a short
distance I made the common error of getting involved in a long, steep and tiresome
traverse. In spite of this toil, we were no better off: we still had to lose the height I had
been seeking to keep and then climb back up. I had often been with skiers who made

Plate 16. Col Pourriac: plates of hoar frost covered the snow reflecting the sun like a mirror, giving it a blinding silvery sheen

these time-wasting and lengthy détours in preference to losing a small distance in height, and here I was, committing the same folly. The Col always seemed to be round the next corner. Fortunately the going was easy and we reached its open expanse, a place so flat that it was almost like a low hump trailing away gradually on both sides. It made such a contrast with the steep passes which we had been crossing further south, yet it nevertheless gave a spaciousness to the view, and it was a pleasant change to be able to put on our skis in comfort. The more usual course is to carry the skis a short way down and kick a small platform in the snow, to stand on whilst putting the skis on; but there is always the horrid thought lurking at the back of the mind that the skis will escape and slip from the grasp, sliding down the mountainside and perhaps being lost forever. I have seen this happen to several of my companions, as well as to me, although we have always managed to find the errant ski in the end.

The slopes on the descent were gentle, in contrast to the peaks in the far distance beyond the Col de Larche, which were steep and broken and dominated by the headland of the Tête de Moyse. But first we wanted our lunch in Grangie. The run down was almost too easy, because in places we had to push with our sticks although the snow was in fine condition. Below us were the houses of Grangie but as we got nearer and nearer so they looked grimmer and more deserted. They were indeed deserted: they were in ruins. So were our hopes of a good lunch. The village must have been bombarded: another casualty of the Second World War?

I was uncertain as to whether or not there was an inn at Argentera but at least we could see the road over the Col de Larche was open, because cars and lorries were clearly visible driving up and down. This is one of the easiest routes through the Alps between France and Italy and many insist it is the pass which Hannibal used in 218 B.C. to bring his army of infantry, cavalry and elephants to the plains of Italy—though there are four other passes which make the same claim. However one warrior seemed to pave the way for others, as certainly it is the route which Francis I used for his invasion of Italy in 1515, and Napoleon later decreed that "the Imperial road from Spain to Italy" should be carried over the Col de Larche, so we were in good company. We soon joined the road and a short stroll down brought us to Argentera—the first village on the Italian side of the Col, thus giving the Col its alternative name, as used on the French side, of Col de l'Argentière.

I thought we had missed lunch because of the destruction of Grangie. I need not have feared: there was an inn and although rather undistinguished, the friendly reception dispelled the tarnished appearance and we were assured we were just in time for lunch. Our kindly hostess, feeling we would be more comfortable, set places for us in the living-room, a small area separated from the kitchen by a screen. Occupying almost the whole of one wall was a tank containing trout caught from the mountain stream behind the inn. We were served with large plates of spaghetti which we washed down with plenty of red wine.

Despite the somnolence due to our generous lunch, I went out to investigate our start for the next day, because precious time can be wasted through casting around for the best path out of a valley before dawn. It was just as well that I explored the way, as I embarked on a low path which petered out into a rocky gorge. By striking straight up over grass and scree I found the true path much higher up. As I followed it back, noting the landmarks with great care, I could see Beryl stretched out asleep on a grassy terrace below me. I soon joined her, as I knew we would have a long and tiring day to follow.

Because the Col was a main route and many travellers must stop by to pass on their news, the inn-keeper and his family were interested not only in us and our project, but also in England. They plied us with lots of questions on a variety of topics, but particularly about our Royal Family. Like many Italians, they seemed to take a deep personal interest in them all.

Our destination for the next night was Chiappera, which would involve crossing three passes and the frontier twice, so that an early start was more than ever desirable. I impressed on the young woman in the inn that we wished to be called at 4.15 and we went to bed early. For some reason I doubted the girl's reliability and of course slept only fitfully, waking several times in the night to check my watch. I woke for myself at 4.15, which was just as well because even by the time we got downstairs there was still no sign of the girl. Nor was there the sign of a key. As we were wondering how we would be able to creep out of the locked inn, we heard an alarm go off in an upper room of the house and the girl appeared, looking very tousled and still not properly awake. She made us coffee and let us out and we got away by five o'clock—not too bad after all.

The path which I had explored the previous day wound upwards in a most comfortable fashion and the weather seemed fair. It was a degree or two too warm for my liking, but I was thankful I had checked the initial stages of the route in advance. We crossed broad patches of frozen snow from time to time. To my amazement, lying in one of the footprints which I had left behind from the day before, was a little black mouse, resting. At first I thought he was dead, as he was reluctant to move and seemed to resent being woken so early, and it was not until I stirred him gently with my foot that he scampered off.

We turned into the Val Roburent, which would take us up to our first pass—the Passo di Rieou Brun or Brown Stream Pass. We broke through the snow crust at every step, which made walking tiring, so we put on our skis and managed to whizz across the steep slope without losing too much height, then once more we had to climb on foot. To our astonishment we came across a huge mound of wool in the snow. We puzzled over its origin and came to the conclusion that it must have been the remains of a wild sheep and that the carcass had been eaten by some sort of predator.

Stopping higher up we could see behind us ridge after ridge of mountains extending to the plains of Italy, but what was more ominous we could see clouds building up once more in the south, their arms spreading across the sky. I hoped that we would be able to race the weather as the sky cleared, but I heeded the warning none-the-less. The route got more complicated as we climbed, and as the result of bearing too far left we arrived a short distance above the pass. Something in the scene caught Beryl's attention and she reached for her camera, but to our consternation she knocked over her rucksack which went bounding down the slope with a fiendish impulsion of its own. Strange how time appears to slow down in such circumstances: we seemed to watch for an aeon in chilling impotence before the rucksack came to rest—and, wonder of wonders! it had not spilled any of its contents.

Looking round after we had recovered the errant rucksack, the view was certainly impressive enough for any photographer to want to catch. The pass was guarded by the red crags of the Tête de Moyse, which towered up impressively. On the far side, the

slopes of the Col ran down easily for over two miles before climbing to our next objective, the Col de la Gypiere d'Oronaye. The peaks of the Aiguille du Chambeyron
seemed a long way off, but we hoped to pass just below it on the morrow. For the
present, we had gentle slopes coupled with a strong breeze in our faces which irritat-
ingly combined to slow us down. When we reached the foot of the next climb we were
glad of the shelter of a large rock. Resting comfortably against it, we had our lunch and
admired the view. Lying back, we could watch the clouds gathering and dispersing,
with winds from north and south striving for supremacy. The south wind seemed to be
winning, its battalions of clouds reinforced with each fresh wave, its minions spreading
further and further across the sky and the fish clouds of lenticular cirrus *(see Plate 11)*
were beginning to group themselves. These fish clouds are a particularly reliable warning of bad weather in the Alps when seen in the south.

The menace of the south wind, with its cohorts of evil, stirred us into action. It was
mid-day, and we still had two passes to cross—a formidable target even without having
to achieve it in haste. The broad depression of the Col d'Oronaye was soon reached and
the towers and battlements of the Aiguille du Chambeyron seemed to have come closer
(Plate 19)...First, however, we had to travel more to the right to cross the Col des
Monges; and suddenly the wind changed through one hundred and eighty degrees.
Instead of blowing cold in our faces, it backed round and buffetted us with warm gusts
from behind. This would have been interesting had we been concerned only with
academic weather features; as it was, the wind change was most unpleasant. Low
clouds accumulated rapidly, the sun disappeared: the very centre of a depression was
passing across us. My forecasting had been accurate, though I could take no satisfaction from this, as it had come a little quicker than I wanted. Here, of all places—just
where the route was complicated, the map was uninformative, and we were getting
tired! We ran as fast as we could to the foot of the snowy ridge; climbed to the most
promising point to cross it; descended briefly; climbed again, this time to the left of a
rocky headland; down we went once more ... and there, through a gap in the ridge, we
could see the chalets of Saretto, a village lower down the valley but close to Chiappera.

Here our mistakes began. The sight of our goal enticed me mistakenly to take to a
broad couloir leading straight down. The angle steepened and we were forced to remove
our skis because the bed was grassy and littered with loose rock, and only patchy snowy
daggers remained here and there on the unexpectedly steep slope. I knew from the map
that it would be steep, but surely not as steep as this! We stopped to look round, trying
to assess the best tactics. We could not change course now because it was already three
o'clock and the weather was closing in. We would press on. The softened but still firm
surface of the tongue of snow on which I was standing invited a glissade. This, in
theory, is a "skilful and controlled glide" on your heels over snow when descending a
mountain, but in this instance controlled it was not: the snow around me started to
move and a small snow slide began to develop. I managed to keep my footing and thus
stepped out of the sliding mass just as it disappeared over a cliff like a soft fleecy
blanket slipping off the edge of the bed. Aghast, I realized what a stupidly dangerous
thing I had done: I had started to glissade when the end of the slope was out of sight. I
can only attribute my unthinking neglect of a fundamental precaution to the fact that
we were approaching the end of a long day and I was lulled by the feeling of security
evoked by the proximity of the valley. It is in precisely such circumstances that

accidents most easily happen, rather than in places where the difficulties are obvious and unremitting care is instinctive.

On my instructions, Beryl came down in the bed of the little avalanche in a more circumspect and orthodox fashion. But our problems were not at an end. The cliff was only about twenty-five feet high, but with all our gear it presented difficulties in the descent. There was a *Bergschrund* at its foot—a chasm which is caused by the snow pulling away from the rock wall—and this was narrow and deep as the heavy snow cover was beginning to part from the mountain like wet cement on a slope *(Plate 29, Chapter III)*. During her descent, Beryl slithered on a patch of ice and her skis slipped from her hold. Fortunately they were tied together but they set off rolling down the steep slope below and we watched breathlessly. They almost stopped and then malevolently resumed their flight heading for another steep gully yet further below and I cannot imagine what it would have been like had the skis been able to take their separate ways! When eventually they came to a final rest, we walked down with care, as though stalking a hunted animal which was about to set off again. At last I was able to lay my hand on them as if I were arresting a fugitive criminal.

Now nearing the floor of the valley we were able to think about accommodation for the night. The inn-keeper at Argentera had told us that Chiappera—the highest hamlet in the Maira Valley—was permanently inhabited, though he could give no information about an inn. We reached the valley between Chiappera, resting on a terrace on our left some distance up the valley, and Saretto which was a short way down on the right. We were pessimistic about finding a place at Chiappera, which looked like a huddle of greystone mediaeval houses; as we turned to look at Saretto a shaft of sunlight appeared through the masses of black cloud and lit up the houses, giving them a much friendlier guise. An additional touch of colour was given to the village by the deep emerald water of a small reservoir and the sound of a dog barking established that there were at least some residents. However, as I looked at Chiappera through my pocket spyglass I could see peasants working in the fields and we decided to explore there first for a night's shelter, even if it was only a roof over our heads, because it was closer to our next start. We shouldered our skis after the last short run down over the broad tracks of old avalanche beds and found Chiappera a delightfully set out place established by a mountain stream, with a tiny but picturesque church at its centre.

There was indeed an inn, but at this time of year it was still shut. Our enquiries elicited that it was common for the parish priest to accommodate travellers. This practice definitely went back a step in time to the days when it was customary for clergy to provide for man's physical as well as spiritual needs, but to our regret the priest was away down the valley on church business and there was no shelter for us at the presbytery. As we wandered round, we saw a man tending his cows and we asked his advice. He apologetically offered us a palliasse of leaves, but was distressed he could not give us even blankets, let alone better hospitality. He was more disconcerted than we were—we had survived the rigours of Callieri. The discussion lengthened and brought his wife on the scene, with the news that the inn at Saretto had just been re-opened after the winter. Weary as we were, we hoped it would be worth the near two-mile trudge down the valley. We reached Saretto after six o'clock—quite an exhausting day! We must have looked bedraggled and dejected, because on our way we met a group of women and one, eyeing Beryl with sympathy, exclaimed: *"Poverina, poverina!"* ... "Oh, you poor girl!"

Having learned Italian initially for the pure pleasure of enjoying and singing Italian opera, it was like coming on stage in the last act of *"Rigoletto"*, as we entered a very primitive inn. The dark, low-ceilinged living-room was occupied by two old women dressed in traditional black. The sinister overtones of the opera setting were rapidly dispelled, however, as we were fussed over and assured of accommodation. The old women were preparing an evening meal of meat and vegetables, but when they saw how tired and hungry we were, they insisted on giving us their food. We all sat down together around the same table. Our host and the two women were content to make their meal off eggs, but we shared a large bottle of the wine which they had been bottling earlier in the day, so it was not long before Beryl and I were floating on air. It was on such intimate occasions that I was especially glad that I spoke Italian, because there is little doubt that we immediately established an empathy between us, to the extent that they made us feel part of the family.

As we were talking, a wizened old woman came in and produced some cream-coloured stockings which she had knitted from goats' wool. They were too small for me, but this was no problem: she left us for a short time and returned with a selection of hand-knitted socks and stockings. The prices she asked were ridiculously low and her gratitude was embarrassing when I paid her a few more lire than she had quoted. After she had left, the kindly proprietress told me that knitting was the woman's only way of supplementing her tiny pension since she had recently been widowed. In these Alpine communities there are not many ways open to the inhabitants of isolated villages for augmenting their incomes.

By now the wind had almost reached gale force; even here in the valley the sturdily-built inn was being buffetted by strong gusts. Great masses of black cloud were riven by the wind as they raced across the sky; the sight and sound gave us a comfortable feeling of satisfaction that we had reached harbour in the teeth of a gathering storm. The primitive black iron bedstead creaked as we climbed in between the covers; we sank into a feather bed which soon warmed up—just as well, because half the window panes were missing and we were almost open to the elements—and it was not long before the rough whitewashed walls dissolved in the haze of sleep.

The gale blew all night and low clouds were still scudding across the sky in the morning, enveloping the mountains right down to the valley. Clearly we could make no forward progress. We decided to utilize the day by exploring Chiappera and reconnoitring our route for the next day—assuming the weather improved, though that was not all that certain. As we strolled up the road to Chiappera we could see the lower slopes of our descent lying just below the clouds. From below it was easy to see why I had made the mistake I did: I should have crossed the plateau completely before turning down, but surrounded by clouds as we had been and in sight of our goal I had been lured to turn down too soon. In the morning light Chiappera looked rather less forbidding, with a great spire of rock, some one thousand feet high, guarding the village like a sentinel. We could see no particular difficulty for our next day's start and we turned to explore more of the valley. We had hoped to visit the priest of Chiappera, but he was still away. There was an absence of children, too, giving a rather melancholy air—indeed, the villagers themselves called it a dying place, for all the young people were leaving to live and work in the towns which offered them greater excitement and material comforts.

Plate 17. Chiappera: Monte Castello, a great spire of rock some thousand feet high guarded the village like a sentinel

Historically "the Alps", to those who live there, were not the mountains but the highland pastures extending along the mountain slopes below the summer snow line. The Alpine Chain is like the backbone of a fish, with a spine but also lateral ribs or ridges. Between the ribs lie the valleys and glens which run up to the backbone giving access to the passes which lead, like vertebral interstices, across the spine to slopes and valleys on the other side. Water has been the chief agent in shaping the valleys and it always amazes me how far it travels in Europe before reaching the sea. Beside the torrent which ran through Chiappera—to flow eventually into the Po and thence to the Adriatic—was a ruined mill, further testimony to the dying of a village which found it cheaper to buy flour than to continue to grind its own grain. Perhaps the purchase by town dwellers of some of the ancient stone houses for conversion to holiday homes would give a kiss of life, but from what we saw, this was being done with rather vulgar taste—carriage lamps, wrought-iron balconies, painted cartwheels here and there looked completely out of place.

Many of these valleys are at heights above three thousand feet, and the architectural styles of the quaint dwellings reflected the need to keep out some elements of the weather. The red-tiled roofs of Saretto were surmounted by square chimneys with the vents at the sides and a lid on top to stop the snow from falling in. They looked like little belfreys. In the small central village square was the church; incongruously, on the other side, was a tumbledown brick kiln, the village incinerator. It was obviously used, as we saw no signs of rubbish dumped in the river, as so commonly seen in the more developed and "civilized" villages in the Alps.

Plate 18. Saretto: the village incinerator

Back at the inn, we found that we had had a four-footed thief in our room and many of our provisions had been stolen. The proprietress shared our anger because she was frequently troubled by marauding cats which took advantage of the rooms being open to the elements. The family had been fully occupied, hard at work all day bottling more wine which had been brought up from Piedmont.

The old woman who knitted socks also returned, all beams and smiles, to show us some wool which she had bought with the extra money I had given to her. It was hand spun goats' wool with the natural oils still in it, and it makes excellent stockings for keeping out wet and cold, similar to oiled Aran wool for our fishermen.

By late afternoon the wind had dropped in strength and patchy clouds were beginning to drift from the north. This indicated that the weather was on the mend, and we planned to leave the next day. Meanwhile the evening was passed in the pleasant company of two young Italians from Acceglio, five or six miles down the valley where they worked in the marble quarries, although they themselves were natives of Tuscany. The interlude was lively, and when we asked for our bill—as we would be away early—the calculation of it was a mammoth computation. With every attempt the proprietor arrived at a different figure and we had finally to agree on a sum which I fear could show him only minimal profit.

Saretto to Césana Torinese

As we expected, the next day was fine and fresh. Our hosts insisted on seeing us off, though we were up soon after four o'clock, and they made us coffee and hot bread to start us on our way. As we strolled up the road, the anomaly of street lights in Chiappera winked at us in the early dawn. Day was just breaking as we arrived and dogs were being put out of doors for their morning exercise, so clearly others too were up and about at the same hour.

It was an easy walk up the lower part of the valley, in a region so far off the beaten track that we imagined we had it to ourselves. However, to our surprise, we were overtaken by two young Italians—most probably inexperienced because they were travelling excessively fast for the beginning of the day: speed should be built up gradually as the muscles warm to their work. The others soon had to stop for a rest and we caught them up. They were well equipped with comforts and they generously insisted that we should take one of their bottles of orange squash.

We stopped for our second breakfast on a grassy bank further up the valley. Little stone-built alp huts were dotted about and the slopes were carpeted with purple crocus. We let the warmth of the early morning sun flood through us as we rested, our eyes feasting on our surroundings and our minds ranging over the routes achieved and yet to come. Fleecy white clouds were travelling fast across the sky and we suspected we would meet a strong wind when we reached the pass. We resumed our climb and once again the Italians caught us up. This time they hospitably pressed us to share some brandy with them, but we declined as graciously as we could. We felt that it might sap our energy, but I think they thought we were teetotallers! The valley was cut into huge terraces and these would make the Italians' return journey really enjoyable, but our route was in a different direction.

The shrill warning cry of a sentinel marmot drew our attention to several of these engaging creatures playing in the sun. They probably had not been out from hibernation for long, for they were quite sleek. These normally plump, thickset little creatures are hunted for their "grease" which is used in the more primitive areas as an embrocation for gout, rheumatism and chilblains, while their pelts are sold to furriers to make winter hats for the wealthy.

We had to press on. We were drawing close to the pass, the Col Mary, and high above our heads we could see the shattered ridges of red granite which swept up towards the Aiguille du Chambeyron but its peak was out of sight behind. On the right the pass was guarded by ribs of equally red rock leading up to the Tête de Cialancion and we climbed up a narrow stream bed which was topped by a spectacular cornice. At the pass we met the fresh wind which we had anticipated and it proffered no temptation to linger. We removed our skins and hastened down the other side until we found a sunny, warm place sheltered from the wind beside a huge boulder. Our frozen faces tingled as they thawed. Above us were the red pinnacles of the Aiguille du Chambeyron against a deep blue sky.

The sun's warmth drove right through our bodies, relaxing our muscles and provoking an intense desire to linger, but the battle with our minds told us that the warmth was also melting the snow. We ran on down the Mary Valley. We were soon looking down on to French territory, where this valley joined the larger valley of Ubaye and on the far side the hamlet of Maljasset. This is one of three hamlets in the area of Maurin, and I had read somewhere that the church had been re-built after being destroyed by an avalanche in the sixteenth century, and it has a niche in part of the churchyard wall for the depositing of coffins in winter when the ground is frozen too hard. I admit that at that moment my main concern was a resting place for us for the night—more important to us than a resting place for the dead, because we had to break the journey at Maljasset before tackling the next stretch: a long day which could take twelve hours. Once again ski tracks lower down reassured us that there must be someone about—and that the skier was obviously a local inhabitant as we saw the footprints of his dog.

We crossed a bridge and made our way to a farmhouse: luck was on our side. The farmhouse, unexpectedly, was occupied and we obtained the even more welcome information that the Club hut was also open.

The Club hut at Maljasset is apparently open all the year round and has a resident guardian as it lies in a key situation close to passes which connect both the Queyras and Ubaye valleys on the French side to the Varaita valley on the Italian side. In olden times this was an important region politically although there are no actual roads across the frontier. The Club hut had been converted from an old farmhouse which had been massively built with stone walls about four feet thick. Inside were vaulted ceilings and small barred windows.

It was a place of great character, and the guardian was also an individual of great character. He invited us into his own room and chatted while he made a meal of spaghetti for us all. He was obviously an enthusiast; a young, refined and educated man, he had chosen the job purely to be amid his beloved mountains, with only his dog for company. His room served him as a bedroom, living-room and kitchen and was sparsely furnished but very orderly. Under the table was a large box, for his old dog to settle in, and as we went into the room he wagged his tail to bid us welcome. Adorning

Plate 19. Two views of the Aiguille du Chambeyron: (top) as seen from a distance from the Col d'Oronaye; and (bottom) as we saw it from below, with the shattered ridges of red granite high above our heads

the walls were mountain photographs, including one of a handsome alsation rescue dog standing on a slope of about 60°—we felt that he really ought to have been wearing crampons, but he was certainly managing incredibly well without them! On one wall gun, ropes and an ice-axe were stowed neatly to hand, while enormous salamis hung from the ceiling and had to be dodged as we moved around the room.

Later, sitting outside, we enjoyed the last of the sun. Clouds were once more forming in the south, not a very good portent for the next day. We were still talking about the prospects when a large party of noisy and rather crude Italians arrived from Ponte Chianale. Because of the increase in numbers, the guardian had to open up the large and impressive vaulted living-room, which had probably originally been a store-room. Only a feeble glimmer of light could penetrate the small solitary barred window at one end. Next to the door was a box, bearing the inscription: *"Pour les animaux"*, into which any suitable scraps of waste food could be put. This was quite unique in my experience and showed the feelings of the guardian who was virtually a St. Francis of Assisi. But the unkindly and crude Italians suggested that the scraps were to feed his dog!

As I had feared, at four o'clock next morning it was raining and the clouds were right down in the valley. Instead of doing the sensible thing and going back to bed straight away, we hung about the living-room. This was depressingly like a dungeon in our mood of chafing itch to get moving again. The Italians either crouched miserably on the benches or prowled aimlessly round the room like prisoners in the Bastille waiting for the tumbrils. It was foolish for us to hang around like this, because it was essential that our next start should be an early one: we would need every minute of daylight for the following stage and even if the weather cleared it was already too late for us to set off. When some of the Italians left to go down, Beryl and I came to our senses and went back to bed. When we left our beds for the second time, the last of the Italians were preparing to go back down to the valley. As the day wore on, the rain turned to snow and then in the afternoon the clouds began to dissolve and the sun suddenly appeared. By evening the sky had completely cleared.

Our plan for the following day was to reach the village of Fontgillarde across two passes, which would probably take us twelve hours, and we were on our way by 4.30, not having lingered over breakfast. A sprinkling of new snow lay round the hut and the air felt fresh though the sky was cloudy. Walking up the valley, the ridges were still hidden by clouds; as these dissolved, the gaps between the wispy edges of cloud widened and when we paused to look back the sun touched the rocks of the Tête de Majour and turned them into molten gold, while the crescent of the waning moon hovered above. The last clouds rolled away and I knew that we would have a fine day.

It was two hours before we obtained any glimpse of our general objective because the valley was long and steep-sided. We climbed in deep shadow and when we suddenly got into sunshine our fingers underwent torments of pain as the circulation returned. This was an opportunity for second breakfast but there was really little warmth in the sun and we were more than glad to get moving again. Ahead of us the valley spread out as it rose to the Col de Longet, but here we had to bear left into a subsidiary valley to reach the Col de la Noire. There are two cols in very close proximity which have the name "Longet"—another riddle we did not stop to solve.

The slopes of the Col de la Noire were steep and fairly recently a big windslab avalanche had fallen. It looked totally different from the wet snow avalanche we had seen above St. Etienne, which had started from a single point. This windslab had broken away in a jagged line from a long transverse crack in the snow, leaving a little overhanging cliff about two feet deep above, while below the loosened snow had slid down in huge angular blocks *(Chapter V, Plate 63)*.

Plate 20. Col de Noire: it was corniced, but there was no difficulty in steering a course between the frozen crests

We stopped for lunch beside a lake and could see the corniced crescent of the Col de la Noire straight ahead. It was a spectacular-looking place, because on the right of it the rocks were black and led up to the even blacker rocks of the Pic de Tête Noire (Black Head!) By contrast, the corniced snowy col swept up to the left, like a slice, to the very bright red rocks of the Pic de la Farneireta.

After a brief rest we tackled the last stretch, but it was an exhausting climb. The slopes lay in full sun and the curved snowfield threw the heat back at us like a mirror. The snow had become damp and caked tenaciously to our skis in huge lumps which not only made them heavy to lift with each step, but hindered them from gliding forward.

We were heartily glad to reach the col and steered a course between the frozen crusts of the cornice. From here I had hoped to see Monte Viso, one of the highest peaks in the region, which lies only ten miles east, but as so often happens it was hidden by closer intervening peaks whereas from a greater distance it might have been seen clearly.

Plate 21. Anthony holding a ski caked with snow: it clung tenaciously to the soles of the skis and prevented them from sliding forwards

The valley in front of us fell away to St. Véran, but because this is not inhabited so early in the year we would have to skirt the valley head and cross another pass—the second Col de Longet—heading for the inn at Fontgillarde. From above it was easy to see where we would have to start climbing up away from the valley because some black cliffs marked unmistakably the site of an old disused copper mine. A small chapel lay by a stream, but who could tell whether it had been built for the benefit of the miners or of the farmers in the grazing alp? On the far side of the Col de la Noire there was perfect powder snow, taking us quickly down to the rocks of the mine.

The slopes leading up to the Col de Longet face south and I had expected hard work in soggy snow, but the humidity was less and the snow had remained dry. This lucky circumstance did not prevent us from a feeling of envy when we saw a chamois bounding up the slopes towards the col: weary as we were, we were almost jealous of his energy and agility.

It was four o'clock when we reached the col—a mere depression in the ridge—and we started down to the valley without loss of time. Unfortunately the snow was crusty and we had to run with care, fatigue catching up as we made our turns, fearful of falling and spilling our heavy loads. What awful conditions to meet at the end of a long day, we thought morosely. Many fairly fresh tracks ran down the slopes: there had recently been a public holiday and no doubt skiers had come up from the valley.

We continued straight down and suddenly there was a transition to splendidly firm fast spring snow, where we could turn without effort; our spirits lightened as we entered a little wood and got entangled in the branches, and we emerged laughing at the twigs enmeshed and sprouting from our hair. Fontgillarde was in sight, a plume of smoke rose straight up in the stillness of the evening, and undoubtedly denoted the inn, good food and wine—so we thought. There was no hurry. We paused to lie in the evening sun, a thick carpet of purple crocus around us, then we walked up to the village. The inn was closed.

We were told there was an inn at St. Pierre, a couple of miles down the valley. Before setting off we took a much-needed glass of wine in a small restaurant and the proprietor offered to give us shelter though he had no spare bedding. We debated on this but decided to walk to St. Pierre. Here we met yet another disappointment: the hotel owner had closed the inn for the day because of business further down the valley.

The choice for us then lay between going back up the valley to the restaurant at Fontgillarde, or continuing down the valley. We took a taxi down to Ville-Vieille: it was at least in the right direction for our route, although it would mean a change of detail. The way twisted down a narrow road and the sky darkened rapidly as we drove. Little scurries of snow fluttered at the windscreen, making us glad that we had at least reached some shelter in time. The distance was soon covered and we received a very friendly reception at Ville-Vieille. At last we were able to sit down to some food, secure in the knowledge that we had accommodation for the night.

In the bar, we made the acquaintance of the local guide, a great mountain lover who had travelled widely in the Alps. He had a chalet at St. Pierre and was accustomed to providing lodgings for mountaineers and could easily have accommodated us had he been there. He was angry with the inn-keeper and he blamed him for what he felt was irresponsible behaviour in not being at home!

The bar was pretty full and several others joined us at the table and entered into the conversation. They were not only very interested in our travels, but anxious to tell us about their district known as the Queyras. They had a lot of visitors arriving by car in the summer as Ville-Vieille is only a short distance from the *Grande Route des Alpes*. Botanists in particular were interested in the abundance of wild flowers and came up from Grenoble, Gap and also from Briançon—our destination which was now only about thirty miles away by road. They told us how the River Guil in the valley wound down to join the Durance below Mont Dauphin and washed down white pebbles mixed with green and red marble. Had we been to the Dauphiné mountains? Had we climbed Monte Viso? We were told of a cavern where cars could shelter in a storm; of limestone precipices seven hundred feet high on either side of the road. The chatter and interest were endless and became increasingly embroidered as the wine sank in the bottles. They were lovely people, but we had to leave them and go to bed: we were very tired and would not be travelling to Briançon by road!

Indeed, the next morning we were still tired and I felt that we deserved to give ourselves a rest day. Although we were nearing the end of our journey we still had quite a distance to go. From experience I have found that if you once get too tired you never seem to recover until the next season.

It was a fine day, and it is normally against my principles to take a day off as it seems to encourage the weather to break. Nevertheless, weighing up the pros and cons we decided to make the exception. We wandered along the mountain path to Les Meyriès. where there was a collection of alpine huts at the beginning of our next route. This preliminary reconnaissance was rewarded as the path would have been easy to miss in the dark. After the previous night's conversation we decided to visit the sixteenth-century church, damaged in the Wars of Religion but re-built a hundred years later. Although I am not religious, I always like to put something in the church box—perhaps it is a mental bribe for our safe return! In the distance we could see the historic village of Château Queyras with the little houses huddled round the old fortress with its mediaeval keep, as though for protection. Unfortunately neither of us had the energy to visit it.

We made our 4.30 start the next day, calculating that we should need five hours to reach the Col de Péas, and I wanted to catch the snow in good condition. The moon was still high and as we walked up towards Les Meyriès the stars began to pale as the sky steadily lightened. We sensed that everyone was still in bed and we crept almost furtively past the clustering houses as though it were immoral for us to be about so early—until somewhere a dog barked and shook our mood.

The next alp, a little plain with a cluster of chalets, was still unoccupied, but it must be a very fertile area to warrant the good mountain road leading to it. As we studied the peaks in the far distance blushing rosily in the first rays of the sun and capped by wisps of pink-tinted cirrus, I wondered if the weather would hold, as it had been so inconstant for most of the way, and we had little reason to expect it to change its ways even though the end of our journey was so close. Our intention was to stay the night in Cervières in the next valley—a village destroyed in 1944 but it had since been re-built. From there we could cross over the mountains to Montgenèvre on our last day.

We turned northwards up a thickly wooded valley deep in snow and heard the muffled roar of the river in full spring spate far below us. Ahead in the far distance we could see the shattered red ridges of the Pic de Rochebrune soaring up in isolated splendour. Walking through the wood was pleasant. We saw tracks where a vixen and her cub had been going in the same direction and they stayed with us for some time. It interests me that foxes, unlike nearly all other wild animals, use man-made paths, when it suits them, instead of shunning them as one might expect. We passed another Alp village before the sides of the valley steepened, and the river below was frozen and

Plate 22. The Pic de Rochebrune: on our way we passed to the right of it
down the valley to Les Fonts

deep in snow. Sooner or later we should have to cross it, so we slid down and side-
stepped up the far side until the angle of the slope eased and we were able to walk
normally. A cable stretched up the valley to some rocks above, presumably to some
mine workings, and it could be used to convey a small bucket to bring down rock or
even wood or hay from an Alp nearby.

We paused for breakfast in a sheltered glen.

It was still quite fresh but great plumes of cirrus stretched up into the sky to
the south, and below them little floccules of cloud were forming, an ominous sign of
bad weather building up especially when developing in the south.

Once again evil was wearing the mask of beauty. The crags of the Pic de
Rochebrune, which we had to pass at close quarters, now seemed near, but the dis-
tance was deceptive because it took us two hours, climbing steadily, to reach the
Col de Péas just below it.

On the far side of the pass the character of the mountains changed once more.
On this journey one of the outstanding features was the variation in the terrain.
Here, in front of us lay gentle undulating snow slopes leading down to a broad val-
ley bordered by the white even snow crest of Dormillouze. We paused to look back
over our route, and there for the first time we saw the elusive summit of Monte
Viso, but it was in the far distance; its lovely cone overshadowed all its neighbours.
So many ridges and valleys separated us and it seemed hard to believe that this
distance had been covered in two days' travel—albeit two long strenuous days.

With an effort I dragged my mind back to the problems ahead and wondered what the snow would be like, because there had been a snowfall three days previously. It usually takes several days for the snow to pack down to a good firm spring crust, by melting in the sun and freezing at night, and it is a very safe snow to ski on. However, I anticipated that it would not have consolidated completely and there would be an objectionable breakable crust, with its hazard of lulling the skier into a false sense of security and then suddenly breaking under his weight.

It was now late April and eleven o'clock: it was possible that the ageing process of the snow had speeded up in the hot sun. If it had, at this time of day, the surface could have melted sufficiently to form a fine powder on the crust and we had the prospect of a very enjoyable and fast run down the valley, which ran roughly from west to east, so that the sides faced north and south. There was a series of shoulders running parallel with the valley, and by keeping on these, ski-ing first on one side and then on the other, we found perfect powder snow on the north facing slopes which had been lying in shadow, and Firn or good spring crust on the south-facing slopes which lay in the sun

Plate 23. The joy of the descent lured us too far down and we had an uncomfortable climb to get out of the stream bed

throughout the day. However, we had to take care in the little valley linking the two slopes as there was a short stretch of the dreaded and anticipated breakable crust.

Here was the perfect example of how the knowledge of snowcraft is of great value to the ski-mountaineer who is aware of what happens to snow both physiologically and microscopically during the ageing process, and can put it to good use by knowing just where to find different types of snow. In this way he can choose a line down the valley which will give him the maximum enjoyment.

Because the inn at Fontgillarde had been shut, we had had to modify our plans, but now, looking up a valley to our right, we could see the Col de Malrif, with attractive valleys leading down. This would have been our original route, but here the two valleys joined and we had no cause to regret our change of plan. Unfortunately the joy of the next descent lured us too far down, into the bed of a stream; the sides got deeper and we realized we should have kept to the slopes above: it was uncomfortable getting out of the gully again.

On the far side of the valley we could see three passes, all leading towards our goal of Montgenèvre, a few miles from Briançon and an attractive finish. On leaving Ville-Vieille we had allowed two days for the journey, with the overnight stop at Cervières now comfortably close. The weather, though, was clearly breaking up once more; the sky was slatey blue and veiled by an opalescent cloud, while the light in the valleys had an unpleasant glaring quality which I associate with bad weather.

This might well be our last fine day. Could we conceivably cross over to Montgenèvre while the going was good? It would mean compressing two days' travel into one, but we were now very fit and I asked Beryl how she felt about it. She agreed to have a try. So near to the end of our journey, neither of us felt like being held up in Cervières for two or three days waiting for the weather to clear merely to complete one day's travel. If we got tired—well, we could always sleep it off in the train on our way home!

There was a choice of passes over the ridge and I chose the Col de Bousson as the easiest, even though we would end up at Césana Torinese—this is further north than Briançon and at the foot of the Italian side of the Montgenèvre pass. On crusty snow we ran down to the chalets of Les Fonts at the top of an open valley of rich pasturage supporting many alp villages. We paused for lunch outside one of the chalets and lay in the sun sheltered from the troublesome breeze which was developing.

We resumed our journey and by three o'clock we had reached the beginning of our last climb. The snow was quite compact, cooled by the dry northerly breeze, but the easy slopes were rather characterless—perhaps an advantage as we wanted no distractions of interest or beauty—although at the top we did see what appeared to be the tracks of many chamois a long way off. As we got close we could identify them as tracks of a snowcat, a motorized snow vehicle, on frontier patrol! We had reached the border and were in Italy again, in a more populated area.

Four o'clock had already gone as we ran down in the murk, through the most appalling breakable crust, to Lago Nero, where the ice was just beginning to melt. A narrow track went into a wood and the last tongues of snow petered out. We took off our skis with relief, though we had an ankle-twisting scramble through the trees. We reached the valley floor to find the river in full spring spate and the bridge marked on the map not in existence! In the distance on the other side we could see the villages perched high up, close to the road to Susa, a famous winter resort: the main road crosses the mountains through the Montgenèvre pass on its way to Turin. There was clearly a road to Césana Torinese from the other side of the river; I hoped we could find at least a path on our side.

It was fortunate that as we reached the valley floor our path got easier, though we could scarcely appreciate then the green fragments of white-veined marble which glistened in the rivulets and pools we negotiated, so tired were we. Beryl, who has always had the power to carry on long after she is tired, admitted that she dared not sit down for she would be unable to get to her feet again, and I too was weary. We had been fourteen hours on our skis, but tiredness no longer mattered because we had reached our goal.

At last the first houses of Césana Torinese appeared and I could ask the name of a simple inn with good food. The recommendations to the Sirena were justified and soon potent Piedmont wine wrapped us in a warm haze which went with us on our sinuous course to the dining room.

And so our journey was ended. We look back with a sense of achievement on nineteen days of most fascinating mountain travel. We had set off eagerly and trudged wearily, we had climbed up and skied down, we had found passes with two names and two passes with the same name. We had crossed line after line of isolated mountains, the two of us alone in a world of challenging slopes, varying snow, threatening avalanches, menacing gorges—but also a world of beautiful valleys, welcoming people, splendid and seemingly endless views, a world of time running out encompassed by the timelessness of the mountains. It had indeed been a wonderful, wonderful "Little Walk on Skis".

Chapter III

1971: Year 2. The Year of Cloud

The Graian Alps

Col de Montgenèvre to Melezet

EAGER to pick up the threads of last year's journey, we stepped out on the platform at Briançon. Outside the station, a minibus was waiting to take passengers up to Montgenèvre, a short distance up the valley. I was surprised and rather apprehensive when I saw that our driver was a young woman, but spotting some sacks lying in a heap I realized that I need not have been anxious, because she also carried the post. It was late April and we were the only occupants as the season for organized winter sport was over. As the 'bus wound its way up the tortuous road, our chauffeuse pointed out a side valley leading to Val des Prés. She proudly announced that it had just been opened up as a Winter Sports Centre. I looked at the steep, thickly wooded lower slopes and decided that they did not afford great possibilities, compared with many other places in the region, which abounded in splendid ski fields. Such is the present-day thirst to jump on the band-waggon and develop unsuitable valleys into ski-ing centres that Beryl and I had often, when we came down from the mountains, passed through these so-called "resorts", which consisted of a single ski-lift and indifferent slopes only suitable for the beginner. So I could hardly share the driver's enthusiasm, but a road rich in hairpin bends is hardly the place to start an argument.

I fell to thinking how strange it was that two hundred and fifty million years ago there were no Alps, and this was but a swampy marsh. Geologists regard the Alps as still young, because they were formed a mere thirty-five million years ago, by a folding of the Earth's crust, which brought to the surface rocks of different densities, folding and contorting the crust into two trenches—the Dauphiné and the Piemonte—with this very ridge in between forming the most prominent frontier ridge between France and Italy. But mountains age the moment they are born and to-day we were climbing one of the oldest and lowest passes in the Alps. It must have eroded a good deal with time. The road twisted and turned around the foot of Mount Janus on our right, from which Col de Montgenèvre had derived its name—appropriately named after the Roman God of doorways, open in war and closed in peace; and, providing the in- and out-coming armies with luck, the pass must have been used in Roman times. Yes! it was all steeped in ancient history.

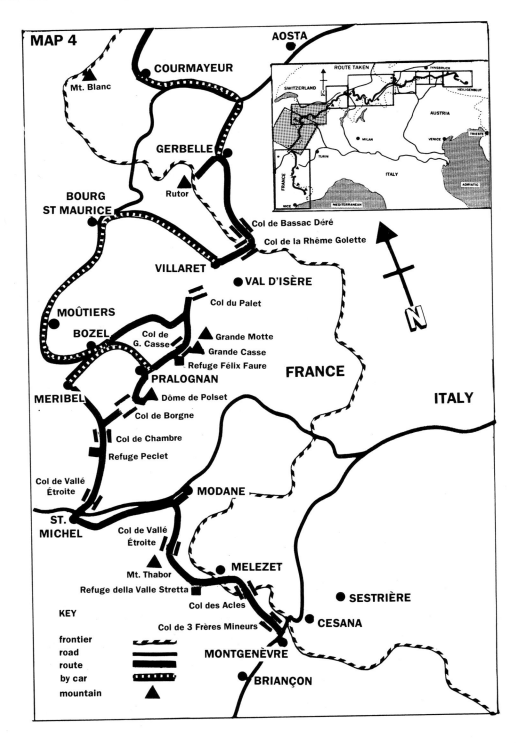

MAP 4

AOSTA

COURMAYEUR

Mt. Blanc

GERBELLE

Rutor

BOURG
ST MAURICE

Col de Bassac Déré

Col de la Rhême Golette

VILLARET

VAL D'ISÈRE

Col du Palet

MOÛTIERS

BOZEL

Col de
G. Casse

Grande Motte

Grande Casse

Refuge Félix Faure

FRANCE

ITALY

PRALOGNAN

MERIBEL

Dôme de Polset

Col de Borgne

Col de Chambre

Refuge Peclet

Col de Vallé
Étroite

MODANE

ST.
MICHEL

Col de Vallé
Étroite

MELEZET

Mt. Thabor

SESTRIÈRE

Refuge della Valle Stretta

Col des Acles

CESANA

KEY

Col de 3 Frères Mineurs

frontier

road

MONTGENÈVRE

route

by car

BRIANÇON

mountain

Inset map (top right):

ROUTE TAKEN

SWITZERLAND

INNSBRUCK

HEILIGENBLUT

AUSTRIA

MILAN

VENICE

TRIESTE

TURIN

ITALY

FRANCE

ADRIATIC

NICE

MEDITERRANEAN

The snow increased in depth as we gained height. There had not been much this season, but Montgenèvre lies at an altitude of nearly six thousand feet and we had no reason to be worried. The village is placed on top of the exposed pass and is an ugly confusion of old and new buildings, as it has been developed rapidly into a Winter Sports Resort. But now in late April it had gone back to its normal sleepy way and there was but one small pleasant inn open, where we were made welcome.

Retired though we were from medical practice, we had had plenty of physical occupation to get us fit at home: exercising our dogs, fencing, sailing, tending a small vineyard and, most of all, mixing mortar and plaster to restore our old house. Indeed, I found joinery good for the arm muscles and it was not unlike orthopaedic surgery—but of course it had the added advantages that the joints did not bleed and I could knock off for tea! So although we were physically fit we decided it would be a good idea to acclimatize ourselves to the height and it would also be nice to make a few short tours without heavy sacks, and thus to find our ski-legs.

We watched the few skiers on the piste using the intermittent ski-lift—they did not seem to be enjoying themselves because the light snowfall left many exposed rocks. So we decided to climb to the summit of Le Chenaillet and have a look over to the Pic de Rochebrun, under which we had passed on our way to Césana the year before.

There was a southerly wind, and within an hour or two clouds began to cover the sky. The glaring light and excessive warmth and humidity dispelled our hopes: signs of bad weather known amongst mountaineers as the Föhn. We were on the little pass by mid-day but the Pic was barely discernible. I made a mental note of the landmarks leading up to the Col des Très Frères Mineurs, as we were due to cross it on our way to Melezet in a day or two.

We felt too lazy to climb the peak and we set off in good snow back towards Montgenèvre. We soon reached the trees: the tree-line is as high as seven thousand five hundred feet, compared with six thousand feet in most parts of the Alps. Perhaps it is this which gives this region its special character and charm, for trees are great fun for the skier providing they are not too close—they add a kind of friendliness to the surroundings and impose a discipline on the skier.

An unpleasant damp wind blew across the pass, and we were not surprised to find the clouds right down the next morning. By the time we had finished breakfast it was raining. We returned to bed, and then passed a lazy day reading, eating and drinking; in a way I liked to think that we were storing up for more frugal days ahead! The weather was disappointing, and very unwelcome—I hoped it would improve as it was a full day's journey to Melezet.

So far, we had been ski-ing together alone, and although we had been held up last year at St. Etienne, this had only been frustrating to ourselves, but it had not really mattered. This year our plans had to be more specific; we were heading for the higher Alps and the complement of glaciers in the Graian Alps, and we would be crossing the Vanoise Massif to reach the south side of Mont Blanc before turning eastwards along the Pennine Alps. I felt that it would be in the interests of safety to have a stronger party, and we had arranged to meet Anthony Gueterbock at Modane. He would accompany us as far as Courmayeur and thereafter we would be joined by Geoffrey Buckley and John Lewis. However, this presented the problem that if the weather delayed us we would be unable to make our rendezvous.

It was clear in the morning, but the snow needed time to settle and we delayed our departure for yet another day, deciding instead to make a short tour to the Sommet des Anges—the Angels' Summit: at least the name was encouraging. The new snow gave a freshness to the scene and the branches on the trees were laden; from time to time they shed their burden with a gentle plop. I had the amusing thought that each of these snowflakes would melt to make a river, as the valley leading up to the summit was the source of the Durance, and I wondered how long each minim would take to reach the Gulf of Lyon in the Mediterranean. On the domed summit were the remains of a broken-down fort, and several huts, as we were close to the Italian border. The wind had veered to the north and the patches of blue sky heralded good weather for our departure the next day.

Sure enough, it was cold and windstill, and we left for Melezet. Stars still twinkled in the sky when we passed the frontier post. The official waved us on: he was not bothering to leave his snug shelter just because we chose to be up before dawn! Below, the lights of Clavière winked at us, and the first rays of sun were already beginning to gild the mountain tops ahead. We heard the harsh scrape of skis on the icy snow as a small party of French frontier troops appeared round a snowy shoulder, high above: they were too far off to hail, but as they had no rucksacks we concluded they must have come from the small village of Nevache and had therefore made a start even earlier than ours. Our route now curved steeply into a deep-cut side valley to the left, which took us below the shadow of Mont Chaberton, and we followed tracks of other Alpine troops, this time accompanied by a mountain dog. We soon reached the Col des Très Frères Mineurs, but the three miner brothers were not there to greet us. They had established their claim to fame many years before, from the small-scale mining which had been carried out in some of these valleys but which had sadly declined in the nineteenth century; and not even their ghosts were there, for we saw no workings.

A tempting, fine corniced ridge swept upwards to our left, its smooth flow broken by craggy spires of dolomite, but no! we must resist the urge to deviate because Melezet was still a long way off. We edged our way gingerly across the icy snow on the top steep slopes. Once over the pass, the surface changed and we were running down in a feathery layer of powder on crust, a skier's dream encountered all too rarely. It is fast and light and at each turn delicate plumes of snow spurted from our skis and the weight of our sacks was forgotten. It was sheer effortless joy. Further down, the gradient eased; we were now in open woodland crossing little subsidiary valleys which called for constant attention to pick a good line, as trees confuse the contours of the ground. Below us, winding along the valley floor, we could see the tracks of the party we had recently encountered. All too soon we reached some chalets. This would be a splendid place for lunch, as it was warm and sheltered. We had been on the move for more than four hours, and we lazed back feeling the heat penetrating our ski trousers as a balm to our aching muscles, and we closed our eyes to re-live the memory of that wonderful run down. But not for long, we still had another pass to cross, the Col des Acles. By contrast, to say that this climb was tedious would be an understatement! The slope faced full south in blazing hot sun, such snow as remained was both sodden and slushy and melting fast, while purple crocus and low bushes of alpen rose thrust their way through to reach the warmth. The streams had unfrozen beneath the trees and with monotonous regularity we took our skis off to cross a stream, and put them on again. We were exhausted, bending, slipping, scraping over small rocks, entangled in low bushes. How we sweated! Determined to end it soon, I made for the lowest point just below some dilapidated army buildings, their intrusion a constant reminder that the frontier was near at hand; but they were uninhabited and merely a desolate relic of the past which told no tale nor any reason, not even for which war they had been built—the frontier had been re-drawn so often.

We lay down on the Col, undisturbed by the least breath of wind. The silence was so intense I could hear singing in my ears. It felt like a vacuum in time. Wisps of cloud, like cigar smoke, hung poised and motionless above us. But we must move—Melezet lay far below us. High up on our left was a shattered ridge of red dolomite fashioned in embattlements, embrasures and turrets, and we named one fantastic cluster "the Castle". We were now on a north-facing slope for our descent: at least the snow made up for our trials on the other side, and we had an exhilarating run down to the valley floor, then made our way as best we could through woods and over old avalanches. We were glad when the red roofs of Melezet appeared ahead, and perched on a shoulder further round was Bardonecchia, a popular Winter Sports area with the Italians—we were back in Italy.

Plate 24. Col des Acles. High up was a ridge of red dolomite fashioned into battlements and turrets: we named it "the Castle"

Outside the first chalets was a frontier barrier, across the road which goes up through a tunnel to re-enter France, but it could not take much traffic as the post was unmanned. We hesitated at the nearby restaurant, but continued down as we needed accommodation for the night, and we soon reached an attractive old-fashioned inn. It was Sunday, and we could hear the loud chatter of the local people even outside, and this lured us in. There was immediate silence as we unshouldered our rucksacks and looked round the smoky, low-ceilinged room. It was packed with typical Italian villagers dressed in their best black suits and black felt hats. They sat at tables drinking wine and smoking *stumpen*—thin peasant cigars with a straw down the middle. They looked at us curiously: we must have looked strangely battered and sweat-stained at a time when the winter sports season was over. What was more, one of us was a woman—and Italians always left their womenfolk at home when they went to the inn. After the initial shock they soon made a space for us at one of their tables, and plied us with questions—where had we been? who were we? where did we come from? ... and they passed round their wine.

The inn-keeper agreed to have us for the night and made enquiries about the Rifugio della Valle Stretta for which we would need a key. He learned that the guardian of the hut was on his way down, as it was the end of season and he did not expect any more people. He normally called in at the restaurant by the frontier post, and we could meet him there. We finished our wine and strolled back to find him. We did not have long to wait. Although I had my Italian Alpine Club card, he was rather suspicious and cross-questioned me carefully before handing over the key. He was troubled because, as in France, there had been vandalism in the Italian huts. However, we sat down for a drink and he soon became friendly; we all pored over the map as we explained our intention to climb Mont Thabor and cross the Passo della Valle Stretta over to Modane. He advised us to take a route which I would never have discovered on the map, and he made a rough but practical sketch. Before parting, he asked me to hand over the key to the Customs Officer in Modane, who was also a skier and a friend of his, and he would send it back by train.

When we got back to our inn a lively game of Moro was in progress. It is one of the most primitive forms of gambling and in most parts of Italy notices are displayed in bars to remind customers that it is illegal. Needless to say the notice was not in view—and had it been there, it would have been ignored, for these players were experts. The game moves at a great pace, accompanied by excited shouts from the spectators. Both players extend anything up to five fingers of one hand, simultaneously calling the number of what they hoped would be the combined total—largely luck of course, although there was a considerable element of psychological anticipation.

The dining-room where we ate was old and low-vaulted, and it was pleasant lingering there chatting to the inn-keeper. He lamented the attractions the young found in unskilled but lucrative jobs in the towns and ski-ing centres like Bardonecchia. This caused problems on the farms because mechanisation was impracticable on any effective scale in these steep-sided valleys. The discussion was resumed next morning as I sat out on a bench in the warm spring sunshine. His three dogs played in front of us, racing over the turf still damp from newly settled snow. He explained to me that one dog was for hunting, one was a guard dog, and the third was a pet: this nondescript little animal dominated the others!

There was no need to start for the hut until after lunch, and we wandered through the village taking photographs. A small group of children was playing in the sun making mud pies to cook in their toy oven. Their old grandmother came out to see who we were, and seeing that we were strangers, told us how a chapel had been built on

Mont Thabor by survivors of a pestilence, in gratitude for their salvation. She glanced quickly at the children and gave me a knowing wink—the stone had been transported to the mountain by a miracle. Two pilgrimages are made every year, though year by year fewer villagers go, and on one occasion the weather was so bad that the men had returned with "candles of snow" in their beards. How often have I suffered in the same way, when my breath had condensed and frozen in my beard, forming stalactites.

We started for the Rifugio after an indifferent lunch. The track went almost as far as the hut, passing by a lake which had been dammed, its deep blue water reflecting a kaleidoscope of colour from the red rock cliffs behind, which were part of a crest called the Three Magi, with three individual peaks named Caspar, Melchior and Balthazar—the three wise men. I wondered if they had been so named by the priests who visited the valley for the pilgrimages to the chapel on Mont Thabor. But it was small wonder that the valley was called *stretta*: deep slopes hemmed us in on both sides, although higher up it broadened into a wooded glade. Here we found tracks of a stone marten in the snow. It is an animal rather like a huge weasel, about three feet long from its nose to the end of its bushy tail, but we did not expect to see him in the flesh as his excursions are nocturnal.

As the trees began to thin out the Refuge came in sight, but Refuge was hardly a fitting word for a splendid two-storey building of stone which blended in well with the surroundings—a perfect spot marred only by crisp papers, beer bottles, and every conceivable sort of hut rubbish strewn indiscriminately around it in the snow. From the balcony ran a steady trickle of melting snow, which we collected in plastic cups, and this spared us the effort of going down to the stream for water, which was some distance below. The general living-room was locked and there were no cooking facilities. The only accommodation we found was a room with four bunks and we heaped on top as many threadbare blankets as we could find. Beryl always carried a meta stove, which was very light and used solid methylated fuel, for such emergencies, and we brewed some coffee. We drank this and ate some sausage and bread, sitting rather forlornly on the floor in the hall. While waiting for more water to drip into the plastic cups we strolled out on the grassy terrace to assess our chances for the next day.

The upper part of the valley was dominated by an imposing craggy rock—Mont Seru—which split the valley into two, and the gentler snowy slopes of Mont Thabor rose to nine thousand feet behind it. The lefthand valley went up to the peak of Mont Thabor and the righthand one to the Col de la Vallée Étroite which we needed to cross to get to Modane. I pulled out the sketch map the guardian had given me. The way he advised us to take down from the peak lay behind Mont Seru, which would bring us to the Col without losing much height, but was narrow and could only be followed in good weather. We could see near the peak the little chapel which the old lady had described but as I spied it through my monocular, heavy clouds were obliterating it and rolling down the valley, grey and ominous: the prospects looked very doubtful.

We collected the water in the plastic cups and made some soup, and as there was nowhere to sit, we retired to bed while it was still light. We were up at 4 a.m. and low curtains of cloud were pressing down. Raindrops spattered on my jacket as I stood looking hopelessly up the valley; even the night had been so warm that our plastic cups had filled. In view of the conditions we would probably have to renounce Mont Thabor, and the most sensible thing was for us to strike direct for the Col and get over to

Modane, where Anthony would be joining us next day. In addition, the guardian wanted his key back as soon as possible, but we would postpone our decision until the valley divided below Mont Seru. The thrill of mountaineering is not only the sensation of achievement but also seeing the magnificent view when range after range of mountains extend into the distance like the waves on the sea, with the added interest of identifying the higher peaks. We had planned to climb specific peaks *en route* to create a diversion from just crossing passes, but it was a pointless exercise when the clouds were right down and there was only the altimeter to tell us when we had reached the top. These decisions have to be made at the time, rather like a military campaign.

We started off through the belt of trees above the hut, but on the way Beryl began to feel sick. It could just be altitude sickness, but on the other hand we had already been at these heights for six days, and the swelling of our legs and reduced urination which we both suffered from for the first few days in the Alps was gone. Moreover, Beryl did not have the splitting headache which we had both experienced at fifteen thousand feet in Kashmir. They are strange symptoms which disappear once you drop down a few hundred feet, and are probably due to oxygen lack. Perhaps it was the indifferent lunch at Melezet, or the melted water from the balcony—which had tasted a bit stale. So we dropped down to a little wooden bridge, the Pont de Fonderie, to refill our water bottles. We were in a wild steep-sided gorge with a few ruined stone huts scattered on its floor: this must be the old foundry which served what was probably an old lead mine on the far slopes, marked "Mine de la Bancha" and now a disordered heap of stones. We could imagine the secluded life of these men, mining and smelting the minerals so far removed from such civilization as even the remote valley below could offer them, and perhaps the Tres Frères Mineurs had come from here. It was warm and Beryl complained of the weight of her load, and she was sick. Should we turn back? She decided it was the extra two pounds weight of the ice-axe, which had taken her over her usual weight limit. She did not really need one, as I always cut the steps on ice, and as she was strongly against turning back, I carried her ice-axe as well as my own—with the mental note that I would send it to England when we reached Modane. I decided to go more slowly, and Beryl gradually felt better.

We struck up through a pleasant wood above the river. It was very still and the silence was only broken by the rustle of our skis through the snow. I rounded a high snowy bank and to my excitement caught sight of the first stone marten I had ever seen, about thirty yards away. He moved quietly off when he saw me, the beautiful curve of his body rippling sinuously. When I reached the place where I had seen him, I saw similar tracks to those I had identified further down the valley, and the imprints were quite unlike any other mountain animal with which I was familiar. But still it was a thrill to see the author of the signature for the first time. He was bold to be out in daylight, and I imagined it was because the valley was so rarely visited.

By now the clouds were very low, and we reached the point where the valley divided: there was no question as to where we should go—we would cross directly over the pass. We halted for a rest on a convenient rock, and we put on more face cream because it is easy to get sunburnt even in mist and cloud. Mont Seru above us played hide-and-seek in the clouds and snow started to fall. I had taken a bearing on the pass with my compass before the cloud engulfed us and according to the altimeter this was the place where we would have descended from Mont Thabor. We should be able to find

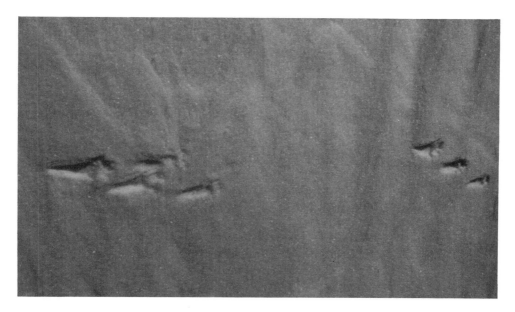

Plate 25. I caught sight of the first Stone Marten I had ever seen. I examined his tracks, but what a thrill it was to have seen the author of this signature.

the pass without too much difficulty, but the mist was so dense that it created in itself confusion. You feel as though you are walking into a bed of cotton wool. At one point Beryl, who was ahead of me, remarked that she could feel warmth on her face and the ground was rising steeply. I suddenly realized that we had walked into a wind scoop: this is sometimes six to eight feet deep and caused by the wind furrowing out an oblong crater in the snow. The warmth which Beryl had felt was reflected from the sides of the scoop as, although the cloud was dense, the sun's rays could penetrate it sufficiently to reflect from the snowy walls.

At last the altimeter and compass proclaimed that we were on the pass, and as it began to fall away I decided that they were correct. It had been a worrying climb and I would dearly like to know what the pass looked like! From the map I knew that we now had to keep to the right of the valley to avoid a steep slope, and we kept our skins on to act as brakes. As we felt our way down the visibility gradually improved. All of a sudden the steep cliffs appeared on the other side of the valley: we were nearly out of the cloud and we could feel the heat of the sun piercing the thin mist above us. But most alarmingly we saw that we were standing on a steep shoulder and the heat was softening the snow rapidly. We must at all costs move off it quickly, first side-stepping very gingerly to avoid dislodging the unbonded snow, and then running in a traverse until we were on easier ground and out of the avalanche zone. It had been a passage of anxious moments because we were far from help of any kind had an avalanche fallen.

Eventually we could see well enough to take off our skins. The valley was very narrow and steep below us, and we looked back to the pass, but the heavy clouds still obscured it, and we could see nothing of Mont Thabor either.

Plate 26. We must have walked into a windscoop like this

Lower down, the valley widened into a small plain where the stream spread itself into groups of shallow clear pools. A series of "plops" drew my attention to a multitude of active frogs: and where could they find a better place to found a froggery? They were doing their utmost to hide themselves from the unwelcome intruders by burying themselves in the sandy floor. Perhaps this was a frog nursery for some gourmets' restaurant? for after all, we were back in France!

Beryl had completely recovered and we rested by a little reservoir for a much-needed lunch. Then we were off again. We reached a military road cut deeply into a tree-clad gorge where we crossed the scarred beds of avalanches. Presently bare patches of road began to appear, and we constantly took our skis off to walk over them—it was all very tiresome—the only alternative was to keep our skis on and lift our feet high like ducks walking out of water, but it did the soles of our skis no good. At last the road was bare of snow though the fields were patchily covered, and the steaming earth produced wraiths about the size of a man drifting along, forming and re-forming in an eerie way. The springy pine needles underfoot seemed to lighten our loads.

We reached the chalets of Charmaix and entered an inn. In a glass case was a stone marten which I could now study at leisure. He was a truly fine looking animal about four feet overall.

The girl told us that we could take the cable-car down to Modane two thousand three hundred feet below in the Val d'Arc, but we chose to walk. Under our feet ran the Mont Cenis tunnel, the first transalpine tunnel, built over a hundred years ago. It carried in comfort its train loads of people and cars from France to Italy; but they missed our view, across to the backcloth of the Vanoise Massif—which was just emerging from cloud—the mountains we intended to traverse in the succeeding days. On this side they were steep and forbidding but to the north they formed a watershed for the Isère river fed by fine glaciers which provide wonderful ski-ing country.

In a group of trees an enormous cross rose boldly from a marble altar, outlined by the mist rising from the valley which had taken on an azure tint with the approaching evening. We passed several more shrines and memorials, one to a soldier killed in the war, another to a forester killed in a nearby avalanche. We crossed a wooden bridge spanning a waterfall; above it was a chapel built into the rock, its walls rising sheer above the torrent. The memorials told their tales of sorrow while the shrines brought hope that the saints would preserve the people in the future.

Modane appeared below us, and after the quiet of the mountains the clanking of shunting trains and the hammering of factories grated harshly on our ears. I delivered the precious hut key to the friendly Customs Officer, who laughed when I offered to pay duty on it! Then we went to the Bureau to send Beryl's ice-axe home.

Modane is on the main rail and road route which connects Chambery with Turin and lies in the valley of the Arc running east-west before turning north to join the Isère. The long ridge of the Grand Massif of the Vanoise bounds the north side of the river. It is broken in one or two places above Modane, which provide passes to the north where we were heading, but all these passes have the disadvantage of lying about six thousand feet above the valley and this would entail a tedious climb without snow and carrying heavy sacks. That would be just the beginning, as once on top we still had further to go. I had pondered over this, and finally decided that the Col de la Vallée Étroite would serve us best. The map showed a road leading some way out of the valley, and if there was no snow, we could take a taxi up it in the direction of the pass; and the town of St. Michel would make a convenient starting place.

Rather incongruously, before leaving England I had chosen from the Michelin Guide the inn where we should meet Anthony. This had naturally met with Anthony's approbation, as we are all fond of our food and wine, and the prices seemed disproportionately low. Our pace quickened as we saw it in the distance, just as with one of my ski-ing friends, who had an unerring nose for material comforts, and I could always tell when the hut or inn was within striking distance, even though it was out of sight, for his pace would increase and he would draw ahead of us, impelled by some inner force. It was like goading a donkey with a carrot.

The inn had outgrown the simple description accorded in the Michelin Guide, and from the outside seemed rather grand for us in our unkempt condition, but I need not have worried because in true continental fashion the proprietors did not turn a hair and made us very welcome.

I had known Anthony Gueterbock since he was a schoolboy. His Brigadier father, whom I had known for many years, was also a member of the Alpine Ski Club; Anthony had undoubtedly inherited his love of mountains from his father and I had toured with him before in the Bernese Oberland with Chris Stocken. While we were waiting for him next day, we stocked up with provisions in the market from a mouth-watering choice of cheeses, patés, dried meats and sausages; and I felt that if I had overstocked, at least Anthony had a good appetite and a strong back.

We tried to get more solid meta fuel for Beryl's stove, but our accents—or perhaps it was our limited French—resulted in our being proffered meat cubes.

Anthony joined us at dinner that evening and was most impressed with our choice of hotel, and we had soon made plans for the next day. I managed to arrange a taxi to take us to La Traverse, which would leave us with a climb of four thousand feet; even this was enough with heavy rucksacks.

St. Michel to Pralognan

Our intention was to make for Pralognan, which is only fifteen miles on the map, and north of Modane as the crow flies. But mountaineers cannot fly like crows; deviations and détours are inescapable when travelling over mountainous country, not just because of the terrain itself, but limitations of daylight, human capacity and overnight stops in suitable refuges—all have to be allowed for. I estimated that we could reach the Refuge Peclet and cross over to Pralognan the next day. Much of this area has peaks and ridges well over ten thousand feet, and working our way over and in between them increased the crow-fly distance in the same way as a dog does walking with his master. Not only this, but we hoped to reach Pralognan by crossing the Col de Borgne, descending to the Gebroula Glacier, and climbing the Dôme de Polset on the way. But at all costs we needed good weather to find our passes, let alone our peaks, and so far we had been hounded unmercifully by clouds.

Next morning we left in the taxi at five o'clock, glad of saving time and labour. It would have been a dull walk to the snow line. Stars were still visible in the paling sky as we shouldered our sacks, and far below the lights of St. Michel glimmered. Anthony led off at a cracking pace up the steep path. I brought up the rear, protesting inwardly, and hoping his legs would soon tire. He possesses an excellent pace, but he was fresh from England, and it takes a day or two to adjust to the discipline of climbing slowly at first so as not to tire when the day may extend over many long hours.

Occasional rivulets crossed our way, the rocks adorned with crystals of rime. Round a corner we surprised a couple of hares, their coats still white. I always find it fascinating how nature operates its camouflage in winter, for hares and ptarmigan turn white to blend against the snow, yet chamois, who roam the same regions, retain their colour, probably because they descend to woods and even villages to look for food in winter.

Higher up tongues of frozen snow made more comfortable walking. We had a second breakfast beside a gurgling stream and we felt that we had broken the back of the journey. Maddeningly, Mont Thabor glowed rosily in the morning sun across the valley, seemingly more than a day's journey but for us untouchable this year; far behind, dwarfing their surroundings, the peaks of the Dauphiné drew our gaze—they were all clear of cloud and the weather looked hopeful. A huge snow bowl gave us a fine run down before we stopped for lunch beside a little frozen lake. We saw footsteps in the snow, made by several men, and from the way they wandered about, it was clear that they had been in mist. The imprints entered a hut, but none came out, and we felt we should investigate as someone might need help. There was no reply to our knock, so we pushed open the door. It felt eerie! Accustoming our eyes to the darkness, we could make out simple furniture, blankets and provisions—but no occupants. Strange. It was rather like a mountain *"Marie Celeste"*—the boat found sailing without passengers or crew. After some discussion we reckoned that the party had spent the night in the hut, but had left in the morning when the snow was still hard, which was why there were no footprints leaving the hut.

The Refuge Peclet lay out of sight in a side valley and we reached it after a tedious traverse in heavy snow. We were relieved to see a group of people standing outside, as we had no key and had hoped that, like the Swiss huts, it would be open. They were a party of French piste skiers and their guides had brought them up to give them experience of hut life as a change from piste ski-ing in the valley. They had virtually taken over the small simple building, and we felt resentful trying to find room on the straw-covered shelves which served as bunks. Nor did they let us sleep, although we were dog tired; even the hard bunks gave them a sense of romance, as they bounced excitedly above our heads sending down a rain of straw through cracks in the boards. It was a novelty for them, but not for us—we were suffering from fatigue after a strenuous day.

Plate 27. Outside the Peclet hut. We were awoken by the dismal cry *"Il neige!"*
Angrily and irrationally I felt the speaker was half responsible

Sure enough, we were awoken the next morning by the dismal cry: *"Il neige!"* Angrily and irrationally I felt the speaker was half responsible. This clearly ruled out our intended crossing to Pralognan, for the route was long and complicated. Moreover, we would have to leave, because the French party were returning to the valley and they would have to lock up and return the key. How we missed the trust of the Swiss, where the huts are left open for mountaineers.

After breakfast the weather improved: it was good enough for us to cross the Col de la Chambre, which was at least in the right direction, and we could make further decisions later. By the time we were away the clouds were lifting, revealing occasional patches of blue sky, but the surrounding mountains remained with their heads glumly buried in cloud. We crossed the pass and ran down through freshly fallen snow to a bowl. Up to the right a narrow valley led to the Col de Borgne and we debated whether to go up. The clouds were right down and with reluctance we gave up the idea, because there would still have been yet another pass to cross and it might be very difficult to find it on a crevassed glacier in the cloud. Though in retrospect I think that we should have gone up to have a look, it would have been another two-hour climb. We continued down the valley for three miles, where we joined the Vallon du Saut. On the far side were some cow chalets and again we debated whether to pass the night in one of them and retrace our steps to the Col de Borgne the next day, but one look at the sky decided us, for leaden grey clouds were accumulating everywhere and had blotted out the patches of blue sky which had sustained our morale; and it began to drizzle. We decided to go down to Mirabel; and we trudged into the village with squelching boots, parched throats, and soaked to the skin.

Mirabel was beginning to be "developed" and we found it difficult to accept change. Row upon row of regimented faceless windows each with its balcony served an ideal purpose for package holidays and week-end flats, but the angular architecture struck a discordant note amongst pine trees and the sleepy chalets of the old village which they had entirely engulfed. There were but few people around and heaps of mudstained snow lay by the roadside looking grim in the incessant rain—it was hardly a welcome!

While we poured beer down our parched throats, we wondered whether to spend the night in Mirabel and have another try at the Col de Borgne next day, as there was no other practicable way over, but none of us was enthusiastic and we decided to adhere to our self-imposed rule of "no going back for a second attempt". If we went round to Pralognan by taxi we could climb the Gebroula Glacier and Dôme de Polset from there, and we would only have missed out the very short stretch over the Col de Borgne. This was really our first major reverse.

By taxi the journey seemed endless as we were skirting the periphery of valley outlets from a centre point rather like travelling along the arc of a circle around a maypole. Passing between some grey industrialized sheds at Bozel the taxi driver pointed out foundries where aluminium was smelted from bauxite and he said it was more sensible to do it here near where it was mined, rather than further down the valley, as its extraction needed vast quantities of electricity, and these valleys with their relatively cheap electric power are a natural choice for these refineries. But we were in no mood to absorb a geological dissertation and by the time we reached Pralognan it was dark—even that was in keeping with the spirit of the day! and all the hotels were shut: it was out of season.

We wandered around disconsolately and met a young Frenchman in similar plight. Beryl had the bright idea of going to the only café to ask if we could find accommodation anywhere. Yes, they would put us up but they could not provide food except coffee and a roll for breakfast. In the meantime the Frenchman had found himself a room with a cooking stove, which he generously offered to share with us if we were unable to find a restaurant; but by this time we had been directed to a stone chalet high up above the village, which we naturally preferred to try. They could only provide cheese fondue and we delved hungrily into the bowl of bubbling molten cheese, thinking how good it was to be in civilized surroundings rather than in the cowshed where we had at first contemplated spending the night.

It rained hard during the night and despite the low clouds which hung motionless in the valley we decided to go up to the Refuge Polset and climb the Dôme the next day—if the weather served. It certainly seemed to be going in alternates, and it is always a good principle to press on when there is a reasonable possibility, as I can remember many glorious expeditions in which we started in unpromising conditions and the weather relented as though stepping aside at our impetuousness.

I think that secretly we felt that we should have some revenge for the setback we had suffered. Armed with a large quantity of French paté, because Anthony said he had never been so well fed in the mountains, we set off. Clouds circled above us in an oily way threatening to shed their load on us at any moment and I was beginning to feel like the Pied Piper of Hamlin attracting his plague of rats. As a thin damp mist obscured everything except the nearest landmarks, it was incredible how we never seemed to be able to shake the clouds off. It all appeared so desolate and unreal. We eventually reached some chalets and I tried to encourage myself by imagining what a peaceful scene it would be in summer, with flowers, cows and herdsmen, but there were none. We took off our skis to cross a wooden bridge and to climb a steep slope on the other side. When we came to put our skis on again, Anthony found that the plate he slid his boot into for climbing uphill was missing. This was alarming, but the best place to look for it would be soon after he had taken his skis off beside the bridge—that is, if it had not fallen into the torrent when he crossed over, as he would never have heard it fall in the water. If he did not find it we would be delayed at least two days, because the nearest town where he could buy another would be Chambery. I watched his figure dwindling into the mist, having considerable misgivings as he went back to find it, but the gods were not entirely against us because I heard a triumphant cry rise up from the valley.

It is extremely tiresome to steer by compass when zig-zagging uphill on the steeper gradients, and we were glad of old ski-tracks to guide us although occasionally we lost them; but at least the business of finding them again provided a diversion from what would have been an interminable time and distance in the unbroken whiteness. At long last we heard a hail from Anthony, who was in the lead: yes! we were there. We climbed up some steps and were confronted by a forbidding-looking iron door, but we had been assured that it would be open, and indeed it was. We found a comfortable little winter room. It was my turn to cook, and the veal steaks fried in butter and garlic won the approval of Beryl and Anthony—but perhaps they were very hungry!

When I awoke I thought: "To-day is the alternate day, it should be fine"—but I hardly dared to look out of the window. Summoning up courage, I dashed to it—the

Plate 28. Séracs: sugar cubes of blue-green ice. The striations register each snowfall like the rings of a tree trunk

clouds completely enveloped the hut—it would be hopeless to start in that. I suppose by now I had almost grown to expect it, but it was still early and we could afford to wait a bit. By seven o'clock the mist began to pale and I stood with my eyes transfixed as the clouds parted suddenly, like the curtains in an Opera House, to reveal sun-kissed rocks hovering above me. Minute by minute the view broadened until we could see all about us. Excitedly we threw all the day necessities into our sacks and hastily set off, for this would be the first glacier climb on our route and both Beryl and I loved glacier ski-ing. We were now in the High Alps, where peaks above ten thousand feet are covered with snow even in summer.

We climbed up the pass, the Col du Soufre, which is a tongue-like couloir leading up the Gebroula Glacier, and once there we stopped to appreciate the scene. About a mile away to the north-east was the elusive Col de Borgne and I thought of the vast distance we had travelled by taxi to meet it again. We agreed that our decision had been wise, however, as there had been two days of bad weather and we certainly would have found difficulty in locating the Col du Soufre in a complete white-out.

We headed south towards the Dôme, on a gentle gradient. The clouds were coming and going, though not in a determined way. We had time to look about us and admire the fantastic shapes in an ice-cliff at a curve in the glacier. An ice-fall lay ahead. We threaded our way through the séracs towering up like mammoth sugar cubes of blue-green ice, and it was interesting to see the varying depths of the striations in their sides, giving a picture of how deep or shallow each snow fall had been in previous years, rather like the rings in a tree trunk (*see also Plate 93, Chapter IX*). It was a scene of exquisite though rough beauty, which I had seen many times before yet which always filled me with awe, for beside these séracs lie crevasses which can extend hundreds of feet into the depths of the glacier (*see Plate 39*) and are often choked with snow or spanned by bridges of frozen snow of indefinite or precarious thickness. No-one could pass by without questioning how they were formed.

We were now above the ice-fall, and the glacier swept up in a smooth unbroken surface to just below the summit, where a depressed wavy line indicated a *Bergschrund* or *Rimaye*—a gap where the glacier pulls away from the ice cap and rocks. We were above eight thousand feet where it never rains but snows, and an average of thirty feet of snow may fall on some mountains during any one year. Yet these mountains do not grow higher: the snow is compressed by its own weight into semi-crystals called névé and as the air is gradually expelled the snow turns into ice, forming an ice-cap which is the source of the glacier. By sheer accumulation it must inevitably overflow from the summit and slide down the nearest gradient; if this is steep it pulls away from the rock face creating a crevasse or *Bergschrund*—as it had done here—and once on the move the ice becomes the glacier, for glaciers are slow-moving rivers of ice. They may not travel more than two hundred and fifty feet in a year, but they obey the same rules as water flowing in a river—except in one respect: ice is inflexible and stiff, and when it flows over a steep or convex curve it cannot bend in the same way as water to accommodate the shape of rocks and gradients in the stream bed and it splits open into serrated rifts or crevasses, and rectangular boulders of ice break off and are thrust upwards in a disordered jumble of séracs to form an ice-fall.

But it was time to take stock of our position, because the south wind had decided to take charge, and dark bands of rolling cloud billowed towards us down the glacier. We

Plate 29. *Bergschrund* or *Rimaye:* a crevasse where the glacier meets the rocks;
in this case it was covered with snow

waited for a while to see if they meant business, for it would be a pity to give up so near
the summit. Occasions like this call for nice judgement on the part of the mountaineer,
in order to steer a course between premature retreat and foolhardy persistence, but the
cataract of cloud continued down the glacier and we turned tail before it, to thread our
way back through the séracs while we could still see; but at least we had an enjoyable
run back to the hut in rather a chastened mood.

 After a bowl of soup we set off for Pralognan. When we reached the valley we were
astonished to meet two Frenchmen on their way up to the hut—they were certainly
late and it would be well after dark when they arrived: they must have known the
district well, but we did not envy them. Back at our café they were glad to see us,
plying us with questions about our trip and the conditions. Mountain folk, like sea-
farers, take a close interest in strangers and are glad to discuss their surroundings.
Then we went back to the restaurant but there was still only cheese fondue on the
menu and by this time it was beginning to pall.

Plate 30. The disordered jumble of séracs and crevasses which form an ice-fall

Pralognan to Tignes

A cloudy damp feeling did nothing to raise our spirits and the barometer was obstinately low—it was a gloomy prospect, but we had at least to make a start. We had eaten all our food and must stock up with provisions for at least three days, as our next stage would be to overnight in the Félix Faure hut and from there it was a long stretch to Tignes, and we did not know what hazards we might meet on the way. Our appetites were stimulated by the wonderful assortment of smoked meats and the diversity of sausages and salami hanging from the ceilings, and by the aromas which are met only in French and Italian shops; and paté—yes, large quantities of it, as Anthony never seems to get over the novelty of eating it in the mountains.

We had a cheerless climb to the hut. The beauty and variety of the ever-changing view, which take the sweat out of climbing uphill, were denied to us by falling snow and low cloud, which prevented us from seeing anything more than a few rocks and slopes immediately ahead. When we reached the hut, the wretched little winter room was damp with puddles from wet clothes and equipment lying on the stone-slabbed floor. A party of Frenchmen, whom we had seen disgorging from a car ahead of us as we started up through the woods, crowded the room and castigated the absent guardian for not visiting the hut to replace the gas cylinder or to provide wood for the stove. But the French had done nothing about it, so we scouted round for ourselves outside the hut and unearthed some rotting planks from the snow and returned in triumph to our quarters. There was hardly an air of jollity and the French were unwilling to talk, so after our supper we retired to the dark, uninviting bunk room feeling most despondent about the morrow.

Our plan was simple, though our route was not. To get to Tignes, at the head of the Isère valley, our way would be across the Col de la Grande Casse, along the Glacier du Rosolin, a short climb up to the glacier of the Grande Motte, and then down to the valley. The Félix Faure hut was well over six thousand feet up, so that once we reached the Col de la Grande Casse it would be mainly downhill running. We were now in the very heart of the Vanoise Massif, in an area completely deserted, yet in the parallel valleys to the north there would soon be hundreds of people ski-ing on the slopes in the emerging development of La Plagne and Bellcôte.

When we left, the French party were still asleep in the hut. At five o'clock the clouds seemed miraculously clear and a thin veil of mist, tinted golden by the first rays of sun, showed a deep azure sky beyond. We reached the glacier of the Grande Casse and saw the Col about two miles ahead, a mere crescent of snow flanked by rocky ridges. The glacier itself was only about half a mile wide and the final slopes were uncomfortably steep though uncrevassed. The new snow had not yet bonded and it slipped off in an infuriating manner from the underlying crust with every step. Having climbed in shadow it was a relief to step into sunshine on the Col, and our first thought was to see what difficulties lay in store ahead. We did not have to search for long. Though the splendid Rosolin glacier promised a three-mile run down, joining its far end the glacier of the Grande Motte had receded and broken off into a very steep ice-cliff. I had read that there was some sort of passage, but even from this distance it looked very daunting. To the right of the ice-cliff was a fine pyramid of the Grande Motte reaching to almost twelve thousand feet, but our thoughts were on the more immediate problem,

Plate 31. We had a long way to go to Tignes over the
Col de Premou (on the left)

and we would have to have a closer view. We ran down across a huge glacier shelf
plastered against the very steep side of the Pointe de la Grande Casse on our right and
from the shelf to our left several subsidiary glaciers ran down to the valley out of sight
below. It was a wonderful situation and the snow was in perfect condition. Strewn
ahead of us at the foot of the Grande Casse were large blocks of ice varying from one to
six feet in diameter. We gave them a wide berth, and with good reason: I suddenly
heard a sharp crack and the noise of falling stones. I looked up hastily at the sheer
rockface of the Grande Casse rising two thousand feet above us.

Bouncing down the slope from the top were blocks of ice, kicking up flurries of
snow, and they joined the others on the glacier beside us. These ice avalanches are not
unlike rock falls, but they are quite unpredictable because they are not dependent on
changes of temperature, and their momentum carries them a long way. There is no
better description as to why they occur than in Colin Frazer's book on avalanches: "Ice
avalanches are almost invariably the simple result of glacier movement; the ice moves
slowly towards the edge of a drop until it falls over it."* In this way it differed from the
glacier flowing down the valley from the Dôme de Polset.

It was not long before we reached the far end where the Rosolin glacier joined that
of the Grande Motte—or so the map indicated. We stood looking up with dismay at a
hanging glacier which rose above our heads in a deterring manner; the snout had
broken off and fallen over the cliff, and where we stood was strewn with enormous
blocks of ice, and their very size must have made the ground tremble when they fell. It
would be suicidal to attempt to climb it, as we would be sitting targets for further falls

*Colin Frazer: "The Avalanche Enigma"; John Murray, 1966

Plate 32. An ice avalanche. These blocks and séracs had fallen from the hanging glacier

of ice. To the right of it we reckoned the slope was too steep for safety, and to the left there was a smooth rocky buttress which could offer a way on to the Grande Motte glacier, easy enough without our equipment, although there were very few foot- or hand-holds, but now impracticable since it would take a long time, especially laden with skis and heavy sacks, and we did not carry pitons, rope ladders or hammers. Our goal was Tignes and although we had been anticipating the wonderful run down the Grande Motte glacier to reach it, we must abandon the idea and it was very disappointing.

However, there was an alternative route; it meant a long détour to cross two passes—the Col de la Croix des Frêtes and the Col du Palet—which would bring us down to the Tignes lake. They were very close together, and the route between them a bit complicated, but as we had good visibility we anticipated no difficulty. Reluctantly we gave up our original intention and skied down the glacier as far as the foot of the valley leading up to the cols, and stopped for lunch before tackling the climb. Despite our disappointment it had been an enjoyable morning's ski-ing and the snow had been good. We glanced back to savour it once more, if only in memory. The very fine wedge of the Pointe de la Grande Casse looked not unlike a scaled-down version of Mount Everest, but even as I watched, haloes of thin cloud began to form above its head and drifted down the valley towards us. It was exasperating. There would be more bad weather and it was arriving at tremendous speed. We scrambled to our feet and set off hurriedly up the valley, for it would take us two hours to reach the first col, and we must beat the weather in order to find the second pass. The head of the valley was soon in cloud which was steadily becoming denser, and we had frequent stops to consult the map.

It was with some relief that we reached the first col and peered over; dimly below we could see a little lake. So far so good, but we must now find the Col du Palet. I decided to make for the lowest point on the ridge up to the right, which should be it. I could see it only a quarter of a mile ahead, and if we traversed round keeping the slope to our right we should find it. We started down the far side without delay because the clouds were boiling up rapidly and obscured our view.

We were now under considerable pressure, and it was the last we were to see of the pass. The visibility had dropped to fifty yards. Beryl was in the lead, Anthony in the rear with the compass, and I was in the middle so that I could consult with him over the map. With Beryl and me lined up in front of him Anthony could steer us by compass and direct our course to right or left.

All seemed well at first, but then the steep slope we were negotiating was constantly pushing us to the right, when according to the map it should be pushing us to the left. This meant we were travelling south instead of east, and of course it was impossible to see why because the clouds were so dense and there was never a moment's clearing. We stopped to consult the map yet again.

"You know," said Anthony, "I think we are going down the same valley."

I was unwilling to agree with him because on these occasions one becomes so disorientated that it is difficult to believe the compass. There was no question of our retracing our steps at this stage, for the visibility had decreased to less than twenty yards in a complete white-out, when you develop a curious encased sensation: there are no contours, no dips, no hummocks, no ridges, no sky, no horizon ... With no horizon to fix the vision, the mind is confused by a feeling of giddiness, so I looked at my feet—they were at least something to focus on and the sensation from them told me that I was standing upright! We groped our way down yard by yard, testing the angle of the slope with a ski stick before taking the next step. Does fear have power to stop the clock or is it danger which drags out the minutes? Gradually the ground began to fall away steeply and we saw boulders and a glacier—surely this must be the way we came up earlier? Yes, we were back at our lunch place, but it was now four o'clock in the evening as we had been floundering about in clouds for a very long time.

Our next problem was a place for the night. The nearest likely habitation was Champagny le Bois, some eight or nine miles off, and our enemy would be darkness; this was the only solution unless we found an alp hut open on the way. Despite the urgency to get down safely in daylight, we stopped for a bite of food as we still had a long way to travel. Once we got off the glacier we ran down in a snow-choked stream bed for some way. The mist was thinner and the sides of the valley steepened: we were entering a gorge and with darkness approaching it might be a trap. Clearly we could no longer continue down it, and we climbed up its bank—a revolting slope of mud, grass and boulders resting on smooth rock slabs. As I stepped on one, it slid from under me, leaving me flat on my face, but I was thankful not to be following into the gorge the hail of boulders which I had dislodged. I picked myself up cautiously, plastered liberally from head to foot in bright yellow clay as if I was a Red Indian on the warpath, but without feathers or tomahawk. The others were kind enough not to laugh, and it suddenly occurred to me that we were supposed to be enjoying ourselves. How odd!

As if we had not had enough for one day, it began to rain, and we finally reached Champagny le Bois bedraggled, cold, our boots squelching, and we were wet through to the skin. There was no inn and we sought for a telephone to summon a taxi. Standing uncertainly in a dim-lit street we saw a slit of light grow into an oblong as a man opened his door, and we asked his advice. He invited us to come in and get warm, and the heat hit us as we crossed the threshold, and looked around. An immense cauldron was suspended over a roaring flame which made our clothes clammier and they started to steam. We stood as still as possible, uneasily aware of the puddles we were causing on his spotless stone-flagged floor. The cheesemaker offered us a barn to sleep in, but there was no hay and the thought of bedding down in wet clothes was distinctly uninviting. He suggested that his wife should knock up the owner of a telephone. I went with her to find a fascinating and kindly little man who possessed the magical power to communicate with Bozel. He set to, vigorously winding the handle of his antique instrument while at the same time trying to hold two separate ear pieces to his ears. Somehow he achieved contact and while we waited for a taxi to fetch us he insisted on my joining him in a glass of wine—we were very soon on common ground. He too was a mountaineer and knew the region well: he was not at all surprised that we could not find our way over the pass in the mist, and our experience was by no means uncommon. This heartened me, for I thought I had made a mess of it.

When the taxi arrived I went to dislodge Beryl and Anthony from the cheesemaker's and after thanking him for his help we were driven down to Bozel.

It was almost bizarre to see the chef in his tall white hat, and spotlessly laundered jacket and apron, step out of the inn door to help us inside with our loads. We must have looked a pretty disreputable bunch, as the rain had failed to remove much of the yellow clay from my face, hair and trousers. The chef's main concern was to please: of course we could have a hot meal, although it was nine o'clock—would we like to go to our rooms first? We were all too tired to realize that this was a tactful hint to clean ourselves up. It had been fifteen hours since we left the Félix Faure hut, and we had had very little food.

"No thanks," we chorused, "wine and food first."

Fortunately there were no other guests in the dining-room and the waitress, although alarmed by our appearance, soon began to treat it as a joke. After plenty of wine and an excellent meal, we were suddenly hit by waves of fatigue, and after a luxurious soak in hot baths we were almost asleep before falling into bed.

Next morning our clothes had dried on the radiator, and I spent some time removing the yellow clay from my trousers with Beryl's hairbrush. It was no longer raining but the leaden sky confirmed our decision to come down, as conditions in the mountains must still be very poor. Anthony had only four days of his holiday left and we decided to go round to Tignes by rail and 'bus, which was an absurd distance to travel when it would have been but half a mile or so over the mountains. But like the Col de Borgne, the Col du Palet had eluded us and this was reverse number two.

I find that the acme of appreciation is contrast: the luxury of hot baths in hotels compared with a cupful of water to wash in in the huts; the delectable meals in the valley contrasted with the rough mountain fare; and so the journey through the valleys on the way to Tignes were highlighted by the throes of early spring—the green fresh fields and newly blossoming trees made an exciting theme and it was in a way like stoking up to meet—well—come what may. Perhaps this is why we do it.

Tignes to Valgrisanche

I had not visited Tignes before and it was impossible to say whether the old village had been submerged by the hydro-electric dam which now spanned the barren reaches of a beautiful wild valley, but there it stood, ugly and surrounded by a hideous clutter of rubbish. Our 'bus driver sensed our recoil from spending the night in one of the barrack-like hotels and suggested that we went a little further along Lake Chevril to Villaret, which would be a nearer starting point from which to continue our journey. He acted as spokesman for us, and achieved from an old crone a reluctant assent for us to have a room with three beds, but food, she said, was out of the question. We had our own provisions so we accepted her extortionate terms. We made use of the rest of the afternoon by exploring the beginning of our next start and climbed up the valley. The sugar-loaf of the Grande Motte was clear of cloud, and we saw with chagrin how easy the route from the Col du Palet down to Tignes would have been.

On our way down we stopped to chat with a young Parisian who lived in a nearby chalet. He gave a gloomy weather forecast, in direct contrast to what we ourselves expected, but our egoes were restored a short while later when a peasant endorsed our views. Whichever was correct, the decision lay solely with us. Our aim was Valgrisanche, an ambitious target for one day, with an eight-hour climb followed by a very long walk after we had descended from the higher regions.

Anthony's alarm watch woke us and at three o'clock next morning, although life is said to be at its lowest ebb at that time of day, our spirits rose. Outside it was delightfully fresh and as we put on our skis the first flush of dawn lit the sky, as though there was an invisible fire over the mountains. Wispy clouds turned rosy and quite suddenly the higher peaks were touched with gold—gone were the clouds: the prediction of the Parisian had been wrong. We climbed for nearly four hours before stopping for breakfast. By the time we had reached the Col de la Rhème Golette at eleven o'clock we felt enough sweat was pouring off us to melt the snow beneath us. The snow had softened sufficiently to cake beneath our skis and this had stopped them from sliding forwards as we climbed, which meant that we had to lift our feet and skis for every step forward—and my word! were the skis heavy with the additional weight of snow dangling from their soles *(Plate 21)*. From time to time we had to bang our feet together to try to knock off the unwanted burden. At the col we paused to check our bearing. We were back in Italy and within a radius of a mile from where we stood were no fewer than fourteen peaks each over ten thousand feet and towering above us; from them glaciers flowed in different directions to form an arc of a circle separated by two rock spines. We were in the heart of a superb ski-mountaineering region which seemed little known and it would be very tempting to explore it in more detail. Ahead of us was the whole chain of the Pennine Alps in the Canton Wallis, spread out from the Grande Combin to Monte Rosa—old friends seen from a new angle—and it was a daunting thought that in three days' time we would be making our way across the length of their glaciers.

We sped down the Goletta Glacier, only to pause and look back to admire the curves of our ski-tracks swinging down the slope and glistening against the sun, before climbing the Col de Bassac Déré. A refreshing breeze revived us at the top, and ahead was our first view of Mont Blanc.

Our stomachs were empty, but they would have to wait as we must catch the snow in the same perfect condition. The broad slopes of the Glaieretta Glacier beckoned us down into a fine bowl some half-a-mile across; it was an amphitheatre bounded by a great circle of cliffs and ridges. Our abstinence was rewarded for the snow was indeed perfect as we sped across a glacier devoid of crevasses, ski-tracks, and landmarks, losing all sense of speed and distance; and it was only when I had to turn that my speed was apparent from the strain it put on my legs.

At last we were forced to halt. The glacier slope steepened and narrowed and we were soon threading our way down through an ice-fall. It required care, as there were open crevasses, but it was not difficult and we did not rope up. It was just a fascinating exercise, weaving a good line, sometimes ski-ing on the glacier, at other times rounding wide open crevasses which forced us off on to the steep slope near the rocks. Once through the ice-fall we sped on to a broad terrace which swept down a sharp incline. Anthony fell, and off came his ski—it swooped down the slope in carefree abandon, dancing, twisting, turning with increasing momentum. We held our breath. It shot in the air and, with a sudden jerk, buried itself in a snowy hummock—and it had not broken! "Phew!" said Anthony, the blood drained from his face, "thank goodness it didn't happen higher up in the ice-fall among the crevasses." Although he had a safety strap to prevent this sort of thing happening, it had broken. He scooted down on one ski until he reached the other. I thought how lucky we were: on a previous occasion when I

Plate 33. From the Glaieretta Glacier we had our first view
of Mont Blanc (seen to the left of the figure)

had been running a touring course in Bivio, I had had to descend a thousand feet to
retrieve a ski, and climb back up again to restore it to its owner.

At last we reached a broad plain with isolated bare rocks; with a simultaneous
thought we halted—food! How we needed it! We lay back in the sun. What a run it had
been, and it was amazing how good the snow had remained, considering it was nearly
the end of April. This morning had made up for our reverses and weather of the last few
days; we were back to our law of contrasts. It was after two o'clock and we still had
nearly ten miles to travel before reaching Valgrisanche, and, unwilling to leave this
valley of wild beauty, we shouldered our rucksacks, negotiated the narrow gorge,
passed some chalets and the Mario Bezzi hut belonging to the Italian Alpine Club, and
soon met a summer path. Half-exposed rocks rasped aggravatingly under our skis and
the snow petered out at Surier, a little summer village at the head of a lake. Here, we
knocked the remains of sodden snow from our skis and shouldered them once more.

The map showed Surier at the head of a long, narrow extent of water, Lake Beau-
regard, with a respectable road running the length of the lakeside for about five miles.
We would soon cover the distance, and mentally we prepared ourselves for the delights
of the valley. The lake had been dammed some time before to make a reservoir, and the
skeletons of a submerged village rose gauntly from the water as a community protest
at the outrageous cost in human terms—for money could never compensate the inhabitants for the loss of their homes where so many had been born and had lived their lives.

The map did not convey reality; we trudged along a muddy track, crossed intermit-
tently by calf-deep snowdrifts, and we climbed over spent avalanches—tiring in the
extreme as we took off our skis and put them on again with monotonous repetition,
relieved only by glimpses of star-shaped pink flowers clinging to crevices in streaming
rock walls along the roadside. We fixed our eyes on the dam ahead but it never seemed

to get nearer; when we did arrive, we saw Valgrisanche below us. Disastrous avalanches had left their marks from the previous year—decaying tips like rotting
corpses of snowy monsters littered the fields, and although tree trunks and large
branches had been sawn and neatly stacked, work still remained as much timber lay
trapped in frozen snow.

We went to quench our thirst in the village tavern, and I enquired about accommodation. "No, regrettably the inn is shut," responded the woman, then she added
encouragingly, "but there is an inn in Gerbelle—*solamente tre passi.*" Only three steps!
Beryl groaned, easing her aching limbs into a chair. It was now 6 p.m., and we had only
had two stops; it had certainly been a long day, though not much longer than I had
planned. After one more beer we were comfortably isolated from the weariness of our
legs. The three paces lengthened to half a mile and Beryl reckoned that they had been
measured in seven-leagued-boots; but it was all downhill and we only had to balance
our bodies on our legs and let gravity take charge.

Valgrisanche to Courmayeur

The Rutor was the highest mountain near Valgrisanche, about eleven-and-a-half
thousand feet high from sea level: it would mean a seven-hour climb from Gerbelle and
it would be quite a "rest day" after our previous exertions! The black-coated locals in
the inn expressed their doubts and in doing so showed just how incredibly little they
knew about the one big mountain and extensive ice-field practically on their doorstep.

As we reached a grassy shoulder next morning, the row of the Pennine Alps
greeted us once again. They glowed golden in the dawn light through a transparent
haze of many shades of blue and purple. They were now immeasurably nearer and we
could pick out details of the individual peaks of the Matterhorn and the Monte Rosa
under the cloudless sky.

We were all slightly astonished that we did not feel the effects of the previous long
day, but we had left most of our gear in the hotel and had light rucksacks—and after all
we were fit. It was a fine fresh morning and there is no doubt that weather has an effect
on the body and spirit for no known scientific reason. At the foot of the glacier we
paused for a second breakfast and looked back with satisfaction at the passes we had
crossed the day before—so far in the distance and seemingly so far in time, because
days packed with interest stretch out the hours in a miraculous way.

The glacier provided a highway to the summit, now clearly visible on the skyline,
but as we got within an hour of the top we saw the weather was breaking fast as clouds
were scudding across with the westerly wind and beginning to envelop our peak.
Unbelievable! Here we were, being overtaken for the second time in three days by a
very sudden deterioration in the weather with scarcely a preliminary warning. Yet, to
be expected, for the high mountains attract the bad weather first and we were near
Mont Blanc the highest mountain in the European Alps. As we looked around, the

Plate 34. The entire range of the Pennine Alps known as the *Haute Route* which
we would be crossing in three days' time

peaks of the Pennine Alps were already collecting their share of the gathering storm.
We might just make it, and we pressed on hot-foot to the final ridge.

The steep face of the main ridge did not afford a passage at this time of year, and we
decided to climb it from the easier, north, side. Finding a small couloir we took off our
skis and planted them very firmly in the snow, for a vicious wind was gusting round the
corner and the last thing we wanted was to see the skis blown off the mountain. We
removed our skins in readiness for a quick run down. The couloir divided the crest in
two. We had no idea which was the higher ridge, but we chose the right-hand one: if for
no other reason, it was the nearest. We scrambled up some easy rocks and snow and
hastened to the top. As so often happens, the wind here was far less fierce. From the top
is said to be one of the finest views of Mont Blanc; I turned instinctively to look for it,
hoping to take it by surprise before it could hide itself—but it was as I had feared: it was
as though Mont Blanc did not exist and there was only white cloud. Staying just long
enough to shake hands and congratulate each other, we then raced down to our skis;
the snow began to fall and we made a hasty descent with the wind behind us and we
were soon in shelter although we could see the wrack driven by wind only a short
distance above us. But it could not destroy the beautiful spring crust and this was one
of the advantages of ski-ing in spring. Just short of some chalets on the summer path
where the snow had melted I was surprised to see a snake. Although I have climbed
and skied since I was sixteen I think it was the first time I had ever seen a snake in the
Alps. It was certainly unusual to see it at this time of year, and it must have come out of

hibernation quite recently. Disturbed by our approach it slithered at speed beneath a nearby rock. We wandered slowly back to our inn, and the lateness of the day confirmed our feeling that we must indeed be getting fit.

Our trip up to Rutor had been planned originally as part of our route, because I intended crossing a pass and running down the Rutor Glacier to La Thuile, in the Val Verney, on our way to Courmayeur; but after the previous day we would have been too tired to do it in one day. However, time had caught up on us and Anthony had to return to England, so the following morning we piled into the jeep which served as the local 'bus and were carried down the lovely valley—and it was a lovely valley, sometimes narrowing to a gorge, with the river far below, then opening into glens clothed in trees of richest green with a few still in their autumn tints for contrast. Further down, patches of apple blossom reminded us that the Aosta valley was near. The freshness and fertility of the lower Val Grisanche are remarkable when one considers the adverse changes generally wrought in Alpine villages by the construction of dams, but here many tributaries join the river below the dam and thus maintain the water level. We said goodbye to Anthony at Arvier and continued on our own way towards Courmayeur. Every inch of the route to Morgex and Pré-St.-Didier was cultivated. Vines, mainly the Pinot Gris grape, flourished on every available patch of ground and at Morgex, some three thousand feet above sea level but endowed with the twin blessings of the shelter of the mountains and the warmth of the Italian sun, the vineyards must surely be the highest in Europe.

We arrived in Courmayeur with mountain appetites and in an attractive restaurant we lunched and had glasses of a refreshing crisp wine from Morgex. On enquiring about the wine I was given a most informative booklet published by the Commune, covering all aspects of the Val d'Aosta, including a long account of the local wine industry—if industry is the right word for what, at its best, is a loving art. Many of the vineyards are still in the hands of local priests—again obviously caring for man's physical as well as spiritual well-being. As we left the restaurant we could feel sultriness in the air and with little else to do we entered the museum. Unlike the Zermatt museum, there was no display of gruesome relics of mountain accidents. The storm broke while we were inside, but I was interested in the section devoted to the expeditions in the Himalayas of the Principe di Savoia, who was an explorer of note, so our short imprisonment was not unduly regretted.

Courmayeur lies at the southern foot of the Mont Blanc range. Both the towns of Chamonix in France and Courmayeur in Italy have developed over the years just because of the Mont Blanc. Every time I visit Courmayeur I find that it has succumbed even more to the tourist trade. The centre has changed very little, but it is now engulfed by an ever-rising tide of modern hotels and expensive-looking tourist shops. Since I had last visited, I found that even the mountain was not sacrosanct: it had not been able to protect itself from the *superstrada* which remorselessly carried traffic towards that feat of engineering, the world's longest road tunnel, seven miles long under the Mont Blanc Massif.

When the guide Jacques Balmat first climbed Mont Blanc in 1786 he had little idea of what an organized tourist trade he would spawn. Saussure, a naturalist, climbed it a year later with eighteen guides! Both he and Balmat achieved their expeditions under difficulties and hardships, for there were no mountain huts or railways and everything had to be carried—tents, primitive sleeping bags, blankets, food and wine—for them these mountains were first ascents. It was a discovery of the uninhabited, things of beauty, a field of research and a desire for further acquaintance, and it was only in the nineteenth century that mountaineering became a field of sport. For us to-day it is made easy—a bivouac is an unpremeditated hardship—but it was not so for them.

By 1899 tours across Mont Blanc were highly organized, and in a Bedeker of that date, which belonged to Beryl's grandfather, there is a note that "tours up Mont Blanc are conducted almost daily in summer". The guides had regulations that each traveller must take two guides (at 100 francs each) and one porter (at 50 francs daily). When food was added and an overnight stay in a hotel, the cost was considerable even at the exchange rate of 25 francs to the £. Many clients complained at the amount which their guides ate, as breakfast consisted of leg of mutton and hot wine and it was often difficult to get them moving until they had made severe inroads into the food.

Plate 35. The Grand Col Ferret with the ridge of the Grande Jorasses on the right

While waiting for Geoffrey Buckley and John Lewis to arrive, we wandered almost due north up the valley. The mountains hung high above us, visible through a fine weather haze fresh after the storm. The ragged red rocks of the Grandes Jorasses peered at us through billowing masses of white clouds but maintained the privacy of the peak. As we neared the shrine of Notre Dame de la Guerison we could see the magnificent Brenva Glacier sweeping up to Mont Blanc, its surface crinkled and seamed with countless rows of crevasses. Above our heads the great obelisk of the Aiguille Noire de Peuterey rose menacingly and possessively determined to obscure our gaze from the summit of Mont Blanc behind it. We looked north-eastwards up the Val Ferret to the Col we would cross the next day, then we returned to our hotel. Geoffrey and John had arrived from Zermatt, where they had been having a few days' ski-ing. Geoffrey we knew well from previous ski-ing holidays both in Norway and the Ortler Alps and—what is more!—he had survived. We had not met John before. It never ceases to impress me how parties manage to link up in some remote place in the mountains by arrangement but as though by chance.

The Pennine Alps

Courmayeur to Zermatt

Next morning we were away by half-past five. We had chartered a taxi to take us up the Val Ferret as far as possible, to avoid a long and profitless walk. The road was clear as far as the hamlet of Lavachey and our driver kept going, in spite of avalanche drifts crossing the road, until he could go no further.

It was a pleasant walk in the freshness of the early morning, with the steep slopes at the head of the valley gradually getting nearer. Two passes led into Switzerland: the Petit and the Grand Cols Ferret. On the far side the two valleys from them unite above La Fouly, where we intended to spend the night. We therefore had a choice; as a gully of unpromising steepness led to the Petit Col, we had no hesitation in choosing the Grand Col, which was steep enough. With some amusement I thought of Töpffer's description of crossing this very same pass in summer. He was on the path which was a bit sheer when he was seized with giddiness—an affliction which plagued him whenever there was a steep drop or a precipitous height, despite thirty years of moutaineering. He attributed it to fear, since despite it he could render useful help to a colleague in danger, on the principle that there is nothing more reassuring than being close to someone who is even more frightened! The human body and its reaction to altitude is unpredictable and no two persons are the same in their response to the thresholds of fear, fatigue or heights,

We had a damp, soggy climb threading our way between streams meandering about the valley floor, striving to keep our feet dry, but higher up, above the trees, it was more comfortable and soon the gradient, which had made Töpffer giddy, began to steepen. We kept well together and despite the easterly wind it was warm and humid, making the snow wet and rotten—it had the very smell of avalanche. We were heartily

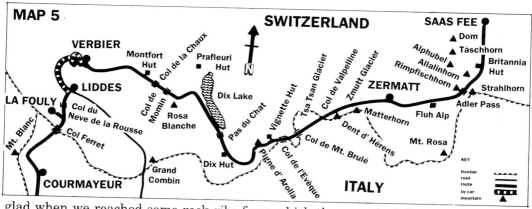

MAP 5

SWITZERLAND

SAAS FEE

VERBIER

Dom

Montfort
Hut

Col de la Chaux

Prafleuri
Hut

N

Alphubel
Täschhorn

Allalinhorn
Rimpfischhorn

Britannia
Hut

LIDDES

Dix Lake

ZERMATT

Strahlhorn

LA FOULY

Col du
Neve de la Rousse

Col de Momin

Rosa
Blanche

Pas du Chat

Vignette Hut

Tsa Tsan Glacier

Col de Valpelline

Znutt Glacier

Adler Pass

Matterhorn

Fluh Alp

Mt. Blanc

Col Ferret

Dent d' Hérens

Mt. Rosa

KEY

Pigne d'Arolla

Col de l'Eveque

Col de Mt. Brulé

frontier
road
route
by car
mountain

COURMAYEUR

Grand
Combin

Dix Hut

ITALY

glad when we reached some rock ribs from which the snow had disappeared, and we
followed them up to the col.

Plate 36. Guarding the pass was a cornice with icicles melting into water

Guarding the pass was a huge cornice streaming with water: the combination of
hot sun and warm wind was having a dramatic effect. It was a warning that most of the
snow around us might be in a similar state, saturated with melt water which would
loosen the bonds between the snow crystals—wet snow avalanches were imminent. We
skirted round the cornice without difficulty and paused for a rest, as trackmaking in
wet snow can be very exhausting. We looked back and to our disgust Mont Blanc still
lay thickly in cloud, although its great Peuterey ridge emerged from time to time.
Shelley must have seen it under similar circumstances when he wrote:-

> "For the very spirit fails
> Driven like a homeless cloud from steep to steep
> That vanishes among the viewless gales!
> Far, far above, piercing the infinite sky,
> Mont Blanc appears—still snowy and serene—
> Its subject mountains their unearthly forms
> Pile around it, ice and rock; broad vales between
> Of frozen floods, unfathomable deeps,
> Blue as the overhanging heaven, that spread
> And wind among the accumulated steeps;
> A desert peopled by storms alone."

Away to the east the Grand Combin, our next project, was visible through a haze surmounted by great turrets and battlements of cumulus, holding the threat of thunder. I looked at the mountain, trying to map out our future route—it would lie a little below its face—a task made more difficult by the haze and cloud.

We could not afford to wait long, for every minute the snow would be getting more dangerous and the valley sides on the eastern slope of the pass were steep. Wet snow avalanches usually start from a single point, very often below rocks where it is particularly warm and fan out like a pear carrying the whole depth of snow with them. The chances of survival if you are buried in one are remote, as there is no air in the water-saturated snow, to breathe and maintain life.

We were therefore pleasantly surprised to find the east-facing slopes were in good condition and we sped down to the valley confidently. Big avalanches had already fallen, clearing the upper slopes of their wet soggy burden and the more recent snow-falls were well on their way to turning into good spring crust. The danger of new avalanches falling was remote, though there was no point in tempting Providence by dawdling.

Lower down, we relaxed in the sun while taking a belated lunch, and I studied the route to the Col des Planards which we intended to cross the next day, on our way to Bourg St. Pierre, which would be the starting point from which to reach the Grand Combin. It was but a short run down into the valley of the Drance and here we met a primitive road, flanked by fields white with spring crocus. Along the way we met a frontier guard, for we were now in Switzerland, and he casually enquired about our route and conditions—more as a fellow mountaineer than in a professional capacity.

The inn at Ferret was shut, which forced us another mile down to La Fouly. It was immaterial, but it would add to next day's climb. To our aggravation, however, the two inns had been taken over by a television team and after lengthy enquiries we eventually found a dormitory where we could sleep. I made a mental note that when the trip was completed I would have to list the different types of sleeping quarters Beryl and I have utilized!

Soon after dawn we started for the Col des Planards. The conditions were totally wretched; a nasty penetrating south-east wind was blowing, bringing masses of low cloud which swirled round the lower slopes and obscured the summits. It was a depressing outlook, heightened by occasional flurries of rain and we were glad to reach the upper snowfields and put on our skis. Clouds pressed down on us, obscuring the pass which lay somewhere in the gloom above. It looked steep and before long we were carrying our skis. As though to add to our troubles, a vital bit of Geoffrey's ski binding popped out in the snow. Unlike Anthony's lost climbing plate, which was about three inches square, this was a small ball-bearing about a quarter-inch in diameter. It was heavy and would bury itself in the snow and searching for it would be like looking for a needle in a haystack. But our luck was in, as Geoffrey found the missing part buried in a footprint.

It seemed unlikely that we would strike the pass and I halted uncertainly. For a fleeting moment I could see below us slopes which I knew led to an easier pass—the Col du Névé de la Rousse. This would take us over, though bring us further down the valley, but we were in no mind to consider such a disadvantage. We hurried down and then started climbing again while we could still see. A broken black cliff loomed up through the mist and I consulted the map yet again. This was splendid: the cliff, which bounded the far side of the pass, would lead us to it. There was a sudden brightness and the clouds peeled away to show the pass guarded by a cornice standing out against a clear blue sky. It was not for long, but at least we had a "fix" and once more the pass reappeared as though playing a game of hide-and-seek.

We turned away from the blasting wind and the black wall of cloud behind us. A broad valley stretched out to hazy green depths below, bathed in sun. Pursued by malevolent gusts of wind we hastened down until we found beside a stream a peaceful place to have lunch. A meandering path took us through woods and open fields to Liddes, where we caught a 'bus up the short distance to Bourg St. Pierre, on the St. Bernard Pass.

Next day, our destination—the Grand Combin, a great ice and snow massif over thirteen thousand feet high—had collected the bad weather in force. The conditions were hardly right for crossing the Col Senodon from the Valsorey hut down to the Cabana Chanrion, because the exit from this hut is difficult owing to fixed ropes and should only be attempted in good snow and reasonable weather. As this seemed unlikely to improve, a more suitable alternative would be to continue our journey from the Mont Fort hut, above Verbier, and rejoin the route to Zermatt by an interesting yet more feasible way. It was a decision which I made with reluctance, for my previous attempts had always been thwarted by similar weather conditions and it was a route which I was very anxious to explore—it is one of the starting points of the famous *Haute Route.*

Our journey round to Verbier was memorable for the oppressive heat in the valley and an unbelievably bad and expensive lunch. A cable car was there to run up to Les Atteles late in the afternoon, from where it would be an easy run down and then a climb to the hut. It was still scorching hot in Verbier and our sacks were heavy as we were carrying food for five days—we needed at least three days to reach Zermatt and a margin in case we were hut-bound by bad weather: we did not know whether or not in this highly-popular and frequented ski-route all the huts would have resident guardians who might provide food. I felt that to walk up, instead of taking the cable car, would be carrying purism too far.

So late in the day we were the sole passengers, but standing on the platform was a knot of workmen. One of them had a small marmot on a string and although showing an interest in the little animal, the workman was hauling it about unthinkingly. I felt sorry for it, and sought to comfort it by stroking its ears. Suddenly, as fast as light, it turned round and snapped at my thumb with razor-sharp teeth. Taken aback, I stood with blood dripping on to the wooden boards. I had imagined that the marmot was tame—but no, as the Italian owner remarked: "I caught him only two days ago." It was futile to explain that it was an act of cruelty to keep a wild animal like that, for the man was quite unimaginative; but looking at the blood on my hand, I was heartened that the sharp teeth would soon make short work of the string and allow the animal to escape.

We set off across a steep slope to the hut. It had been lying in full sun. Serious avalanches had already fallen, but small snow slides constantly crossed our path—Beryl rode across one, for all the world like surfing on snow.

So near Verbier, the hut was crowded and the living room thick with smoke and heat from accumulated bodies. The guardian, presiding over a cooking stove, greeted us—if a grunt can be properly called a greeting—and half resentfully made it clear: space would be allotted if it could be found. We fled outside to wait. The sun was setting and spectacular banners of transparent clouds, tinged with blue and purple, lay over the great chain of mountains which culminated in Mont Blanc. It grew cold and we returned regretfully into the heat and smoke.

Ahead of us we had a long distance, which involved crossing four passes to the Cabane de Dix, and we were anxious to get away early to allow for any hazards on the journey. There were no self-catering facilities in the Mont Fort hut and we hung about impatiently waiting for the guardian to rouse himself and give us breakfast. He eventually arrived sleepily and much put out because we unreasonably were not returning to Verbier with the rest of the crowd, starting much later; but we got away by five. The morning was beautifully fresh and as we climbed, I cast sidelong glances towards the great ridges of the Mont Blanc as they cast off their mauve haze and sprang to life, one by one, at the golden touch of the early sun. We soon reached the Col de la Chaux and basked in the sunshine before running down to a blue lake. Across the valley rose the snowy pyramid of the Rosa Blanche tinged with early morning gold. A short run down and another easy climb took us to the Col de Momin, where we rested, lying back against sun-warmed rocks. The Rosa Blanche was now much nearer, and within an hour we stood below its final slopes. Leaving our heavy rucksacks in the snow we felt weightless and seemed to gallop up the final ridge to the summit. I remembered the fantastic view I had enjoyed on the last occasion, but the thrill was not to be repeated. The Grand Combin was still wreathed in cloud which obstinately refused to clear, but we contented ourselves with the little white pyramid of the Combin de Corbassière, which is two thousand feet lower and normally overshadowed by its great neighbour and is therefore overlooked. For one moment we all went mad, exhilarated by our achievement: Geoffrey, John and I imagined we were the Three Musketeers and playfully fenced with our ski-sticks on the peak! So free, without the weight of sacks, it was a carefree run down crossing ripples of snow to the laughter and loud hail of "Water!" as in a sailing race, when the point of collision came near. It was fun.

We stopped for a rest and to pick up our sacks. It was not yet one o'clock, the day was young, and it was a pity to waste a good afternoon. I put the alternatives to Geoffrey and John: should we go down to the Prafleurie hut which was privately owned and might not be open, or should we press on to the Dix hut, a good four hours away? We were enjoying ourselves, the weather was fine, and we did not anticipate any difficulties, so we agreed to go on to the Dix hut. We ran down the Prafleurie Glacier

Plate 37. The Rosa Blanche: it was now much nearer and within an hour we stood below its final slopes

and climbed a little pass about nine thousand feet high which looked over the Dix lake—nearly five miles long and now covered with shattered green ice. The track beside it, which looked so enticing from above, proved to be muddy and encumbered with sodden patches of snow and the going was not easy.

John began to lag behind and we had to wait for him from time to time. I asked him if he was tired.

"No!" he said adamantly, "I prefer to go at my own pace."

At the end of the lake was a steep pass, the Pas du Chat, which needed the cat's wary tread to avoid dislodging a crazy mass of boulders and ourselves down the mountain. We waited for John at the top. It had taken us some five hours to cover the length of the lake. I was beginning to get anxious as our waits were becoming longer and daylight was waning fast. We were at the foot of the glacier, and although it is not particularly crevassed we had to travel up it to find the hut; and I had no mind to spend the night sitting on cubes of ice if we failed to find the hut in the dark. I looked round—there was no reasonable shelter and the snow was too sparse and sodden to build a satisfactory bivouac.

Geoffrey and I sat down to discuss what to do: he was nonplussed. He knew John well, and had done a good deal of walking with him in the Welsh mountains, when he had always managed to keep up a cracking pace; furthermore, up till now he had always kept up well with our party. Why had he slowed down? It was true we had had a long day, we had been travelling for thirteen hours, crossed four passes, and never dropped below seven-and-a-half thousand feet, but he was physically fit and insistent that he was not tired.

I cursed myself for not having realized the cause before: at home he lived at sea level, and he had not been at any great height until he slept the night in the Mont Fort hut, which is nearly eight thousand feet above sea level. The Rosa Blanche, which we had just climbed, was eleven thousand feet, and the "fencing" match on the peak and climbing the nine-thousand-foot pass had tipped the balance. Whilst he was physically fit, it wwas still possible for him to be unacclimatized to height, because the body needs time to manufacture more red blood cells to carry oxygen at the lower barometric pressures of altitude; and of course exertion uses up oxygen more rapidly.

This mild mountain sickness is due to oxygen lack which assails ski-tourers rather than piste skiers because of the added exertion of walking uphill. Each individual has his own symptoms—some have lack of energy, others nausea, sickness or a blinding headache; but the commonest symptom is irritability or a temporary personality change which I had frequently encountered when running the touring courses for the Ski Club of Great Britain. I often teased Beryl that I had no need to look at the altimeter at ten thousand feet because she always lost her temper until she became acclimatized, and on the Dufourspitz—which is thirteen thousand feet—she admitted that she felt sapped of energy and did not care if she fell off the mountain! I was mentally glad that she had become acclimatized soon after we left the Valle Stretta, as out of a party of four two people with mountain sickness might have caused real trouble.

Ten thousand feet is the generally accepted level when the body begins to protest, although it naturally varies in different individuals, and the higher you go the longer it takes to acclimatize. The symptoms pass off rapidly even after dropping down a few hundred feet; nevertheless the sufferer is often mortified by the disturbance caused when he reverts to normal after rest.

Apart from oxygen lack, there is probably another factor—a disturbance in body fluids. Both Beryl and I have noticed that when we arrive in the Alps we pass very little urine for the first three or four days and our feet and legs swell; then urine is suddenly passed and the swelling disappears. A temporary accumulation of fluid in the brain may explain the headache and personality change, as it rapidly passes off if a diuretic pill is taken to excrete the excess fluid, and some doctor skiers I know take a diuretic pill the moment they arrive in the Alps as a precaution against the headache.

Although all this provided the theoretical explanation, it did not produce the immediate solution, as we were making things worse for John by climbing higher; but we had burned our boats now—it was too late to turn back to the Prafleurie hut (and in any case it might be shut): we must press on to the Dix hut but the problem was how to get John to move faster.

I suddenly thought of the Ski Touring Leaders' Course which Beryl and I had attended. One of the students was similarly afflicted at eleven thousand feet—he said he was not tired, yet he was lagging behind. Hermann Steuri, the famous Grindlewald guide, who was in charge of the course, said: "It's a form of mild mountain sickness—there's only one thing to do: insult him—it always calls forth a spark of energy."

It was worth a try. I was very rude to John, suggesting he left his rucksack, and we would come back for it the next day. To my astonishment it had a miraculous effect. More than a spark was kindled: he picked up his rucksack and shot up the glacier like a scalded cat. The boot was now on the other foot, and it was we who were trying to keep up, and he was soon out of sight. In the Mont Fort hut I had dropped my torch and broken the bulb, and unfortunately John was unaware that he had taken the only functioning torch with him.

There was no moon, and by now it was pitch black, even the snow seemed black: we would not be able to see any crevasses. Neither could I see to navigate with compass and altimeter. However, St. Jude, the Patron Saint of lost causes, must have been with us. There were some old frozen ski tracks which we followed by listening to the scrape of our skis in the ruts: the sounds were different when we strayed.

We came across John trying to make a bivouac on the glacier. I looked at my altimeter by the light of his torch—even in good weather the hut is not easy to find, but judging from our height we must be nearly there.

Suddenly Beryl cried out—she had seen a light high above us; it had wavered and gone out. Surely the hut could not be up there? Clouds hung low over our heads, played on with an occasional flicker of lightning—and we heard thunder—it could have been that.

I racked my brains in an effort to remember the exact position of the hut, as the 1:50,000 map shows little detail. We felt our way round the rocky headland. Where could the hut be? It must certainly be near at hand.

Plate 38. The Dix Hut: surely the hut could not be up there

"There it is," said Beryl, pointing upwards at a large shadow.

"Just a big rock," was our reply, as it is so easy to be deceived in darkness. John scrambled a little way up the moraine.

"Yes, it's the hut all right," he shouted.

We followed upwards, scrabbling up loose boulders, as we could find no path. Soon the hut really did loom up. There were no lights, and all was silent. We pushed open the door and entered. Our throats were parched and we crept into the kitchen to find water. Quietly the guardian appeared. He had just gone to bed when he heard us come in, but he made us welcome by bringing glasses of foaming beer.

"Much better than water," he implied.

He was not surprised that the journey had taken us so long, because the melting snowfield makes the going harder. It was his torch which Beryl had spotted, as it was his custom to walk on to the promontory overlooking the glacier and flash a light before going to bed. This was for the benefit of any belated mountaineers, as he was aware of how difficult it was to find the hut.

We gave John a diuretic pill to get rid of any excess fluid in his body, and after a night's rest he was back to his normal cheerful self. The diagnosis of mountain sickness had obviously been correct, and so we decided to take the day off to give him more time to acclimatize fully.

I sat outside the hut and saw the minuscule specks of skiers descending the glaciers and running towards the Pas de Chevres, a cleft in the rock which leads down to the village of Arolla, and as I watched with my spyglass I saw them climbing up to the pass on iron ladders which have been put in the rocks, as they would be difficult to climb with heavy sacks and skis. You only find this sort of thing on very frequented routes.

The guardian came out to share the afternoon sunshine with us. He was a mine of information regarding the local mountains. He told us of experiments he had made in choosing a suitable source of water for the hut, which would provide a good supply throughout the year. Many of these guardians have a true sense of vocation in serving, helping and advising their guests; most of them are retired guides and closely understand the problems of mountaineers. It is only when the guests are few that they have a chance to relax; for the rest of the time they are constantly busy, and a hut full of mountaineers all coming and going at different hours must be a true trial of patience.

We spun out the remaining hours looking at the hut book: in it are inscribed the names of those using the hut, with their expeditions and comments. It is always fascinating to see who has been doing what during the previous seasons, and to search for names of friends and climbing acquaintances, and there is usually some comment or other to add to the amusement. We did not have far to search, for there was some man apologizing for breaking the axe, ruefully complaining at the hardness of the wood!

The guardian cooked us a splendid meal of goulash and served us with plenty of red wine: we were well stoked up to continue our journey next morning to the Pigne d'Arolla and then down to the Vignette Hut.

We were away by five. Banks of very heavy purple cloud hung in the east. They threatened no immediate evil, but held hidden menace like the low warning growl of an animal against intruders. The easy climb up the Glacier du Cheilon was followed by a steep climb beside an ice-fall into a little plateau. Straight ahead of us spectacular broken ice-cliffs hung from the face of the Pigne d'Arolla. They looked intimidating, but this was not our way for the mountain can be climbed from the rear up gentle snow slopes, as is so often the case. We put on crampons and climbed up to the lefthand side, which offered a safe but impressive route and John was climbing well. Clouds had been

Plate 39. A crevasse: these may descend hundreds of feet into the glacier

gathering quietly and we could no longer see the summit nor the unnamed pass which we had to cross to reach the Otemma Glacier. The peak was only twenty minutes away and perversely we climbed the final stretch without even discerning it. The slope finally flattened out, the height of 12,372 feet corresponded with my altimeter, so we reckoned we must be there at the top—perched forlornly like despondent chickens, surrounded by whiteness. But even so there was an immense satisfaction in having captured a peak and scored off the weather.

Mist looks much the same anywhere and we skied over to the crossing point to reach the upper slopes of the Otemma Glacier, then as we descended it the visibility improved. The glacier was comfortably steep and old ski tracks were of great morale value; we crossed and re-crossed them in the mist. I remember one hasty stop just above a crevasse which almost spanned the width of the glacier. It was all of twenty feet wide and very deep—the edges curved over into the abyss shading into blue, navy blue, and then to black in the depths. It could be as much as two hundred and fifty feet deep—who knows, except a victim whom it might have claimed but would he have lived to tell the story? We skirted round the crevasse and sought a way down to the valley because of the steepness of the slope. There had been new snow and at one point my skis cut through the surface and set off a small powder snow avalanche below me. This is one of the commonest ways they start, but fortunately there was no other person in the way to become involved. This type of avalanche is not sodden with water like the wet snow avalanche we met near the Col Ferret. New snow contains air; it is in this type of avalanche that a victim stands the best chance of survival.

We saw the Vignette hut perched on a rocky headland with a sheer drop of about a thousand feet to the glacier below—it is not exactly the place for sleep-walking! It stood out, surrounded by a sea of glaciers and fragmented splits of ice made into fanciful translucent shapes against the gloomy sky. Carrion birds circled below the headland waiting for droppings from the kitchen and the "thunder boxes" which are precariously and draughtily poised over the abyss. However, the other approach to the hut is an easy four hours' walk up the glacier from Arolla, which is one of the highest and most popular ski-ing resorts in the Canton Wallis. There were only four other skiers in the hut, a party of friendly Bavarians who had come up from the Chaurion hut. They, too, had had an attempt on the Grand Combin but had turned back and decided to return to Zermatt.

We had now officially joined the classic "High Level Route" across the Pennine Alps which is an expedition that even some hardened piste skiers have an ambition to undertake. The guardian warned us that as it was Saturday there would be an influx of people from Arolla, and he quickly allotted us bunks in the dormitory. It was as well, because during the afternoon a constant stream of skiers arrived, as he had predicted, and they overcrowded the small living room.

It was a clear star-lit night and I was hopeful that our journey to Zermatt would be uneventful. No sooner were we asleep, however, than a noisy unpleasant party of Swiss invaded our dormitory. Not only did they trample around the room in heavy hut boots, banging doors as they moved about, but they started a noisy conversation and it was only after protests from the other occupants, including ourselves, that their voices subsided into a half-complaining mutter. How we longed for the other huts where we had known solitude!

Plate 40. The Vignette hut is built on a rocky ridge above an impressive drop to the glacier below—not a place for sleepwalking

At 3 a.m. the cry "All parties for Zermatt!" awoke us; it was like announcing the departure of a train and even at that hour it struck me as being comic. Three parties, the Bavarians, a French party and ourselves, assembled rather crossly at breakfast, since 3 a.m. is hardly an exhilarating hour to start the day, but we all had a long journey ahead of us.

Our day—if it could be called such! started in brilliant moonlight which picked out clearly the undulations and hummocks. The air was crisp and fresh, the snow squeaked under our boots—it was in perfect condition. We slipped on our skis and sped like demons down to the valley floor, our speed enhanced by the surrounding darkness. It was so exciting that we felt like thieves stealing their booty without getting caught. What a wonderful way to start a journey.

We halted and put on our skins just as the dawn was breaking across the Rhône valley to the north of us. The peaks of the western "tail" of the Bernese Oberland began to catch the light reflected from the sky, glowing orange from the still invisible sun. Horizontal bands of black cloud added to the theatrical effect, which might have been staged especially for us. Yet hanging above Mont Collon, the moon was high, like some ethereal lantern, disappearing and re-appearing once more as we climbed in the shadow of the peak. We had been first to leave the hut and as we threaded our way through an ice-fall I prayed that I would make no mistakes in the route, as that would be ignominious in the presence of the other nationalities! As we gained height a little pink cloud like a translucent flamingo's wing hovered over the pass—the Col d'Eveque—and as we reached it the sun was born and cast long shadows of our bodies

Plate 41. Col d'Eveque: dawn was just breaking

across the snow. We paused to look back; there we saw the Pigne d'Arolla for the last time—a snowy pyramid, coldly aloof in the early dawn without a cloud, supported at its base by the Otemma Glacier like frozen surf: how different from yesterday! Around us lay the confusion of peaks and ridges of the Pennine Alps, but my gaze was riveted on the Matterhorn, fifteen thousand feet high and standing alone, poised like a sea-lion waiting for food such as lives it had claimed; a collar of cloud swirled around its neck, a source of sudden storms, lightning and snow. It was a mountain feared in the last century by peasants and guides alike, convinced of the presence of djinns and effreets which hurled down rocks; a restless mountain; the last of the great alpine peaks to be scaled.

Plate 42. The descent from the Col d'Eveque into the Arolla Valley

Meanwhile the other parties had passed us, and it was time for us to be gone as well: I hoped that it would not turn into an international race. Despite the fact that it was now the middle of May, we surprisingly skied on powder snow down to the mainstream of the Arolla Glacier. Once more we halted and put on skins to climb the Col de Mont Brulé, a small indentation in the ridge which lay ahead, and the Bavarians, who were now in the lead, were making towards it. It was baking hot, the sky clear blue; it was a pity that none of us marked the position of the Col more carefully, for as we climbed clouds suddenly billowed over the pass and cascaded down towards us. The air struck suddenly chill and within a few minutes we had put on pullovers and anoraks. It was a curious sensation. We could still see down the sunny Arolla glacier, the pale disc of the sun hovered above us, and we caught occasional glimpses of blue sky.

Plate 43. Col de Mont Brulé. As we set off clouds began to tower behind the Col
and cascade towards us

I had a feeling that the Bavarian party had struck off too far to the right and before long they returned saying they had reached the Col de la Tsa de Tsan which would have taken them into the wrong valley. We consulted the map with the French and bore away to the left. Suddenly the clouds parted and we saw some old ski tracks leading up to the pass. We soon collected together on the top, as though an intangible bond had formed between us, as we all had something to contribute to the collective strength. While waiting for the last man to arrive, I wandered around the col and found an old bivouac hole where someone had been caught out in bad weather. I could well imagine what a cold night he had passed, which would add to the anxiety of wondering what sort of weather the next day would bring and how long his food (if he had had any) would last.

There was a slight movement in the mist, which began to clear, and we started down the slope anxious to take the advantage of the lead. Suddenly we found ourselves in a sun-drenched valley free from cloud. The Tsa de Tsan glacier clings to the side of the mountains to form a semi-circular bowl. It was a spectacular amphitheatre formed by a fine crest running from the Dent d'Herens and culminating in a series of peaks, all close on thirteen thousand feet high, before falling away into the upper Italian valleys. This was the place for lunch—and the other parties thought so too, but we separated once more into our little national groups: to preserve our individuality? National behaviour is a strange thing!

Plate 44. The Tsa de Tsan glacier clings to the side of the mountains
to form a semi-circular bowl

We now had to cross the glacier to reach our third pass, the Col de Valpelline, and the French took the lead. They found their way skilfully and without a pause through the mist-enshrouded upper slopes, where once more we found ourselves all together. The next stretch lay down the Stockji glacier which leads into the Smutt glacier at the base of the Matterhorn and is heavily crevassed. On the col the Bavarians decided to take the lead and roped themselves together, since it would be easy to fall down one of these crevasses in the mist. The rope would check the distance of the victim's fall and then hopefully be used to haul him out. The rest of us followed in their tracks unroped. There were several sets of crevasses which we all skilfully avoided and we were soon out of the cloud; the spine of the Matterhorn suddenly appeared floating above us. Off with the rope and we were all running freely. We were approaching the Matterhorn from the famous west side—the squatting rump of the lion; above us was the Col de Lion from where Whymper had had seven unsuccessful attempts to scale the mountain.

All difficulties passed, our parties separated in the same way as they had been drawn together. The Zmutt Glacier was relatively flat, as it had receded considerably and the melting snout was pitted with "mill races", those holes through which water rushed turbulently. The snow around was speckled grey with chips of grit and ground-up rock which had been mostly thrust to the sides to form the high banks of moraine which gave some idea of the glacier's original height. These were the aftermath of centuries of erosion by the ice on the valley's floor. We took off our skis and trod carefully over rocks polished smooth by the glacier now gone, and we picked our way through tiny streams which meandered about to feed tufts of grass and spring flowers. We soon reached the chalets of Stafel and it seemed a good place to take a short rest before walking down to Zermatt.

I suppose the Matterhorn was my favourite mountain, and I had climbed it with Felix Biner when I was a medical student, before I was married. Instinctively I looked up at it, for it was from here that Edward Whymper had studied the profile of its east face, to see if it would provide an easier way for his eighth attempt on the summit. I pointed out to Beryl the difficulties which had beset him in his previous efforts as he had always tackled it from the west side—the lion's rump. What we saw from here was the east face lying back at an angle of 40°, which was not nearly so steep as it appeared face-on in the classical photographs. The stratified rocks sloped obliquely and almost formed a staircase from this side, whereas on the west the rocks overhung. Nowadays the ascent is made easy by the presence of fixed ropes over the more difficult places. I could not but admire Whymper's fanatical and dogged persistence, and it was only tragic that the final successful ascent had become an international race and that Whymper's party—which was an amalgamation of three English parties—was far too large for safety. When Whymper reached the summit he peered over; he saw the Italian guide Carrel (who was the only other man besides himself who really believed that the Matterhorn could be scaled) with six other Italians climbing up from the Italian Col de Lion side. He shouted to them to show that he arrived there first, but as they took no notice he hurled down rocks on them until they fled. When the Italians reached the valley they blamed the spirits on top of the Matterhorn for throwing the rocks.

But this was not all. On the descent, Croz—one of the two guides—was leading and Hadow, the weakest member of the party, was behind him. Hadow slipped and pulled himself, Croz, Hudson and Douglas off the mountain to their deaths. The rope between them broke, leaving Whymper and the two Taugwalders (one of whom was also a guide) to face the enquiry in Zermatt.

It is greatly to Carrel's credit that he successfully climbed the difficult Italian route from the west side three days later, despite Whymper's seven unsuccessful attempts.

We decided to spend the night at the Bahnhof Hotel in Zermatt. It is an institution of note for all climbers and was run by the guide Bernard Biner for many years, providing a warm welcome, friendship and advice for mountaineers from all over the world. Beside a number of bedrooms, it has dormitories and a kitchen for climbers who do not wish to maintain an expensive hotel room while they are in the mountains. Sadly, Bernard died some years ago, but the Bahnhof was still run on exactly the same lines by his sister Paula, a lady of great charm who continued the same spirit of homeliness and friendship. She told us that no-one had been across the *Haute Route* for several days on account of the weather. We had made it just in time: already the sky was covered in a blanket of high cloud and next day all was grey and the Matterhorn had vanished. What is Zermatt without the Matterhorn?

I took the opportunity to call on Felix Biner, the old guide who had taken me up the Matterhorn before the War. He was now in his eighties, hale and hearty, and still went into his beloved mountains to climb a minor peak or two. We were equally delighted to see each other and over a glass of wine spent a long time talking about the climbs we had made together. It seemed strange how he could recall details of minor incidents that had occurred so long ago. No-one can deny the spirit of comradeship and under-standing which can exist between professional and amateur which is based on mutual respect; it is a pity that present-day economics have made it so difficult for amateurs to employ guides for one or two weeks, as they did in the past, for they are now denied these agreeable lasting friendships. Beryl, who had been shopping in Zermatt, came in later to meet Felix, bringing with her a magnificent alarm watch—a thing I had wanted for years. No longer would I have the anxiety of oversleeping in the huts, which makes the last hour a fitful pretence of sleep, a dozing wakefulness. Old Felix was delighted that I had a wife who could share my interests.

Next day, although the Matterhorn still remained obstinately in cloud, the great ridges of the Mischabelhorn appeared cloudless and plentifully adorned with new snow, and Paula told us that it was locally regarded as a yardstick: for once it was clear, the weather was likely to change for the better. We would now be leaving behind the *mont, vallée, col, glacier* and *cabane* of French mountaineering but find instead *horn, tal, joch, gletscher* and *hutte* of the German-speaking Swiss at Zermatt alongside the Ita-lian *punte, valle, passo, ghiacciaio* and *rifugio* when we consulted the map.

Zermatt to Saas Fee

Saas Fee was our final goal for this year and my original intention had been to stay at the Monte Rosa (otherwise known as the Bétemps) Hut. It lies in a superb situation above Zermatt and at the foot of Monte Rosa and we had used it several times to climb the mountain in the past. I had my doubts as to whether Beryl would be willing to tackle it once again—she had suffered so badly from the cold on the last occasion, and a cold mountain it is, surrounded closely by many peaks over thirteen thousand feet and itself the second highest mountain after Mont Blanc. However, in view of the uncer-tainty of the weather, I decided to take the direct route up the Findeln Glacier and over the Adler pass. The Fluhalp Inn was closed but we managed to get the key in order to spend the night there. Geoffrey and John decided to take the cable car up to Blauherd so as to save a three-hour walk and we gave them our skis and sacks and walked up the snow-free summer path. It was wonderful to be unencumbered with baggage and we remarked how difficult it was to alter our walking rhythm, as we had both become so accustomed to carrying heavy loads. We met the others, shouldered our sacks and found it surprisingly easy reverting to our old rhythm. We unlocked the Inn and soon had the wood stove burning, but ominous growls of thunder and flashes of lightning lit the sky as we crawled into our bunks.

A buzzing on my wrist early next morning got us on the move and we soon cleaned up the Inn. We all have our altars, and for a moment I stood outside looking about me. Strangely, the Matterhorn had shed its shroud to bid us adieu. Memories brought back sentiments of the happy hours Beryl and I had spent ski-ing here and climbing some of these vast gigantic peaks—Castor, Pollux, Monte Rosa, the Stralhorn. Every mountaineer has his special mountain—even Christian Almer, the famous guide who had climbed most of the peaks in the Alpine Chain, had his cherished mountain, the Wetterhorn in the Bernese Oberland; at the age of seventy he, and his wife aged seventy-one, ascended it on their Golden Wedding Anniversary—perhaps I will take Beryl up the Matterhorn on ours!

We walked along the lateral crest of moraine above the Findeln glacier searching for a way down, as it was strewn with boulders and ankle-twisting, half-frozen mud; and being heavily laden we took added care over a short scramble which in summer time would be no inconvenience to any mountaineer. Once on the glacier it was comfortable walking, though I constantly stopped to test with my ice-axe the security of the snow bridges spanning the many crevasses. All of a sudden the wind rose and feathery cirrus covered the sky. I looked across to Monte Rosa but it was invisible in an enormous bank of lowering cloud—we were in for a storm. A low rumble of thunder echoed across the glacier, ricocheting between the peaks. I took a quick bearing on the Adler pass, but the first snow flakes fell before I could put the map away. Clouds steadily outflanked us and visibility was down to a hundred yards. The rumble of thunder came nearer and the electrical atmosphere charged up rapidly—the storm reached us. We had been climbing on crampons, because the underlying snow was crusted and hard, and carrying our skis; but some of us had metallic skis and even the ski bindings began to sing in a sinister way. We put our skis on as the electrical tension built up and crackled and thundered around us: we saw no reason to act as lightning conductors. There was nowhere to shelter, and what could I do with the ice-axe which continued to supply me with unwanted background music, attached as it was to the rucksack on my back? I tried to be objective as I noticed how the pitch of the singing note increased with the intensity of the storm and I hoped that the risk of being struck by lightning on the glacier itself would be less than it would have been had I been high up on the pass. Suddenly the silence was intense, broken only by the hiss of our skis on the snow and the occasional squeak of our bindings. The slope steepened abruptly and we took off our skis. Silence, yes, but not for long—a sudden gusty wind blew down the pass which numbed our fingers even through two pairs of gloves. The visibility was down to fifty yards; were those footprints ahead?—they were, though half snowed in. We could just see the col above us—so near and yet so far—as the gusts tore at us violently, threatening to blow us off balance. With each battering we were forced to stand still in the snow steps, anchoring ourselves by planting our skis in the snow and leaning against the wind. We finally reached the pass and found two other parties sheltering behind some rocks, debating whether to return to the Britannia Hut or continue their planned route to Zermatt. When they heard our report they chose to return to the hut.

Still relentlessly pursued by wind we descended, but at last the clouds were above us and we felt warmth once again. We stopped for food and a well-earned rest in sunshine—we had been on the move for seven hours without a pause and not one of us had flagged. The words of Whymper came to my mind:—

> "We who go mountain-scrambling have constantly set before us the superiority of fixed purpose or perseverance to brute force. We know that each height, each step, must be gained by patient, laborious toil and that wishing cannot take the place of working; we know the benefits of mutual aid; that many a difficulty must be

encountered and many an obstacle must be grappled with or turned, but we know that where there's a will there's a way; and we come back to our daily occupations better fitted to fight the battles of life and overcome the impediments which obstruct our paths, strengthened and cheered by the recollection of past labours, and by memories of victories gained in other fields ... we value those noble qualities of human nature—courage, patience, endurance and fortitude."

The Britannia Hut was crammed full. We still had a day or two to spare, but the weather was clearly still unsettled. Why not end on that note? A run down on splendid spring snow took us to the top of the cable-car run. As we rode down, the snowless slopes and red roofs rose to meet us and the smell of grass wafted up as we walked across the meadows still damp from the melted snow. We were back on earth.

In retrospect we had experienced a very varied tour; we had stumbled on a game of chance played by the peasants, been lost in mist and encountered the kindly help and hospitality of the villagers, been relentlessly pursued by cloud, skied by moonlight, been caught in an electric storm. We had skied from the solitude of the little-known to the historical and most popular mountainous area of the Alps, and had experienced various forms of altitude sickness. Indeed, I have described John's symptoms of mountain sickness in some detail as it may be a trap for others and it could happen to anyone. I have since found, too, that such symptoms are not uncommon in skiers who live at sea level and, however fit, go straight out to traverse the higher peaks. Peter Hackett, in his book on mountain sickness, writes that the susceptibility to mountain sickness varies enormously in different individuals, and that younger people are more readily affected than the older ones. Chris Bonnington tells us that even if the individual has a high degree of physical fitness this does not affect his susceptibility to mountain sickness. The earliest symptoms that most mountaineers encounter are lassitude and a personality change in the form of irritability and depression. It was therefore greatly to John's credit that he kept up well with us for the rest of the journey and proved to be not only an asset but a good companion.

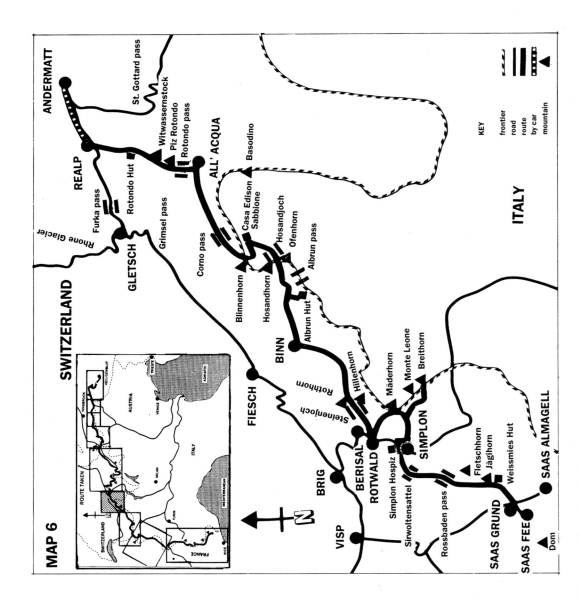

Chapter IV

1972:   Year 3.   The Year of Frustration

The Pennine Alps

Saas Almagell to Simplon Hospiz

THIS year we made our way back to Saas Fee. We proposed to limber up and acclimatize ourselves to the altitude by spending a few days at Saas Almagell. It lies above Saas Fee and is the last village at the head of the Saas Valley. It seemed that the weather was prepared to make amends for the previous year as the sun shone from the cloudless blue sky.

As we stepped from the 'bus in the little square Philip Booth and Jeremy Whitehead were there waiting to greet us. They were both keen ski-tourers and were members of the Alpine Ski Club. I had previously met Philip in one of the Austrian huts, touring with some of his friends. I had read articles in journals by both Philip and Jeremy about ski-tours, but had not skied with either of them before.

I introduced them to Beryl and we spent the afternoon "piste-bashing". This exercise merely strengthened my dislike for mechanical transport in the mountains, because the rocks and snow around the top of the ski-lift were littered with chocolate papers, beer cans, cigarette ends and all kinds of rubbish. I watched the skiers pouring off the lift in droves like chickens dropping off a conveyor belt and without even a glance at their surroundings they hared down at speed, at times clipping a slower competitor in passing and knocking him over. With demonic fervour their main purpose was to achieve as many runs as they could in the shortest possible time. Yes, they were "battery-skiers", but they could have been in the middle of Hampstead Heath for all they cared about mountains. Still, each man to his own pleasure, for our worlds were poles apart: it was time for us to explore the local peaks and passes.

During the night we could hear snow dripping off the eaves and chunks of snow sliding off the roof as it melted and it started to rain. Next morning, after it had stopped raining, we walked to the end of the village and wandered up the Almagell valley; we were the only people there—which surprised us, as the head of the valley is dominated on the left by the south face of a very fine mountain, the Weissmies, over thirteen thousand feet high, and on the right by the Sonnighorn. Anyone wishing to stray from the piste can climb three thousand feet to reach smaller peaks and passes which join the two mountains in an arc of a circle, with downhill running over a very nice glacier. But we did not claim a peak or a pass, as in the upper slopes we met the fury of the anabiatic wind from above and willy-waws of snow flurried and chased each other across the slopes: the weather was unsettled.

The next day was more promising and we set off to climb the Jazzihorn in the adjoining valley. It would be a four-hour climb and again it was deserted. Squirrels, disturbed by our presence, scampered ahead of us as if they had never seen man; they took refuge behind boulders and peered at us cautiously: perhaps, after all, the ski-lifts had a purpose in protecting their privacy. Somewhere a fox barked and we heard the answering call of the vixen in higher pitch: both seemed to be a warning, perhaps to their cubs. They had no need to smell intruders: they could hear them. The silence was so intense that even the first snowflakes falling on my jacket sounded like a stone dropping into a pond—yes, it was snowing again, but only lightly! Some way up the valley the Jazzihorn buried itself in cloud, and so we decided to make for the Antrona pass which was about thirteen hundred feet lower and almost free of cloud. I was curious to see over, as both this pass and the Monte Moro pass, which lies at the head of the Saas Valley, have great historical associations, as they provided a direct trade route between Domodossola and the Rhône Valley in earlier times, and it was interesting to see what difficulties and dangers must have been endured by merchants in those days. Since it was also the frontier line it was of course a constant source of disputes between the Swiss and the Italians in the sixteenth century.

What a pass! Precipitous slopes led down some two thousand feet to a little lake which had been dammed, and beyond we could just make out the deep green woods at the head of the Antrona Valley. But perhaps in those earlier days it was not so steep, because in 1642 there was a landslide which destroyed the greater part of Antrona village.

The wind drove us down, back to our valley, to find somewhere to eat our lunch and then we had much fun on the way back ski-ing in and around trees, which some people aptly call "birds'-nesting"!

With no more short tours to make from Saas Almagell we felt we were sufficiently acclimatized to set off on our journey next day. We could afford to start late, as it was only a four-hour climb up to the Weissmies hut from Saas Grund, a village further down the valley.

Whilst having breakfast we were astonished to see water pouring through the ceiling. The proprietor, who was leaning against the bar thumbing over his newspapers, seemed totally unconcerned when we drew his attention to the deluge. He casually looked up and said: "Oh, that's good!" and ambled off to fetch a bucket.

"It's often much worse than that," he muttered resignedly and went back to thumbing his newspaper without a word of explanation—he was obviously so used to it happening that he saw no reason to enlighten us as to the cause, and we could only surmise that his wife, who was amply proportioned, was taking a much-needed bath. Whether on account of the flood or not, the proprietor became much less reserved, and even cheerful, as we said goodbye, and he asked us to send him a postcard from England about the outcome of the trip.

We had time to wander round Saas Grund and we were fascinated by the gnarled dead tree branches arranged in a line above old cartwheels outside the church. They were fanciful natural carvings reminiscent of Trolls in Norway. Unfortunately the village was invaded by French hippies and gramophones playing the latest "noises" made it intolerable. Our shopping completed, having bought food for several days, we sped up the path pursued remorselessly by the cacophony.

Plate 45. The Allalinhorn, Alphubel and Taschhorn above the Saas Valley

The path zig-zagged and around each bend the giant peaks of the Mischabel group gradually came into view as though they too were climbing the ridge on the other side of the valley—all of them over thirteen thousand feet high: the Allalinhorn, Alphubel, Taschhorn, Dom and Lenzspitze forming a palisade along the top of the western curve of the Saas Valley. Although we had climbed most of these mountains individually in the past, and looked across to an adjacent peak, it was an unusual view to see them arranged like sentinels for us to judge which was the highest. They beckoned to us, but we turned our backs on them, entering a sheltered side valley which took us to the summer alp of Trift nestling in a bowl.

The angular twisted remains of the pylons of a cable railway brought down by an avalanche (or was it an Act of God?) lay like distorted orange monsters in the snow, reminding us that some prefer to take their mountaineering the easy way, but for us the satisfaction lay in stretching endurance to the limit and battling with the elements. We climbed long and hard, our rucksacks heavy with the weight of five days' food: the Weissmies hut never seemed to get nearer until we spied the rocky pyramid of the Fletschhorn soaring up loftily.

The Weissmies hut was an ugly square grey stone building, but the winter room was small and inviting. Two young Germans, the only other occupants, had been watching our approach and judging that we might be thirsty had thoughtfully boiled some water for tea. They had been up there for the best part of a week and had only managed to climb the Weissmies and Langehorn as the weather had prevented them from achieving more. They were glad of new company, since conversation between two people is likely to run out after a week. Like us, they hoped to climb the Fletschhorn the next day. There was very little wood left for the stove and frying our steaks over the feeble heat was an art, and I could sense the impatience behind me. Beryl was attempting to boil rice and Jeremy—who was a bachelor schoolmaster and knew nothing of Beryl's prowess as a cook—was giving her detailed instructions with sixth-form precision, much to her and the Germans' amusement.

As night fell I went out on to the balcony to look at the weather. Coloured lights of Saas Fee began to appear, twinkling in the valley below. The star-spangled sky promised a fine day. It was indeed clear, Venus appearing from behind the Jägihorn like a second moon. The giant peaks were now but shadows in the sky. Having just left the tumultuous world of the rat race, the noise, and man's apparent necessity for constant background "music", I reflected on what a privilege it was to be here, surrounded by glaciers covered with virgin untracked snow, and to know the meaning of real silence: here there was a sense of peace and time to think. To be dwarfed by the splendour of those giant peaks was in itself a challenge to conquer them, spurred on by the cat-and-mouse game with the weather, whose purpose it was to hinder.

We awoke to a grey dawn. The Germans were away before us, but the high peaks were already putting on their fluffy hats, and it was warm. This would make our attempt on the Fletschhorn a hit and run affair. We reached the Trift Glacier and were confronted by a huge ice-fall threatening in the gloom as the clouds closed in. Below it, enormous blocks of ice had broken off and were strewn over the snow. Ahead, the ice-fall was encompassed by two rocky cliffs and there was no passage around the side. The jumble of séracs was heaped like chunks of broken green-blue ceramic blocks with one monster about sixty feet high poised precariously. It may have stood like that for many years, locked in its menacing stance, but one day the glacier would move and topple it over. The passage upwards through the séracs was steep and narrow and new snow slipped off the underlying ice with every step. It was impossible to contour or zig-zag uphill in the normal way, so we put on crampons to get a grip and carried our skis.

There was a hail from above, and the two Germans appeared out of the murk, skiing with immense skill down a 45° slope in short swings and jump turns. They reckoned the weather had broken and we reluctantly agreed, so we carried our skis down again! It was a sad decision with the summit only half-an-hour away, but none of us relished the idea of ski-ing back through the ice-fall when unable to see. The Germans had already left when we arrived back at the hut, but like true mountaineers they had left us plenty of melted snow for cooking and drinking. We were short of wood, however. After searching round in the cellar we found a rotten plank and we had no compunction about using it for firewood.

Taking advantage of our absence, black velvety choughs were searching outside for scraps of food. They strutted along the low stone wall with complete lack of shyness and looked like real Walt Disney birds with their legs brilliant red against the snow and toes upturned as if to keep them off the cold stone—though they should be used to it since their nests are built in rocky crevices.

We woke at 5 a.m., and it was bitterly cold. We needed good weather to continue our journey to the Simplon Pass as the route was complicated. Fortunately the wind had dropped, leaving whorls and streamers of blown snow like icing sugar around the hut. In view of the intense cold and the possibility of frozen fingers, we postponed our start until seven o'clock, by which time the sun was gilding the peaks on the opposite side of the valley. A run down in light powder snow took us to a broad exposed terrace which contours the southern and western shoulders of the Jägihorn. It was a spectacular situation: ribs of rock radiated down from the peak like outspread fingers crossing our path. We picked our way over patches of snow between the boulders, from time to time having to carry our skis over them. After three hours we halted for lunch at a rock which gave us a viewpoint of our first pass, which was a mere dent in the Rothorn Grat, nameless but dignified by a spot reference on the map, and certainly difficult to locate in bad visibility. I glanced anxiously at the sky—we were in for a warm front and we cut our rest short, setting off hot-foot for the pass.

At the top, far across the Rhône Valley, rose the great peaks of the Oberland, grey and uninviting; below us, we looked down into the steep-sided bowl of the Mattwald Glacier, already filling up with billowing cloud. We were aiming now for the Rossboden Pass, a point where two glaciers meet, and if they meet head-on it is tantamount to a traffic pile up, splitting the ice into crevasses and séracs. We looked at the map: wiggly streaks intersecting the contour lines told us there was a steep ice-fall there on the left which would be an embarrassment—we must avoid it at all costs. We ran down into the cloud, but as we descended through it visibility began to improve and we found ourselves beneath an ice-cliff, a sheer wall of blue ice stretching upwards some two hundred and fifty feet into the gloom of the cloud above us. Even without the sun it was an impressively beautiful sight. We passed below it and, skirting the broken surface of smaller ice-falls, a steep run down took us to the Oberfoulmoos, an imposing rocky headland on the valley floor and a sentinel between the two meeting glaciers. We entered the valley for our final climb to the last pass, the Sirwoltensattel. The far-off Oberland peaks were now shrouded in a glaring yellow haze which looked sinister, since these high mountains attract the first of the bad weather and nearby peaks were beginning to collect their share. As we reached the top the snowflakes began to fall, and we heaved a sigh of relief that we had negotiated this difficult and complicated route without mishap.

But we sighed too soon, for as I swung down the slope on the far side, my ski-binding cable broke, although the ski did not plunge away as it was tethered to my ankle with a safety strap. I was glad that they were old-fashioned bindings, as I had a spare cable in my sack, and it was also fortunate that it had not occurred earlier ... we were nearly there. Below us lay the Simplon Pass, a road built by Napoleon because of its strategic value. Before then, the pass had been little more than a track leading up to the Hospiz.

Since the thirteenth century the Hospiz has been a rest house for travellers passing from Italy to Switzerland, but it had been taken over by the monks of the Order of Austin Canons after the Battle of Waterloo. We debated. Would the Hospiz be open at this time of the year, and would the monks admit Beryl for the night? We would be reaching the road at Niederalp on the south side of the pass, and it would mean walking three-quarters of an hour up the road to the Hospiz. The alternative was nearly five miles downhill to Simplon village. Rather than face the disappointment of having to make a second journey if we were turned away from the Hospiz, we opted to go to the village. Food and drink were uppermost in our minds as, hounded by bad weather, we had had very little of either.

The Post Hotel had been built to the orders of Napoleon, presumably when he built the road across the pass. Although it had been partly modernized in very good taste, much of the old structure remained. The walls were decorated with old prints and photographs of the Simplon Pass, though these were too modern to show the barracks which Napoleon also built, but the impressive high-vaulted stable which now housed our skis had once accommodated the conscripts.

Neither Philip nor I approved of modern ski boots and bindings, as they appeared much too clumsy for the ski-tourer, and how could one possibly climb rocks for the final peak in a boot which came half-way up the leg and was totally inflexible? The ski binding which went with it was not only heavy, but did not allow the same excursion for raising the heel when walking uphill. For this reason we were both dubbed old-fashioned. Some years ago, when these boots and bindings came on the market, Philip wrote a cleverly worded letter to the Ski Club magazine discussing the type of oils required for these new bindings. I realized he was poking fun at them and I entered into the correspondence in similar vein. Thus we were in like mood when it came to filling in the documents for our overnight stay at the hotel, which eventually went into the police records. They are a tiresome occupation as you are always asked to fill them in when you are having a meal and of course your passport is upstairs in the bedroom—as on this occasion. We decided to sign them all "Charlie Chaplin", and even the grave Sabbath faces of the other diners began to relax in veiled amusement while the hotelier accepted them without question.

There were differing opinions in the hotel as to whether or not we should find the Hospiz open, let alone women admitted, which explained why I had been unable to obtain positive information from the Swiss Travel Bureau in England; so we decided to take a 'bus up and see. The journey seemed short compared with our trudge down the night before. It is not a steep pass, and it was understandable that it held so much strategic value for Napoleon. Even before he built the road it must have been frequently used as a cart-track before the Hospiz became a monastery. The Hospiz now is a huge oblong building built of stones of the most attractive peach colour. As we arrived, a group of young schoolgirls was returning from the ski slopes, and thus dispelled our fears on the admission of women.

The reception office was down a high, solid stone-flagged corridor and the young monk gave us a friendly greeting. He seemed surprised at our lack of dismay when he apologetically explained they only had dormitories with long bunks and did we mind all sharing the same room? As for washrooms and showers, it would be quite all right for Beryl to use the monks', since the schoolgirls had all the other accommodation. The Hospiz was run as a simple mountain hotel, many of which are "super" huts and there is plenty of good cheap food and wine. There were only about half-a-dozen monks running the Hospiz; they wore ordinary suits and could be distinguished solely by their high-necked black pullovers and crucifixes. They were remarkable for their serene expressions and great sense of fun. The students who occupied the rest of the building were very well behaved but lively French schoolgirls and the monks were teaching them to ski. There was only one thing lacking—light reading matter: the library held nothing but religious works and Beryl, who had gone there in search of a novel, came back disappointed.

Next morning we set off full of hope for Monte Leone and there was a large party of the schoolgirls with the same object. It soon became an endurance race, as I dislike giving the impression—even if a false one—of hanging back to use other people's tracks. There was a fair amount of new snow and when we had to cross a steep couloir we took the precaution to spread out: although the snow was reasonably consolidated, if it did avalanche it would only involve one or possibly two of us. A superb glacier leads up to the north face of Monte Leone, but the final slope is a steep ice wall not practicable so early in the year. The winter route, which we were taking, lay up the Hohmatten glacier to a col on a corniced ridge lying between Monte Leone and the Breithorn.

We were now well behind the French party as Philip was having trouble with his skins and his slow progress could be judged by muttered growls and curses. I turned round in time to see one of his feet slipping backwards as he stepped up a steep slope. The skin came off and he balanced precariously on the other foot while he tried to stick it on again, but it would not adhere. He tried to warm it inside his anorak, for he was using the original sealskins which are stuck on with wax. They really *had* come out of the Ark! Strangely enough, they had not given trouble before on the earlier part of our journey. These skins are ideal when in good humour as the snow does not collect in large globs between the skin and ski even if the snow is soft and wet, and they have the added advantage of allowing short distance downhill running without being taken off. This is particularly useful when covering gently undulating ground. But wax is not the ideal adhesive: it can be the very Devil as it goes solid in the cold. Philip had my profound sympathy as I had used such skins for many years, but Beryl had persuaded me to move with the times after we had had similar trying experiences and I had abandoned their virtues in favour of the type she was using. These were made of a plush-like fabric which tied on with straps, but these too had their disadvantages as we were always repairing the straps where the sharp edges of the ski cut through.

By the time we reached the col both summits were in cloud and we were all a bit unenthusiastic; whichever cloud-enveloped peak we reached, we would not be able to see much. The Breithorn was nearest and only two hundred feet lower, so we decided to climb it instead of Monte Leone. A few steps cut with the ice-axe just below the summit brought us to the top. As far as the view was concerned, it made no difference: all I can remember was Simplon village in shadow far below seen through occasional holes in the cloud. I was beginning to resign myself to unfulfilled hopes!

Back at the Hospiz, Philip found that his brand-new skis had disintegrated, which confirmed our ideas that perhaps after all it was better to be old-fashioned and let someone else try out the new-fangled ideas first! It was not practicable to get them repaired and, having left some business worries behind him, Philip decided to go home. We were sorry to see him go, as he had been good fun.

That evening Jeremy and I discussed with the monks our plans for the next day. The monks told us that there was no accommodation at Berisal, where we had planned to go, and so we decided to cross the Mäderlucke Pass and spend the night in Rotwald, where we knew there was an inn.

Plate 46. *Skavla*: ripples of wind-swept snow on the pass below Monte Leone

The Lepontine Alps

Simplon to Binn

When the thick mist began to dissolve next morning, we set off. High up near the pass we were again in thick cloud and many were the halts to check our direction by compass, because the pass was just a gap in a rocky ridge. We reached a point where we knew we should double back, but it seemed all ridge without a gap. If only we had a moment's visibility ... and as though to answer our wish, there was a sudden clearing and there was the pass barely a hundred yards above us. We hurried up as fast as we could go, but before we reached the ridge we were again enveloped in cloud and a confused and frustrating half-hour followed: the compass always seemed to be pointing the wrong way! At last we found a gap. Surely this *must* be the pass? and we peered down into the gloom below, where a few rock ribs disappeared into the swirling mist. It looked intimidatingly steep. We waited a while for another sudden clearing, but never a chance did we get. We had to move sometime and, shouldering our skis, we walked down the broken rocks which might have been the summer path. It was! We must be on the right route. I felt thankful that we were going down and not up: the snow was well bonded despite the steepness and for safety we continued to walk straight down the snow slope until we were out of the clouds, for steep slopes like this are more likely to avalanche if you ski across them. At length it seemed safe to put on skis and we swept past the Mäder Hut with only its roof and chimney showing, and the rest of it buried in deep snow: it struck me as faintly comic that in planning the tour I had considered using this hut!

We were given a warm welcome by two middle-aged ladies who ran the Post Hotel at Rotwald, and they understood our needs as breakfast was waiting for us outside our bedrooms at five o'clock next morning.

It was as well we had not counted on Berisal for accommodation, as we found it a sad collection of derelict cottages—a pity, because it lay at the mouth of the valley where we turned off towards the Steinenjoch to go over to Binn. We followed a wooded path printed with a confusion of marmots' tracks: they must have been having fun, circling under and around the rocks and back into a muddied snow-hole which marked their front door. Unusually, one intrepid little fellow had strayed well above the tree line as if to lead our way, but I wondered what attraction there had been to take him away from the others and to go visiting so far afield.

We walked comfortably up a stream bed, knowing that somewhere to the left we had to climb into another valley, but there did not seem to be any promising way and eventually we found ourselves in a steep-sided ravine. On one side an overhanging crag topped by a stunted tree reminded me of a print by an imaginative artist of more than a century ago. We emerged above it on to a sunny shoulder, congratulating ourselves that the Steinenjoch was only two hours away—just round the corner—and comfortably we sat down to eat some food. We started off again and suddenly the thought dawned on me—the conformation of the ground did not agree with the contours on the map. Where next? After a consultation we were forced to the conclusion that we had passed the narrow entrance to the Steinental and come up the wrong valley. To return

Plate 47. Marmot tracks: one little fellow seemed to lead the way

to the main valley and look for the entrance was unthinkable—we should lose at least two hours. Was there a way across higher up? A low rock ridge separated the two valleys and the map showed a summer path: it must take us across—we would just have to go and see. Fortunately the ridge was fairly free of snow and we walked down the steep slopes into the floor of the Steinental, thankful to be on the correct route. However, we had lost not only time, but also height: by now we should have been on the pass. It was close on mid-day and the heat was intense; up and down, we had climbed some three thousand feet in the frying sun for three hours. The magical sound of trickling water led us to some mossy rocks and a tiny stream rippling over them. We had been conserving our water supply, but now we could drink our fill. It was like coming on an oasis in a desert.

Steep slopes led up to the Hillenhorn on our right. I had thought to climb it on the way, but now we were so hopelessly behind schedule we must attempt the impossible and make up for lost time. We pressed on to the pass. We paid dearly for those two lost hours as the snow on the far side was beginning to freeze in the evening shadow and we were soon scraping across the most evil breakable crust whereas had we not lost time the snow would have been perfect. It is extraordinary how one mistake in the mountains can create unforeseen difficulties, for not only did we have bad snow but the additional tiredness diminished care. Below, enormous avalanche fields forced us to take off our skis on a steep slope. While Beryl removed hers she accidentally dislodged her rucksack. It came bounding towards me—a quick leap across snow blocks and a flying tackle and I was able to grab it, counting myself lucky indeed not to have been impaled on the ice-axe and crampons which were attached on the outside.

Plate 48. The Steinenjoch. We were glad of a rest as we had been frying in the sun for the past three hours

The track down to Binn seemed never-ending, and by the time we reached the village the lights were already twinkling in the windows. We were all very tired and ready for food. Entering the only inn we expected the usual friendly mountain welcome, but no! it was out of season and they would not put us up. We felt angry as it was clear that the hotel was being managed by people from the valley whose main purpose in running a hotel was probably geared to a week's stay on a summer package tour, and their concern did not extend to the hungry and weary traveller. However, the girl in charge, sensing our anger and frustration, directed us to a nearby *pension* which we found was run by a ruddy-faced mountaineer and hunter, who only too gladly made us welcome. His eyes twinkled with amusement when he heard of our meanderings up the wrong valley and agreed that the entrance to the valley we had missed was difficult to find as it was steep, and it was easy to go astray. His wife had no meat, but cooked us a large omelette. Unlike her husband, she was very shy but tried to practise speaking English, which she was learning from the television.

Binn to Andermatt

Binn was comparatively low-lying at only four-and-a-half thousand feet. It was not a ski-ing centre because the valley is steep-sided. We planned to walk up to the Albrun Hut to spend the night and this would take four or five hours. There was no need, therefore, to start early and so it was a real luxury to get up late. There was time to stroll around the very unspoilt village which boasted only one shop, where we bought provisions. I then sought out the guardian to get the hut key and to find out exactly where the hut was, as it was not marked on the map. It had recently been given to the Swiss Alpine Club by the Army. The guardian was away, but his wife—who handed me the key—had no precise knowledge of the hut's whereabouts and waved her finger over the map which might have led us to believe the hut occupied half the mountainside! But at least I had some idea of which valley bowl it was likely to be in, and at what altitude. While Jeremy and I were doing this, Beryl walked up to the first village—Giessen—which would be on our way. She wanted to get the straps on her skin repaired and she also had a strong desire to drink some creamy mountain milk. When we joined her she was lying basking in the sun on a meadow strewn with purple and white crocus and listening to the chorus of birds who were glad to see the sun and spring: they knew they would be safe in this area because it is part of a Nature Reserve. It always saddened us that so much of Europe which has the most lovely countryside has no birds because they are hunted, and to come across them in these Reserves makes them stand out as something unusual.

We started off, a little reluctant to leave this bird paradise, and trudged up into the snow by way of an easy path. It was pleasant until the sun abandoned us and the further we climbed the more sharply gusts of unpleasant damp wind assailed us. I looked back down the valley with some anxiety, to see masses of dark cloud sweeping up the valley and about to overtake us, and then it soon began to snow gently. It was worrying because we did not know the exact whereabouts of the hut, but we reached an open summer grazing pasture and it was likely to be fairly near by. There were a few alp huts clustered together and I made a mental note of them as they might be useful in an emergency. We stopped and had a look at the altimeter: according to our height, the hut was about three hundred feet higher up the valley, and although the weather was closing in, we were nearly there. It would be pointless to return down the valley to Binn. We continued on in the gathering whiteness, the visibility now down to a hundred yards, the snow blowing horizontally, driving snowflakes stinging our eyes. We bent our heads down and leaned against the wind, but the further we went the more obvious it became that we would only find the hut if we stumbled on it by good fortune, as we could see nothing. Our tracks were rapidly becoming obliterated by the wind and snow and it would be prudent to retreat to the alp huts while we could still see the tracks to serve as our guide. We would probably have a miserable night, but at least we should have shelter and be out of the biting wind.

We searched round the alp huts; they were all firmly barred, except one: it had a broken window and we climbed through. It was part of a lean-to shed which was used for cheese-making. A large black iron cauldron stood against the wall with a hood over it. There were a few wooden benches and to our delight a pile of firewood in one corner. The walls were blackened and the roof was ill-fitting against the house. A large drift of snow occupied one end of the room and with each gust of wind shivers of snow descended on us from under the eaves: it was a draughty place! With a few flat stones we built a little fireplace on top of the cauldron and soon got a small fire going; the smoke billowed up into the blackened cowl, but occasional gusts of wind swirled it back into the room. We huddled round, warming our hands. The fire would do for cooking a meal, but it would be unsafe to keep it going during the night—I had seen too many Arabs in Iraq poisoned by carbon monoxide fumes from their charcoal stoves in winter. We warmed some soup in a tin, as this was hardly the place for *Cordon Bleu* cookery, and ate some sausage and bread, then reluctantly had to extinguish the fire, as the smoke was too dense.

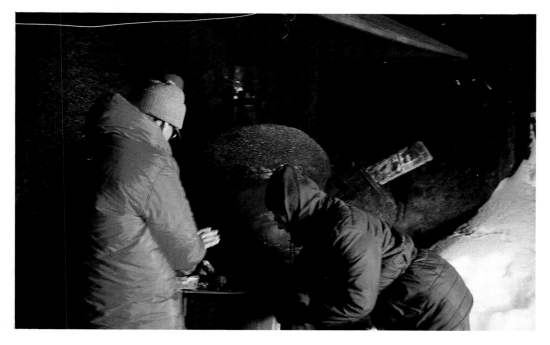

Plate 49. The bivouac in the cheese-making room.
Hardly the place for *Cordon Bleu* cookery

Bed time came. The stone-flagged floor was uninvitingly icy and we laid some churn covers over it with sticks of firewood to fill in the gaps—at least that would be a warmer bed than the stone floor. Putting on all our spare pullovers and clothes we snuggled down and went to bed. Jeremy was slightly better off: he pulled on a windproof kagool which reached to his knees and climbed into a nylon bivouac sack. But even he did not have much sleep: just a fitful doze. The howling wind and the cold were now intense and Beryl began to shiver. Suddenly Jeremy woke up and banged the churn covers smartly with his hand and flashed his torch round the room to frighten off imaginary creatures.

"The mice are eating our bread," he cried; but it was only the chattering of Beryl's teeth!

The roof creaked ominously and I wondered if it would hold in this howling gale—the prospect of being left roofless was uninviting, though at worst we could dig a snow-hole in the drift in the corner. From time to time we got up and stamped our feet to restore the circulation to our toes which, despite our boots and two pairs of socks, were numbed with cold and inactivity.

Dawn came at last and we got the fire going again. It was a faint glimmer, but at least it gave us a psychological feeling of warmth. We toasted some cheese in the empty soup tin and with a drink of coffee made on Beryl's meta solid fuel stove some of our stiffness began to wear off and we felt a little more cheerful as the wind was abating. By ten o'clock there was a welcome clearing outside with glimpses of sun and it was good enough for us to go and look for the Club hut. Within half-an-hour we spied a flag-staff—and only a flag-staff—some way up the valley and this clearly must mark the location of the hut, though we could not see any building. It was not surprising that we had not been able to find it in the storm, as it was almost completely buried in snow and as though to emphasize the frequency of such a circumstance, a large shovel hung from the flagpole. It took us nearly an hour to dig down some eight feet to find the front door and we let ourselves in.

It was most attractive inside—one little room with everything necessary and in spotless order: two tiers of long bunks which would accommodate about a dozen people, plenty of wood, paper, matches and a saw. and snow already melted on the stove (the depth of snow above the hut had kept it from freezing). What a contrast with some of the huts we had visited, and it really did us good to see it as we were all feeling jaded.

From the hut book we noticed that the last visitors had been in residence ten days before and there were frequent remarks in earlier records of "digging the hut out" as it lay in a wind bowl. One thing is certain: we would never have found it the previous evening and I would certainly not recommend anyone to try to find it except in good visibility.

The first thing we needed was a hot meal, and then we rolled ourselves up in blankets and made up for lost sleep. When we awoke late in the afternoon the weather was clearly on the mend, though fearsome crackling noises from the polythene windows emphasized that the wind had not completely dropped. It was Jeremy's birthday and to celebrate it he had carried a fruit cake all the way from England. What a treat! It crowned our evening meal, our tiredness went, and we could relax once more in the knowledge that the night in the cheese-maker's lean-to was now but a bad dream. As always after a climax of some sort, we fell to reminiscing about climbs and ski tours, and comparing notes, because Jeremy spends all his school holidays in mountains. He is an active leader in unguided mountain climbs and tours for one of the Ski or Alpine Clubs. He knew the area around Andermatt and I felt this would be useful as it was a part of the Alps I did not know well. However, neither of us knew the region between here and All'Acqua, for which we were bound, proposing to spend a night at the Sabbione Dam on the way.

The Sabbione Dam is in Italy, only a stone's throw over the border and we were used to zig-zagging back and forth over the frontiers, but one of the difficulties lay in finding out—since I had no key—if there was a guardian in the hut in winter. We hoped there would be someone in residence; if not, at the worst, we would have to break in because any other habitation would be ten miles away as the crow flies.

We left at five o'clock and a short run down took us to the Talli Glacier and it was a steep climb up to the pass, the Hohsandjoch. The snow had been badly crusted by the wind and would not support the weight of our skis; at times we broke through and alternated this with slipping on glassy ice when the skins failed to grip. It was tiresome—just the place for using harscheisen *(Plate 13),* but only Jeremy had them and he forged ahead. I mentally thought what a luxury it would have been to carry them, but the infrequent occasions when we needed them did not, to my mind, justify the extra weight of nine ounces each. My rucksack was already too heavy with food, rope, ice-axe and shovel, to the extent that a bivouac sack should have greater priority and would have been welcome in the cheese-maker's hut. I had always relied on my ability and judgment to find my way to shelter for the night even in a white-out.

The fine peak of the Ofenhorn towered above us and the lower slopes were liberally strewn with huge blocks of blue ice fallen from the hanging glacier clinging to its flank. We had intended to climb it from the other side, over the pass. The pass itself was steep, the lowest point on an unbroken rocky ridge joining the two adjacent peaks, the Ofenhorn and the Hohsandhorn. On the left the ridge was a cockscomb of rocky black spires (or "gendarmes") perched like a row of policemen in readiness to topple over and arrest us, their appearance made more ominous by a pall of grey cloud.

Plate 50. The gendarmes, perched like a row of policemen waiting to topple over and arrest us

Plate 51. The Sabbione Glacier: it ended abruptly as a sheer ice-cliff such as I had seen only in Arctic waters

From the pass we turned right to climb the Ofenhorn, the sun glittering and gleaming yellow off the glossy ice. It was sheer ice all the way to the peak and steep at that. Although it would have made a wonderful run down in good snow, there was no hope of the skis gripping and a fall near the top would entail a precipitous slide to the bottom, a distance of over six hundred and fifty feet. Footsteps had been cut with an ice-axe by others, and led upwards: undoubtedly these conditions had existed for some time. Should we walk up and walk down? Below us we had a good view of the lake and the Sabbione Dam, but a grey haze was spreading up the valley behind us and blotting out peak after peak: we would soon have snow. We had better find the hut by the Dam while we could still see, as we did not want a repetition of the night in the cheese-maker's hut.

The snow was good and we sped nearly three miles over a gentle Sabbione glacier unbroken by crevasses. Suddenly, ahead of me, I saw Jeremy sweep round in a sharp curve then stop. The glacier had ended abruptly as a sheer ice cliff about a hundred feet high, dropping straight down into the lake. It was as well we had decided to come down in good visibility as we could have skied over the edge! In normal circumstances the glacier would have gradually petered out. For us, this ice cliff was totally unexpected. I had only seen such cliffs in Arctic glaciers where they meet the sea: the sea water has a lower freezing point and erodes the ice. In this case at Sabbione there was little doubt that the raised water level due to the Dam (as the lake was man-made) had melted the snout of the glacier in summer and formed this cliff. We contoured round the mountain-side and found our way down on to the lake where the glacier had receded naturally through the passage of years. Looking up at it, the ice cliff was an unusual sight—the ice blocks no longer angular but moulded and rounded in fanciful shapes by irregular meltings: a rival at any time to Henry Moore sculptures.

It was snowing lightly as we crossed the frozen lake and we were glad to see that the blue shutters of the house belonging to the Dam were open: it must be occupied. Then we saw two figures cross the slope on skis and go in. This was surprising, because the hut is so isolated and people rarely go there in winter. We knocked on the door to ask for the key of the hut, which lay further up the mountainside. A shy, reticent little man came out, and he was delighted to see new faces, and reluctant to part too soon.

"You know the hut will be cold," he volunteered, inviting us in for beer. "Take your boots off," he added thoughtfully—not because they were snowy and wet, but because he intended us to stay. He could not miss the rare chance of a convivial evening. It would be warm and comfortable inside, and we did not need any persuasion

It was clear that we were back in another bachelor establishment. Whereas in the Simplon Monastery the emphasis had been on Godly things, and the schoolgirls were seen in the eyes of the monks as Children of God, here in this establishment woman was depicted in realms of fantasy and dreams of the unattainable. Although on the walls there were a few photographs of the dam under construction and groups of mountaineers and ski teachers, all other available space was occupied by large posters and pictures of nudes and semi-nudes. They were even on the backs of doors, dish cloths, antimacassars on the chairs. There was an abundance of bric-à-brac, working models and ash-trays all with the one theme—nudes. They stood as monuments to deprivation and dreams. The Dam-keeper made an abortive attempt to telephone his superiors to obtain permission for us to spend the night on their premises, but I strongly suspect that he had one finger pressed on the hook for fear they would say "No": at all events, he returned to the room saying that he could not get through.

He told us that he was a guide in summer, but in the winter it was very lonely. The two men whom we had seen crossing the slopes were his nephews. They had been out collecting meteorological information, as in winter there was no work on the dam. Every two weeks they all went down to the Central Establishment in the valley and by rotation went to another dam, then back to Sabbione. To them it must have been a monastic existence despite the nudes.

While our host went into the kitchen to cook us a meal—which he insisted on doing unaided—Beryl picked up one of the magazines lying on the table: it was the Italian equivalent of *Playboy*. I heard her chuckle at the contrast between the reading matter in this bachelor stronghold and the religious books she had encountered in the Hospiz.

The meal was excellent. The Dam-keeper really gave us his best Italian cooking accompanied by very good wine. By now we were all at ease and the conversation broadened—they felt at home with us because I spoke Italian. They told us that they all preferred the simple life rather than earning more money in a factory, because they loved mountains and Nature. It was a beautiful spot in summer, with many wild flowers.

Before we retired to his "real" and very comfortable beds, we went out to look at the sky. He promised us a fine day and advised us to climb the Blinnenhorn as from there to All'Acqua we should have a ten-mile run down except for a small climb up to the Corno Pass on the way. We went in and had a look at the map. He explained that the best way was to cross the lake and get on to the Hohsand Glacier, and then it would be important to turn right, up a small valley, to cross on to the Gries Glacier which led up to the peak. He stressed that there were two little valleys and we must take the right one, as otherwise we would find ourselves on the wrong side of a rock ridge which separated the two glaciers.

"In their own way, these two bachelor establishments are both dedicated," said Beryl as we got into bed, "the one on a spiritual plane and the other to the love of mountains, flowers and nature in the raw. They both have their virtues. The monks showed serenity, but on the whole I think I prefer the earthy attitude—our friend the Dam-keeper has been so incredibly thoughtful and kind."

Indeed, he was up early to give us breakfast and to see us off. It was a perfect dawn as he had prophesied: the peaks at the head of the valley shone ghostly in the early light and stillness hung over the mountains like a halt in time. Our host was unwilling to accept any payment for his hospitality and we left with the promise that we would send him the biggest English nude picture that we could find, to add to his collection. (This eventually turned out to be a large poster: the back view of a kneeling woman, with a calendar printed over her toes and the soles of her feet. We could imagine his pride when he showed it to his friends.)

Armed with his instructions we set off across the lake and when we reached the point where we had to turn off we stopped and debated. There were two or three little depression-like valleys, nothing very definite and the map was not much help. We chose the one which looked most suitable and climbed for two hours in boiling hot sun. Jeremy was in the lead and as we came over a brow I suddenly heard an angry scream, and Jeremy was stamping his skis in frustration: we were below the rock ridge which separated us from the Gries Glacier and had taken the wrong valley! Thwarted, we only hoped our friend was not watching our progress through his binoculars.

The ridge was about three hundred feet high and quite impracticable to scale with our heavy sacks and skis. There was nothing for it—we would have to descend in order to round its foot. The run down would have been enjoyable under any other circumstances, as the snow was in perfect condition, but our minds were filled with disappointment at losing a thousand feet in height and the prospect of another hour's toil up in the frying sun. When we did find the right valley the entrance to it was so steep it was easy to see how we had missed it. Eventually we crossed over to the Gries Glacier by a corniced snowy ridge blown by wind into frozen plates of *skavla* like the foam of crested surf.

My body seemed to gain four inches in height as I took off my heavy sack and we all dumped our gear to climb the final ridge on foot.

From the eleven-thousand-foot summit we gazed with awe at the great length of the Gries Glacier, a silver carpet spread out below us for nearly five unbroken miles. I had seen the larger, impressive Brenva Glacier in the Mont Blanc range and the Aletsch Glacier in the Bernese Oberland which is fifteen miles long and a mile wide, but the Gries Glacier was for me at that moment the most perfect and compact, for around us the Formazza peaks were spread out to the east and the fine crest of Basodino like the edge of a saw was near at hand. It is a splendid area for ski-mountaineering which we must surely explore another day.

For once the clouds played fair and we started down, our earlier frustrations recompensed for by powder snow on firm crust—a skier's dream. It was very fast and we sped over slope after slope, terrace after terrace, with complete abandon, the feathery snow spurting from our ski tips like the chips from a woodworker's lathe ... down, down, down ... All too soon we reached a frozen lake, where we rested to gather strength for a last hot climb to the Corno Pass. What a run it had been, one which will remain forever in my memory.

It was now three o'clock and time to get moving. It would only take us half-an-hour to get to the top, but the sun drained us of every ounce of energy. Jeremy filled his white linen hat with snow which, he assured us, was very refreshing, but as we never wore sun hats we had to take his word for it.

We paused at the pass to look back. The glacier burned silvery in the late afternoon sun, clouds of cumulus billowed over the peak and rolled down towards us—for once, only once, had we cheated them!

We ran down another mile to the Corno hut where we hoped to find water, as the frustrating climb up the Blinnenhorn had exhausted our water supplies and our mouths were like sandpaper; but we were out of luck, so we pressed on spurred by the thought that the quicker we got down the sooner we would find a drink. We reached the road which runs down from the Nufenen pass and connects the Rhône Valley with Bellinzone and Lugano. The pass was not yet open but this part had been snow-ploughed to give access to the villages above All'Acqua. Fortunately the road was not gritted and we careered at speed, our skis clattering over the frozen surface. From time to time, however, we *had* to stop to rest our weary legs. Then we had to move again, the beckoning valley stretching deep green below in the evening shadow while high up above the peaks, capped with their films of cloud, glowed like gold in the falling sun.

Plate 52. The Gries Glacier burned silvery in the late afternoon sun

It was after six o'clock when we reached All'Acqua—twelve hours of mountain travel, but what a day it had been!

Apart from a few chalets there was only the Hospiz, which I had firmly believed was another monastery, though we found it was now a hotel. They accepted us doubtfully as they had no guests and were packing up to go down to a hoteliers' celebration in the valley next morning, but on hearing that we would leave for the Rotondo hut at 5 a.m. they made us welcome. Their Great St. Bernard was sprawled in front of the door and having a great fondness for dogs I went to talk to him. He was a fine animal but in bad humour—perhaps he sensed the departure of his master. I had the indignity of being bitten. Fortunately his teeth were blunt and my trousers at least were undamaged. But there may have been another explanation ... had he drunk the contents of his flask of brandy?

All'Acqua is not high—only just over five thousand feet—but the night had been cold and we were glad to find the snow hard. The well-trodden track as far as the Piansecco hut saved us time as it is about an hour's walk up the valley and it would have taken us longer had we been making tracks. Above the hut there is a broken cliff which straddles the side valley leading up to the Rotondo Pass. Jeremy and I debated which line to take and as we could not agree we each decided to take our own line, it would be safe enough for us to part as it was just an unpleasant rocky scramble and Jeremy is a first-class rock climber. In any case it would speed up our progress as it is always tedious following another. After Beryl and I had struggled up for half-an-hour looking for hand- and foot-holds safe enough to bear our weight, we strangely met Jeremy, more or less face to face round a ridge at the top of the rock face. On comparing notes it seemed that he had chosen an even worse line than mine! By now the mist of course had descended but the wind was light and, keeping together, we only knew that we had reached the pass when the ground began to fall away. I was glad that Jeremy knew this stretch of the journey as we now had to contour round the base of Piz Rotondo and find the Witenwasseren Pass over a mile away at the head of the valley, somewhere in the mist.

Toiling through mist always makes time go slowly and distances seem greater, because you are constantly wondering if you are on the right track and there is nothing interesting to look at to while away the time. As though to encourage us, there were occasional clearings and glimpses of a fine rock ridge bristling with spires, or gendarmes, stretching up to the peak of Piz Rotondo, and I thought what good rock-climbing they would make particularly in summer.

We reached the pass at one o'clock. On our right we knew there was the Witenwasserenstock towering up to ten thousand feet although we could not see it clearly. From this area run tributaries and melt-waters which form the head sources of three of the most important European rivers: the Rhône flowing to the Mediterranean, the Rhine flowing to the North Sea, and the Ticino via the Po to the Adriatic. Though not a particularly imposing mountain, who can deny its importance in the scheme of things? As if to remind us of its distinction, the wind met us in full blast on the other side of the pass, bringing with it snow which lashed our faces and clouded our goggles. Just to prove that it was such a significant watershed, a great deal of new snow had already fallen on this side of the pass. The snow came up to our knees and considerably slowed our descent. The visibility had not reduced sufficiently for us to rope up, but we kept as close together as possible. Roping-up is always an unpleasant business because unless the skiers are all equally adept—which they never are! and those following behind the leader make their turns in exactly the same places, you end up with a lot of bodies jerked on to their backs and lying in the snow. As it was, from time to time one of us disappeared from sight and I had anxious moments while I called out for everyone to stop so that we could be reunited.

Lower down we saw the tracks of a "snow-cat" and its tank-like imprints told us the Swiss Army had been there, as they have a large headquarters in Andermatt and frequently use this area for manoeuvres. We eventually sighted the Rotondo hut perched on a shoulder at the side of the valley. It was splendidly appointed and is very popular with ski-tourers as there are a number of excellent expeditions to be made. Jeremy told us that the guardian was an extremely nice woman who was held in high regard by the skiers. There was nobody there when we arrived so we made ourselves at home for the night.

Three feet of new snow had fallen by the morning and it seemed pointless to stay any longer, so we decided to go down to Andermatt. The snow was so deep that we could not ski and we had to push ourselves downhill with our ski-sticks. Visibility was still bad and occasional wind scoops and cornices, which involved each one of us in turn in a tangled mass, provided no hazard but almost light relief. Towards the valley we heard sounds of mortar fire, although there were no warning flags: I doubt if anyone was expected to come from above in such conditions. Then we met the Swiss Army face to face, just as a soldier was loading a mortar. He obligingly held his fire while we passed, but I was glad that they were probably only using dummy shells.

The snow soon became wet and turned into muddy slush churned up by army vehicles. We trudged down to Realp and lunched there while waiting for the 'bus to take us to Andermatt.

It was the end of Jeremy's holiday and as the weather showed no sign of improving we all decided to go back to England. On reflection we seemed to have achieved quite a lot despite the bad weather conditions.

I thought of Mummery's words written a century ago: "The true mountaineer is a wanderer, whether he succeeds or fails he delights in the fun and jollity of the struggle." Mountains do not change, nor does man's approach. We had not succeeded in all our targets: we had planned to climb seven peaks and achieved only two—and only seen the view from one! But we had had fun with Philip in the Post House at Simplon and Jeremy's birthday cake at the ex-Army hut, experienced monastic simplicity in the Simplon Hospiz and true hospitality at the Sabbione Dam. As for struggles ... I shall always think of churn covers when I sleep on an uncomfortable bed and of mice when I hear a clattering noise—or perhaps I shall think of Beryl's teeth!

Chapter V

1973: Year 4. The Year of Progress

The Lepontine and Adula Alps

Andermatt to Vals

WE RESUMED our tour on April 1st and I hoped that the weather was not going to make April Fools of us and thwart our plans.

Philip Booth joined us again having tried, he said, to build up his fitness to match his enthusiasm. He brought with him a friend, Jim Mason, a slim wisp of a man with legs as thin as matchsticks. I was a bit shaken, but Philip assured me that Jim would be all right, and as events turned out his appearance belied his mountaineering capacity and determination.

We embarked without delay. There was an early morning freshness in the air as we stole through the silent streets of Andermatt, bound for the Vermigel hut. Not far outside the village, where we had to turn up a path, a notice informed us that the hut was *"belegt"*. We sought in our German dictionary for the meaning: it might be covered, received, invested, billeted or—grim thought! bombed out. We decided to go and see which of these unattractive alternatives was correct.

The day was set fair as we walked up the valley, a whisker away from the cable car to the Gemsstock above Andermatt from which, tourists can tell you, six hundred Alpine peaks can be glimpsed, though I have never checked it personally and I am sure that it is only the summer visitors who count them. The sun was getting up and we stopped to put on face creams. While Philip was searching for his, he laid the contents of his rucksack, neatly done up in plastic bags, on the hard snow. In a moment, a faint stir in the breeze sent them flying down the slope into a ravine. With grave misgivings we peered over to see the bags strewn haphazardly over rocks and terraces. Fortunately we were only going up to the hut, about a three-hour climb, but even so the delay while we collected the packages caused a much more tiring journey in the blazing sun. Before the invention of plastic bags we carried our gear in linen bags which did not easily slide over the snow.

When we reached the hut it was buried deep in snow, deserted and abandoned, because higher up on a shoulder was a new but only half-built hut. So this was the meaning of *"belegt"*—a puzzle solved but another problem created. What now? Where

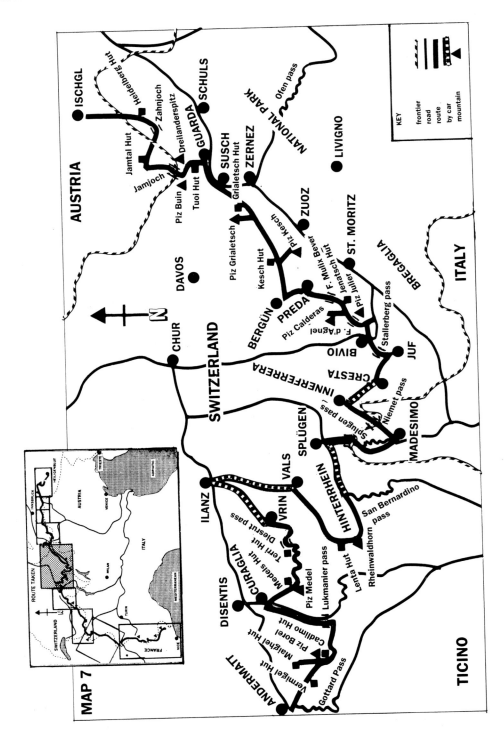

to spend the night? There was the Maighels hut in the next valley, which we could reach by the evening if we climbed the Maighels pass, another fifteen hundred feet above us. On our way up, a group of Germans came swinging down from Piz Borel, a peak to the right of the pass. They had had a splendid day and their comments interested us: we too planned to climb this peak the next day—although at that moment it was but a dim shadow in haze and the prospect was ominous.

An easy run down on fast snow brought us to the hut and a Swiss Ski Club flag fluttered outside. There was no sign of occupation so we inspected the wicker baskets in the pigeon-holes on the wall—yes, there must be quite a large group of people as the baskets were filled with personal belongings and tins of food. The stove was still warm, so that the other occupants could not have been gone for long. We were soon brewing tea—we were very thirsty. Shortly afterwards a group of fifteen men and women returned and we had to take it in turns to cook our evening meal.

We were surprised to find that, although there was no guardian in the hut, we could buy tinned food, beer and wine. Food we had brought with us, but wine ... that was something different and a luxury. A box and a tariff were provided for payment. Beryl and I had encountered this practice in Norway, but never before in the Alps. The Swiss told us that it was an experimental innovation being carried out in the remoter Alpine huts on the assumption that visitors would have a high standard of integrity. This may be so: genuine mountain travellers are unlikely to abuse the privilege—indeed, they often leave behind their food in case the next occupants are snowed in for a few days. This system, however, would not have worked in the Vermigel hut in the first valley because it was too accessible to day trippers from Andermatt, who have no concept of the occasional plight of mountaineers.

Philip looked distinctly pale, and retired early to his bunk, refusing food as he said he felt sick, but Beryl took him some soup and insisted he drank it, because the day had been long and he must have lost a lot of fluid sweating uphill in the blazing sun. The old guides had a formula: drink plenty of tea when you return to the hut and do not eat food for about an hour,

As a doctor, Beryl's medical curiosity was aroused and she questioned Philip further. He admitted that he had found the day long and tiring, but attributed his sickness to the height. We were now above seven thousand feet and it always took him two or three days to acclimatize. He usually spent these two or three days in the lower altitudes of the valley before attempting the peaks, but this time he had thought that would not be necessary as he had been training by deep-sea diving. This, of course, had had the opposite effect to acclimatizing for altitude: when you consider that the barometric pressure on the peak of Monte Rosa (which is fourteen thousand feet high) is half the barometric pressure at sea level it is not surprising that in the mountains the air is rarefied because the oxygen pressure is low. There is thus a need to generate extra red blood cells to carry sufficient oxygen for the body's needs, particularly under stress. In effect Philip had accustomed himself to *high* barometric and oxygen pressure instead of low, and it was not surprising that he felt ill.

The following morning Philip was a little better and wanted to carry on, but we decided to renounce Piz Borel as in any case a gusty wind from the south foretold bad weather. We set off for the Cadlimo hut across the Bornengo pass. Here we met an extraordinary sight—great plates of ice, about a foot or more across, hurled high in the

Plate 53. A steep gully led up to the Cadlimo Hut; a track of footsteps was already there

air by fierce gusts of wind as though thrown straight at us by an invisible giant hand—something which I had never seen before. We were thankful to reach the comparative stillness on the far side of the pass. Across the valley a long steep gully led up to the hut. We were lucky to find a track of footsteps in the snow, as this would save a lot of time in cutting steps ourselves, but even then it was a balancing act as we carried our skis up the steep slope and extricated our legs which got snowed up to the knees when some of the steps gave way.

The Cadlimo was a pretty little stone-built hut with blue and white striped shutters. It was partly submerged in drifted snow and we effected our entrance up a ladder into an upstairs window. We soon had the wood stove going and the appetizing smell of frying pork filled the kitchen. We intended to spend the night there and have another attempt at climbing Piz Borel the next day before running down to Curaglia. After our meal we started to play chess, but every time I glanced out of the window the sky became more leaden and the clouds began to thicken. It looked as though we might have an enforced stay, snowed in in the hut for several days ... surely the sensible thing to do would be to sit out the bad weather in the valley—it was more comfortable. What time was it? ... three o'clock ... yes, we could reach the Lukmanier pass before dusk, where there was a Hospiz.

Plate 54. The Cadlimo Hut: the winter entrance through an upstairs window

Having eaten a good meal Philip said he felt better and we all agreed to go down to the Hospiz. Pursued by thickening cloud we skied down, buoyed up with the prospect of warm beds and wine; we might even get as far as Curaglia and hear the rattle of dominoes and the clatter in the smokey bars as the peasants played cards. We reached the valley floor. It was flat and there were no landmarks—it was as well we had decided to come down, as navigation would have been difficult in bad weather. We could now see the Medel Valley below us: oddly enough, the mountains above it were still in sun, although all about us was gloomy murk. "Their turn next," I thought, grimly, as the snowflakes began to fall. To reach the Medel Valley we descended a steep slope. The snow was soft—oozing wet—rotten to the point of avalanching, but it was held back safely by broken terrace-like ridges.

When we reached the head of the Medel Valley leading up to the Lukmanier pass our luck ran out—there was only frozen water. We had bought new maps but even since the printing a reservoir had been built. The Hospiz, which used to be open during the winter, was now under water. To reach the road, which we could see on the far side of the valley, meant an extra mile or two détour. However, our spirits rose. A new Hospiz had been built and surely the occupants would carry on the old tradition. It was shut! The new grey granite and decorative stained glass windows mocked us in their affluence.

While snowflakes swirled around us we stood disconsolately munching chocolate, quietly cursing the occupants for not being there, and hoping that they were offering up prayers for those in peril. Dusk was descending and it would be a nine-mile walk down to Curaglia. At least it was downhill and we resentfully shouldered our skis, following a line of obscene electricity pylons across to the "galleries" of the new road. Some of these half-tunnels were cut out of the rock face with concrete window frames. They should provide easy walking on a road clear of old avalanches and rock falls, and shelter from the driving snow: although "progress" had let us down, it also had its advantages—or so we thought.

It was now snowing hard and rivulets of melting snow trickled off my skis and ran down my neck, but we should have the wind behind us. Confidently we entered the first tunnel. It was dark. There was a chorus of dismay: like skittles in a bowling alley our feet shot in the air, we landed on bruised elbows and bottoms and slid for some distance on a sheet of sheer ice. Our skis, clattering and bouncing, tangled us in a heap. Gingerly we picked ourselves up to our feet—it was the end of the ice, but Philip suggested that if we met any more we should wear crampons.

By this time his nausea had returned and the fall had not helped. He was in bad shape and his retchings echoed with hollow frequency in the tunnel. Despite the nausea, he plodded on, encouraged by the thoughts of lower altitudes: sign of the true mountaineer, who schools himself to carry on even when tired. Beryl and Jim were also tired but neither complained; it must be a survival reaction—better to plod on than spend the night in a cold, draughty tunnel or a bivouac.

As we came out of the tunnel we found the road choked here and there with snowdrifts, and the occasional SOS telephone box taunted us in useless silence as we knew that no rescue vehicle could negotiate the road in those conditions. It was now dark and the surrounding snow was a dim dark grey. We trudged down, down, down. At every turn in the road we had the impression of glowing lights—a mirage in a snowy desert. At last, there really *was* a glow, but it was far off. We came to a little village lit by a solitary lamp. There was no inn, nor had we reached Curaglia, which was a further three miles away. We wandered round, soaked through, looking for a light in a window, but all was black. We went back to the lamp, thinking that we would have to carry on down the road, but Beryl noticed some telephone wires attached to a house. We knocked on the door, hoping we would be able to telephone for a taxi.

Dripping though we were, the householders invited us into their spotless kitchen and they telephoned the Scopi Inn at Curaglia to reserve beds for us. That was not all, for they insisted on taking us to Curaglia by car, which involved two journeys because of our gear. This was true mountain hospitality. Our luck was in! At the Scopi Inn we drank wine with our benefactors, our minds in a haze. It had been a fourteen hour journey, which was a long way for a second day. We dropped into bed, our bodies bruised and aching but with the comforting thought that tomorrow it would be snowing.

"It isn't easy, travelling with the Wilberforce Smiths," murmured Beryl as she tried to find a more comfortable part of her anatomy to lie on in bed.

We had a day of enforced break from our route and in spite of the snow we took the opportunity to buy some chocolates for our benefactors and then to explore Disentis. Dominated by its renowned monastery, it is a large village in the valley of the Vorder Rhein. Here, nearly two hundred years ago, a Benedictine monk called Placidus à Spescha earned the title of "Father of Modern Mountaineering". He tended the sick in the neighbouring valleys for seventeen years until the authorities, in their ignorance, thought his wanderings in the mountains meant he was spying for the French; then the French came and destroyed all his manuscripts and scientific collections. In spite of all his mountaineering, climbing many peaks, he appears rarely to have set foot on a glacier.

Returning to the Scopi Inn we had a cheerful greeting from the proprietor, inviting us to try his own honey and local cheese derived from pastures above the village, which he proudly asserted were the finest in the district. We felt his pride was justified.

We were delighted to awake to a fine morning, the new snow giving freshness to the fields and slopes above the village. Unfortunately Philip surprised us by saying he could come no further. It is true that he had not been feeling well, and the descent of three-and-a-half thousand feet and a fourteen-hour day had been too much. We were disappointed both for his sake and our own, particularly as he had a marvellous sense of humour. However, ski-touring requires prudence rather than foolhardiness and as we would once again be high up in remote glacier regions his decision was wise. Jim seemed to have survived the long day and was keen to carry on, and we were glad to have his company.

We set off for the Medels hut and a returning party of Dutch skiers warned us it was cold there. As the valley broadened above the trees we crossed the pastures but there were no cows there now to provide the delicious cheese. An impressive gully led up to the hut, which was perched on a shoulder above the pass—the Fourcla Lavaz—a more windy site could not have been chosen on which to build a hut. The Dutchmen had been right: it *was* cold and another reason was the high cost of wood—four Swiss francs a bundle and the slivers were thin and rapidly burned through. After a huge meal of bacon and eggs the cold drove us to our bunks and we piled on as many blankets as we could find. During the night the wind howled round the hut and the cold affected me. I had difficulty in passing water, but at the time I had no idea of the crisis it would create later on.

The cold inside was unpleasant; outside it had its advantages because we knew that the snow would not soften too quickly so there was no urgency to start for Piz Medel. Climbing the glacier we passed a huge outcrop of rock called the Refugi de Camutschs (Chamois), but we saw no chamois taking refuge, it may just have been a fanciful name—although the numbers and spread of chamois have diminished in Alpine areas over the years.

The summit of Piz Medel is ten thousand five hundred feet up and when we reached it, ridge upon ridge of fine mountains stretched on all sides like waves breaking on a shallow shore, and I marvelled how at one time all this had been covered with ice. Many of the peaks I could not identify, and it was too cold to make a prolonged study of the map. To the south were the Adula Alps and the Canton of Ticino, the only Italian-speaking Canton in Switzerland, the River Ticino flowing into Lake Maggiore and out again towards the Adriatic. To the north, headwaters of the Rhine begin their long journey to the North Sea.

Plate 55. Piz Medel: the reward from the summit

A clear starlit morning greeted me as I looked outside, the crescent moon hanging over the peaks, but somehow we did not leave for the Terri hut until half-past seven—far too late. After a short run down we had to turn into a side valley, but listening to Jim and Beryl in the guise of Devil's Advocates I turned into our side valley too soon and later I cursed myself for not having had the courage of my convictions. We found ourselves on a broad shelf and an impassable cliff separated us from the valley floor below. Thwarted, I gazed across to our pass—the Fuorcla Sura de Lavaz: we could not afford to waste time as the slopes on the far side were already in full sun, yet we would have to retrace our steps. Although this time-consuming diversion gave us an amusing run down, we were now two hours behind. This meant a long hot climb up the breathless valley and there is nothing more frustrating than hurrying against time and weather. It was made worse by a formless cloud growing ahead of us and collecting on the pass, accentuating our mistake. Our progress seemed snail-like, and we did not reach the pass until mid-day. The rocky wedge of Piz Güda faced us across the valley to the west, far beneath us a green valley led through the haze down to Olivone in the Ticino and far away to the east we caught our first glimpse of the Rheinwaldhorn. In profile it looked impressively steep from this side—we would be climbing it in three days' time, we thought optimistically. We did not stop long on the pass as the nearest mountains were losing their form in the heat haze and a halo of cirrus surrounded the sun and produced a circular rainbow: every indication of bad weather. There was now no time to climb Piz Valdraus and we hastened down to the Plaun la Greina on surprisingly good snow. A little stream wandered about the plain and it seemed incongruous that its waters would soon join the Rhine. Here we had a short stop for lunch.

Entering a narrow valley, now deep in shadow, the snow was already crusting over and it made a treacherous run down. The Terri hut was perched on a domed hillock at a confluence of valleys like a mediaeval fortress guarding the way. Though it was being rebuilt during the summer months, it was now deserted, but we found all we needed and used up Philip's unwanted provisions. It would be difficult for anyone travelling down the Vorderrhein road and looking up at the south-leading valleys to have any conception of what lay behind—we were in a remote triangle encompassed between the Lukmanier and San Bernardino Passes and yet we were in a place almost inaccessible in winter. There had only been one party in the hut that year. Thoughtfully they had left their bread and spaghetti behind, assuming that the next party, if any, might be snowed in. They were—the mice had eaten the provisions!

I was glad of the companionship of Jim and Beryl, for although we were only six miles from the nearest habitation we felt the loneliness and isolation such as people must feel at the North Pole. I had plenty to worry about because the eastern way out from the Terri hut lay over the Diesrut Pass, which is narrow and flanked on either side by the steep slopes of Piz Tgietsehn and Piz Stgir and very avalanche-prone. I had known this from the map when pre-planning the route, but since weather and snow conditions vary so do the dangers. The air was warm, which added to my anxiety, so after a meal I went outside to study the area close at hand with my little monocular spy-glass.

The "pimple" on which we were perched was the centre of a three-pronged star. To the north the Sumvitg Valley led down to the Vorderrhein. This had steep walls prone to avalanches and was probably the reason why the hut was seldom used in winter as this was the nearest access. The way we had come, over the Plaun la Greina in the west, was safe but it led in the wrong direction down to Italy. The Diesrut Pass would take us eastwards, the way we wanted to go to get down to Vrin. The lower half of the pass looked horrible, even steeper than on the map and by now we well knew that it may have changed since the map was printed. It was almost a wall flanked by avalanche-prone slopes and thus with a two-day-old cover of snow it was out of the question, far too dangerous under present conditions. However, I saw an alternative: we could retrace our steps to the Plaun la Greina and join the pass higher up.

That night the banging of a loose shutter and the whistle of the wind in a cracked window reminded me of our isolated position and I slept only fitfully.

We made a four o'clock start. The sky was dark and the stars twinkled. It was still warm, but the snow should be freezing at that hour and unlikely to come adrift. I heaved a sigh of relief—it *was* freezing and we climbed in shadow on crampons

Plate 56. The Diesrut Pass: as we neared the crest our figures eclipsed the sun

startling Schneehühne, or rock partridges, from their rocky cover; though their flight was noiseless, I sympathized with their complaining and protesting whistle.

The night sky was paling and as we reached the crest of the pass my figure eclipsed the watery rising sun and cast a long shadow on the snow. Beryl, who was directly behind me and as usual carried her camera at the ready, raised it in an instant and took a picture which later became a prize winner.

Across the valley rose the pyramid of Piz Vrin, its base cushioned on a boiling sea of cloud. We ran down a narrow stream bed choked with three- and four-foot blocks of snow fallen from recent avalanches. My anxiety was over, as they would be unlikely to avalanche again. Nevertheless, crossing these large blocks of snow was not easy; the skis dug in then fluttered up and down as if we were riding the waves of a rough sea.

We reached the alp village of Puzzatsch. It was uninhabited but footprints in the snow told us that peasants had already visited the chalets to prepare for the spring, and we could not be far from habitation because the whine of a sawmill rose up through the mist. The pasture was extensive and the well-built chalets were an indication of prosperity.

A last rush through sodden slush brought us on to a muddy track and down to San Giusep. There was a cheerful clanging of bells as the leaders of a herd of sheep rounded the corner in front of us. They eyed us suspiciously, refusing to let us pass despite our peaceful overtures. They remained stubborn and we had to climb up the bank to détour round them. Further along, a group of sheep huddled outside a door of one of the chalets, as though seeking admission. We did not stop, however, as it was beginning to snow, we were very thirsty, and we were not far from Vrin.

While we were having a meal at the inn in Vrin, some peasants were playing "Jass", a Swiss card game, and I noticed that they were speaking Romansch. I vaguely expected it because of the curious spelling of the local mountain names such as we had encountered around the Terri hut—Stgir and Tgietsehn—which were neither German nor French, and must be Romansch. Though strictly speaking this language is limited to the Grisons Canton it is heard as far west as Andermatt and east to the Austrian border, but I did not expect to meet it until we reached Bivio and the Engadine Valley. Here, however, the Luminez Valley was an isolated pocket and one needs to examine the geography of the Swiss Alps and some of the history of Switzerland to understand why no less than five languages are spoken.

Nearly one quarter of Switzerland's land area is High Alps, forests or barren rocks, and it is largely the direction in which the main valleys and mountain ranges run that has kept the languages separate. The north of Switzerland is lowland and it is easy to understand why German is spoken as a result of early Alamanni and later German invasions from the north.

The southernmost part of Switzerland, the Ticino, is Italian-speaking, again understandably so, as it is a "Swiss wedge" driven into Italy. If mountain ranges and rivers are natural frontiers, then this area should theoretically be Italian, because it is bounded in the north by the Lepontine and Adula Alps and the Ticino river, and the access to Switzerland is over the St. Gotthard Pass. However, the Swiss nationality of the Ticino dates back to invasions by the Uri and Schwys Confederates between the years 1400 and 1500, the Confederates winning it from the Duke of Milan, and it has never been reclaimed. It is quite a large area extending from Lake

Maggiore in the west to Lake Lugano in the east, and southwards almost to the town of Como.

In the west of Switzerland, French is spoken and to the east, German. From Mont Blanc travelling eastwards the Alps are split basically into two parallel chains by the rivers Rhône and Rhine, which, although they run in different directions, split the Alps in a straight line. To the north of the rivers are the Bernese Oberland and Glarus Alps, and to their south are the Pennine, Lepontine, Adula and Bernina Alps. It is easy to appreciate how the Burgundians and later the French invaded the Rhône Valley to the west, as the river eventually discharges itself into the Mediterranean and French is spoken west of a line running north-south from Neuchatel Fribourg to Sion. Similarly, German is spoken east of this line and was probably introduced up the Rhine Valley which runs eastwards to Lake Constance.

What about the fourth language, Romansch? It is a language of the Canton Grisons and we know that it was spoken in this region until as late as the seventeenth century. It is still taught in the schools but has latterly become the Grisons' second language to German. So what is its origin? The eastern part of the Grisons was invaded in 600 B.C. by an Etruscan Prince named Rhaetus who gave it his name—indeed, the Alps south of the Engadine Valley are known as the Rhaetian Alps.

There was one mountain road used by the Romans to reach this region, and in the year 15 B.C. the Emperor Tiberius invaded across the Maloja and Julier Passes, introducing the Lingua Romana, or common Latin language then spoken. Romansch is a combination of Rhaetian and Lingua Romana and it is due to the confines of mountains and isolated valleys that it has been able to survive as the fourth national language of Switzerland.

There is the fifth language, Switzer-Deutsch, which the Swiss speak colloquially between themselves. It is derived from the very first "High German" spoken by the Alamannic and Swabian tribes who crossed the Rhine in the fifth century and settled in Switzerland. But even this dialect may vary from town to town, valley to valley, as the Swiss are very individual, and a large city like Zurich has differences in the dialect from one end of the city to the other. As Switzer-Deutsch is not a written or literary language, French, German and Italian are used for business and political purposes and since 1937 Romansch has also been recognized as an official language for these purposes, whilst encouragement has been given to developing its literature.

There were no suitable shops in Vrin and a high rock ridge separated us from the parallel Vals valley where we wished to go in order to climb the Rheinwaldhorn. So we took the 'bus down to Ilanz, but found the shops there shut and our thoughts of getting further supplies were still-born, and it was after dark when we alighted in Vals. The garish lights of the Kurhotel blazed through the falling snow—Vals was a fashionable Spa. It was dispiriting, but we found the old village of Vals lay half-a-mile up the road and here we discovered an old-fashioned inn frequented by local people who were pleased to see us and anxious to talk to us. Here in *this* valley German was spoken—not because of the Spa but because of geographical history, they told us. On our way up to Vals from Ilanz in the Rhine Valley we had passed through a long narrow gorge which had sealed off the Vals Valley before the road had been built. The hotelier explained that most of the social contact had been over the high or inhospitable passes in the south which led to the German-speaking Hinterrhein Valley. This isolation had affected not only the language but also the architecture, which was distinctly teutonic in style and quite different from the Italianate houses and chalets in the north. The inhabitants were still strongly individualistic, and even now quarry and trim their own slates and make their own milk churns from soft wood.

These two parallel valleys demonstrate admirably how language and intense individuality have been preserved by geography and history.

Since the road was built, the prosperity of Vals rests on the exploitation of the magical charms of the natural springs and although the "Spa" was out of season, we met groups of foreigners only too willing to discuss their complaints and they tried to convince us that carbon dioxide given off by the pine trees had health-giving qualities! And all the while, lorries trundled bottles of liquid gold down the road.

After several days of incessant snow the housetops were thickly covered by white overhanging caps resembling old French duvets. Stephen Leslie once wrote: "The next best thing to good weather in the mountains was really bad weather". This may be true for a day or two if the mountaineer is warm, well fed and snug in the valley, but I began to wonder if he was ever weather bound for a week. It had upset our plans—we were now three days behind our schedule as we were due to meet Richard Brooke in Splügen. Poor Jim, who had enjoyed the tour as far as it went, wisely left us for some resort where he could get some piste ski-ing. I telephoned Richard in England and asked him to join us at Vals. While we waited for him we explored the valley.

In the little village of Cumbals down the road real skulls were perched in recesses above the church door, looking as grim as shrunken heads from Ecuador. It seems that parts of skeletons had been unearthed during ploughing nearby; the bones had been given burial, but the skulls had been displayed as a gruesome reminder of man's limited span of life. They, too, had been weatherbound as if they had died waiting for the snow to stop.

We capitulated to tourism by visiting the spa-water factory. Visitors watched the various processes from a comfortable lounge high above the factory floor. Samples were available for tasting. On the principle of trying anything once, I succumbed, but I decided I preferred wine!

On the way back, a bulldozer was hard at work clearing the snow. Passers-by prudently gave it a wide berth, but the village priest, determined to hold his course like Pharoah, defied its progress, holding up his hand in admonition as it rumbled towards him and it came to a snorting halt a few yards away. Children glissaded down the piled-up snow, watched by the statue in the village square of the Madonna cradling her Child from the elements.

Plate 57. Cumbals: real skulls were perched in recesses above the church
door—a reminder of man's limited span of life

Vals to the Julier Pass

The last time I had skied with Richard Brooke had been on a combined Alpine Club/Alpine Ski Club meet in the Bernina. When he joined us this time, he told us he had had no difficulty in locating us in the Inn—he had simply observed the hotels from the outside and decided they were all too grand for the Wilberforce Smiths!

Richard is a first-class mountaineer and had been with Hillary in the Antarctic. His experience in snow-craft and climbing would be a great asset. Laced with humour, he shows an instinctive unflappable approach to mountains and we have similar ideas on how to climb them; his love of mountains mirrors my own.

Plate 58. Richard Brooke at the tree line where the snow petered out

The weather was on the mend and we decided to start the next day for the Lenta hut to climb the Rheinwaldhorn on our way over to Splügen and the Julier Pass. When I announced our intention, the proprietor looked very solemn and shook his head gravely. I could hear him thinking and I knew what his comment would be. In the meantime Beryl returned with the provisions, rather worried because she had been advised by the shopkeepers that it would be suicide to go.

"The way to the Lenta hut is very dangerous with all this new snow," the innkeeper said, now that he felt that he had allies. Then as an afterthought he added: "Why not cross the Tomul Pass?"

Richard and I looked at the map. The valley to the pass was very steep and even narrower and it only took us into the next valley and not in the direction we wanted to go. The innkeeper was not a mountaineer nor was the shopkeeper; their advice was obviously well-meant but ignorant and we knew that by now the valley snow was well settled. The proprietor seemed somewhat mollified when I promised to turn back if conditions were unsafe, but we could hear his complaining mutter to a friend as they sat together over a glass of wine. After every accident there is certain to be one or more persons to testify that they "told him not to go".

"You'll be all right," said a roadmender who was drinking at the bar. "You're mountaineers." He was one himself and in the course of conversation we agreed that the advice given by uninformed villagers is frequently wrong and we preferred to take encouragement from one whose occupation took him into the mountains.

Next morning a taxi arrived at dawn to take us up the road as far as the dam, and this saved us two hours' walk. We put on our skis and started climbing. Conditions were wintry all right: the cold north wind numbed our fingers and our ski bindings creaked with frost. Underfoot the snow was well settled and as we walked through the trees we could see the sun-gilded spire of the Zervreilahorn. Our path contoured above the artificial lake, a dam not long built with the chalets of Zervreila now beneath the water—such is progress, but it always makes me feel sad. We reached a notice which starkly informed the traveller that he proceeded at his own peril—bears, wolves, dragons, who knows? Perhaps it was only as far as this place that the Kurverein (a local council responsible for paths) was insured—or was this the point for our suicide predicted by the hotelier and shopkeeper?

At the end of the lake the path dropped to the valley floor, which now began to narrow. Alp huts had been built, many of them backing on to large rocks to protect them from avalanches. There had been only a few inches of new snow, which confirmed our belief in the difficulty of judging snow conditions in the mountains when there had been such a heavy snowfall in the valley—but then one so often sees from mountain tops in full sun the cloud sea, or *"nebelmeer"* lying in the valley where it is either raining or snowing. One or two avalanches had come down but they were too small to reach the valley floor: so much for suicide—and we certainly saw no dragons.

The Rheinwaldhorn appeared at the head of the valley: insignificant at such a distance it lay at the end of a fine glacier, and before long we were at the Lenta hut. It was newly-built, for the old one had been destroyed by an avalanche in 1968. The new site had been chosen on a safer slope and to make doubly sure the present hut was incorporated in a huge boulder which formed part of the structure. A large fresh snowdrift obscured the door and it took us a long time to dig it clear. It was cold inside

Plate 59. The white patch in the centre distance is a sea of cloud or *Nebelmeer*. People living in the valley do not appreciate the weather conditions above the clouds

and it did not feel as though the hut had been used recently, so we threw open the shutters to the warm sun and brought the blankets out to air.

It was barely mid-day and over a leisurely meal we basked outside in the sun. It was a wonderful situation: the north-facing Lenta Glacier curved up to the peak of the Rheinwaldhorn in a series of steep slopes and terraces, broken by the crevasses in deep blue shadow, while the pale blue-green séracs forming their upper lips caught the slanting sun. I was reminded that the first ascent of the Rheinwaldhorn was made by Father Placidus à Spescha nearly two hundred years ago. It amazed me to think how far he was from his native Disentis and how difficult it must have been. In those days there were no Alpine Club huts to provide an overnight stay and shorten the journey before climbing the peak, which was one of the loftiest in the eastern half of the Lepontine Alps. Towards Vals, down the valley, we watched a party of five Swiss toiling up in our tracks. We could tell they were Swiss by the way they followed each other regimentally and climbed in unison at fair speed. They were heavily laden, as they intended to stay five days we learned, and were obviously going to make themselves comfortable. When they unpacked their rucksacks it was plain that meals were to be accompanied by an abundance of wine and Richard's envious glances were understandable.

The lengthening shadows and the cold drove us in.

Soon after dawn we started off for the Rheinwaldhorn, threading our way through the lower part of the glacier which is steep and crevassed. Stealthily a mist rose from the valley: the mountains appeared like ghosts through the veil of cloud and the hollow disc of the sun came and went until there was a stirring above us and the mist lifted to reveal an almost clear blue sky, We had been in comparative shelter on the glacier and watching the clouds torn to shreds on the ridges above we braced ourselves for the cold we would surely meet. The icy wind had frozen the snow hard below the summit and we stopped to put on crampons—an evil job in the biting cold and our fingers stuck to the cold iron as we fumbled with the straps. Leaving our skis and rucksacks we walked to the top. It was nearly windstill—a phenomenon commonly met in the mountains. I remember one occasion when we climbed in a fierce, freezing wind and yet on the top I struck a match and the flame needed no protection.

Plate 60. The summit of the Rheinwaldhorn: this is why I love mountains

For once I knew why I loved mountains. Wave after wave of snowy peaks, passes and valleys ... Piz Medel now far distant both in space and time ... at our feet the olive-green valley of Malvaglia plunged over six thousand feet into the depths and a little stream of meltwaters wound its way through the valley to join the Ticino river ... and to the east were the mountains to come.

A sudden evil, chilly wind bullied us down reminding us that it had already spoilt the snow. The Swiss had been watching our descent from a neighbouring mountain and were unimpressed with our skill—but then how could they know that such a vast expanse of snow below them was so treacherous at close quarters?

We were pleased because we had achieved a very fine peak and at the same time the tracks we had made would serve us next day for our journey over to the Rheinwald Valley—the crossing point over the Lenta Lücke Pass lay on the shoulder of the Rheinwaldhorn not so far from the summit.

It was a clear dawn and the Swiss had left before us, carrying light loads to climb the Rheinwaldhorn. To our surprise, despite our heavy loads, we soon overtook them on the steep crevassed part of the glacier. The reason was immediately all too clear. The girl in the party was transfixed, trembling and with tears pouring down her face. A rather ineffectual young man was trying to comfort her but was offering no helpful advice, although the sight of the crevasses had completely unnerved her. We made some suggestions and gave her encouragement, but it struck me that it was pitifully irresponsible to take a relative beginner on such ground, as it might deter her forever. As we continued upwards, instead of counting steps or mentally humming tunes, it was a change to have something to muse on, and I contrasted how this poor woman had been introduced to glaciers and crevasses with the way in which I had trained Beryl. At first I carried her rucksack until she got confidence in negotiating all types of snow, and then I gradually weaned her on to more difficult rock climbs and snowfields, always encouraging her and telling her where to put her feet, and how to cope with the difficulties. Fear is a reaction to the known from experience, or to the unknown by expectation. You can walk along a plank on the ground and not fall off, but raise it a few feet above the ground and the element of fear of falling off is introduced. It was unfortunate that Beryl had fallen off a mountain in Skye when a rock hand-hold gave way, and from then on she had a genuine fear of steep rock faces and snowy knife-edges on mountain crests *(Plate 102, Chapter X)*. Nevertheless, with encouragement she would forge ahead if she had to. For us, the element of fear was always a challenge and it made ski-mountaineering more exciting. I suppose I had learned all this from a Zermatt guide, who was well accustomed to hauling the greenest of mountaineers up the Matterhorn, for in reading the entries in his Guide's Book I saw: "Hermann, you're just wonderful. I'm normally giddy if I stand on a chair!" He must have given that climber great encouragement, and certainly earned his money to have got him up the Matterhorn!

Plate 61. The north-facing glacier which leads up to the Rheinwaldhorn is the Lenta Glacier.
The gaping crevasses unnerved the young woman

However, for this poor young woman, suddenly deposited on a glacier and not forewarned, it must have been a terrifying experience to look down a wide gaping hole, disappearing hundreds of feet into blue-black darkness *(Plate 39, Chapter III):* her sense of fear would be similar to one when facing a shark with open, snapping jaws, yet the sight of a crevasse would not affect the peasants who lived in the mountains, were used to them, and hung their meat in the ice caves and crevasses before there were refrigerators.

It is just possible that her young man was not as thoughtless, for living with a person at close quarters and under stress in the mountains soon determines whether you respect them or whether they have irritating habits such as sucking their teeth and nose-picking—situations which could cause marital disharmony! Perhaps he was putting her to the test or trying to shake her off!

We reached the pass—a flattening on the shoulder, for the true pass is a bit lower and not practicable in winter—and far in the distance was the San Bernardino Pass; but nearer at hand were some dreamlike glaciers specially made for the ski-mountaineer: the Paradies Glacier—its name is so descriptive! We were soon strung out on a steep slope looking for a feasible way down, but the broken ground provided a good anchorage for the snow. Entering a stream bed in a narrow gorge just below the Zapport hut, we found it was choked with old avalanches and as a reminder a cascade of wet snow tumbled down and rumbled after us. It was not the place to linger.

As we reached the open plain of the Rheinwald Valley we could see the St. Bernard tunnel and the drone of the traffic was audible even five miles away. It was a toilsome flat plod along the valley to Hinterrhein at the mouth of the tunnel. A luxurious-looking inn at the roadside raised hopes of a gourmet meal, but all they could offer was cheese and beer. I telephoned the hotel at Vals to tell them of our safe arrival and we then took a 'bus up to Splügen. Rucksacks under ten kilos travelled free, but there was no nonsense about weighing our considerably heavier sacks as the conductor was a mountaineer.

Splügen appeared little altered, from my memories of many years ago, but our inn had become a hotel. The stone-flagged floor, from which the snow never melted, was now replaced by one of polished pine, but the welcome was just the same. The proprietress remembered us, as we had been there one Easter when there were no other guests and Splügen was still unknown. She remembered drawing faces of "him" and "her" on the eggs which we had found in our packed lunch! These mountain people have a refreshingly simple humour.

We had planned to go round the Surettahorn, which meant crossing three passes, to get to Innerferrera. As we stole out of the hotel at 4 a.m. rain drops pattered on my windjacket. There was a sprinkling of new snow in the street. Two men passed us going fast, and to my friendly enquiry I had the laconic reply: "In the hills". Whether they were smugglers or just peasants going to work we shall never know.

It had become warm and misty before we struck into the hillside to find our first pass, and it soon turned to snow. We stopped to consider—we should need better weather than that. As if to help us make up our minds, a weasel peeped shyly from behind a rock, at the same time frightening a ptarmigan which flew off in the direction of the Splügen Pass which led over to Italy. Yes! we would cross it too, spend the night in Madesimo and find another way to Innerferrera the next day.

It was a dull walk up the snow-covered road and snowdrifts would make the road impassable for many weeks. We comforted ourselves with thoughts of hot coffee when we reached the village of Monte Spluga, on the Italian side of the Splügen Pass, at the head of a lake with a dam at the end. Despite the hydro-electric scheme, however, the inhabitants had fled, leaving only a few workmen digging out the abandoned village and clearing the road. A lorry crept up behind us and we gratefully accepted a lift on top of mounds of road grit; we were transported the length of the lake to the dam, and climbed down from the lorry. The driver grinned as he drove away: perhaps he thought we were smugglers—no sensible people would be crossing from Switzerland in that weather! In fact, we wanted to look at the Niemet Pass. It looked dispiritingly steep in the wan light, but it could possibly afford a way over to Innerferrera next day.

Madesimo was a queer mixture of old and new buildings and expensive-looking shops: it was a newly-developed ski resort. It was still sufficiently unspoilt, however, to have a good inn, the Cacciatora and to underline its name "The Hunter" it was full of stuffed animals; and the gourmet cuisine gave us regrets at having to return to Switzerland. We ate so much that after lunch we retired to bed; we got up for dinner and went to bed again—a curious day!

The next morning, at the foot of the Niemet Pass, we shouldered our skis and started to climb steeply, as we had foreseen. The snow was too soft to bear our weight—just what we might have expected. Richard took the lead and was going fast. Occasionally I glanced back. The clouds were gradually covering the sky. Then the gradient became really steep, giving the erroneous impression that it was nearly vertical: we could put out our hands and touch the slope. By this time we were mid-thigh deep in snow. Richard was still leading, but, finding it exhausting, he gave me his rope and ice-axe. We pulled one leg out and bent the knee to ninety degrees before plunging the foot in again, our heavy rucksacks throwing us off balance. To steady ourselves, we planted the skis firmly above us, and even bushes were not ignored, as make-shift hand-holds. It was like wading through deep thick mud, made worse by the steepness of the slope. It was curious to think that in summer it would be a simple zig-zag path. At last the gradient eased. We sat down for a rest, but not for long as the weather was still chasing us, occasional patches of sunlight accentuating the general greyness. As we passed the deserted frontier shed back into Switzerland, a great curved cloud was being driven towards us, its edges frayed by strong wind. We hurried along a narrow icy rutted path through the woods above Innerferrera. It became steeper and once launched on this "toboggan track", with skis planted in different ruts, there was little we could do except hope that there was nothing fearful round the corner! At length this became too hazardous and we took off our skis and trotted down sedately.

There was a rushing sound, like a river in full spate. The tempest hit us. Tree tops swayed violently, pine trees bent almost in half like jumpers' poles, clouds of snow whirled horizontally stinging our eyes and lashing our faces unmercifully. We leaned against the wind with all our weight and pushed on down to the denser trees in the forest below. By the time we saw the roof tops of Innerferrera we were deep in the valley: the wind had dropped but it was snowing heavily. We crossed the river, here fed by the waters of the Lago di Lei—through some quirk in the international boundary line they are the only Italian waters to flow into the Rhine.

Thankfully we entered the little inn and dried our clothes on the stove, but our hopes of a hot meal were dashed as the inn was otherwise almost in a state of hibernation. We could be provided with soup to help out our own provisions, but, as the old lady in charge explained, there was very limited traffic going through these days. While we were waiting for the 'bus to take us up to Cresta, she told us that there were other, similar, villages which had become a sort of no-man's-land between the towns and ski resorts, lying in a state of suspended animation as their purpose had now gone. We had a long wait for the 'bus as the service is infrequent and unpredictable—a strange thing for Switzerland.

It was late afternoon when we arrived in Cresta, over four miles up the valley. The Easter holidays were just beginning and the hotelier was not very pleased to see us, explaining that we should have to give up our beds in the morning. This looked serious as there was little likelihood of an improvement in the weather. A group of young Germans casually mentioned that they were living in the *Matrazenlager,* a multi-sex dormitory of two-tier bunks. This was news to us and as there were plenty of spare bunks, we quickly arranged a transfer before more guests arrived.

I was relieved to find Cresta unspoilt: one hotel and one shop. Plans had been under way to develop—or to spoil—the village but fortunately an *impasse* had been reached: the ski-lift builders were unwilling to risk their capital before there was more hotel accommodation, while the hoteliers would not build until the ski-lift was there. In spite of a rather grim extension, the fine old inn still retained considerable character. The old salon transported us back a century: the finely panelled room was stiffly furnished with Victorian sofas and plush armchairs, in beautiful rosewood and in a theme of green. Aspidistras and antimacassars completed the scene. The antique wall clock was silent: the stationary hands had probably indicated the same time since the turn of the century. In this atmosphere of changeless years we read and played chess until I decided to look at the weather—which brought us back to the present. I looked out of the window and saw the strong wind blowing the snowflakes horizontally down the valley. Yes, the wind was strong—this was disturbing—what would it do to the snow? From past experience I knew that the Stallerberg Pass had a reputation for harbouring wind-slab snow on the Juf side, as the wind usually whistles across it from Bivio, making it a lee slope. This was the reason why Beryl and I had never skied over to Juf from Bivio, as the wind-slab might well avalanche. This time we proposed to cross the pass in the opposite direction, from Juf to Bivio, and at least we would be climbing up the slope and we would be able to assess its safety far better than if we had been ski-ing down it. However, it was necessary to try and find out if there was any possibility of wind-slab having developed below the pass: and to do this I had to know from which direction the prevailing wind had been packing the snow during the winter months, as this is the time when the slab normally develops.

I sought out the hotelier, as there was no-one else to ask, but wind was just wind to him, and as for its prevailing direction, well ... it just made him cold! The next best thing was for me to go outside and find out for myself. I examined boulders, pebbles, tree stumps and all the small projections I could locate to see how the snow had drifted on to them, as the snow builds up into a small cliff on the windward side and trails off to a point to leeward. It seemed that the prevailing wind had come from the south-west, and as the Stallerberg Pass faces south-west it had been lying to windward and to my

Plate 62. I examined tree stumps to determine the direction of the prevailing wind

joy I felt that the snow would be well and firmly packed and that there would be no danger of slab formation. It is essential for the ski-mountaineer to know why wind-slab is dangerous, and how it is formed, because then he knows where to look for it and is able to give it a very wide berth.

Plate 63. A windslab avalanche: showing the line of cleavage (C-C) and the smooth underlying surface (S) where there is no anchorage

The Stallerberg Pass itself lies above seven thousand feet and at these altitudes the snow lying nearest to the ground is comparatively warm, and hardly varies in temperature being plus or minus 5°C throughout the year. However, the snow deposited on top is not only colder, but is also cooled by wind and it forms a surface crust which bonds

Plate 64. Bivio: an old haunt of ours. It was like coming home

well on a windward slope. On the leeward slope the ground-level snow, being warmer, gradually sublimates or vaporizes into the cooler snow lying above it, and forms hoar frost crystals which have no cohesion as they are cup-shaped and slippery, like grains of rice. On the windward side of the pass, when there are blizzards and high winds, the new snow is quickly fragmented and packs well, forming a stable, bonded frozen crust. But once the snow reaches the comparative shelter of the leeward side, the wind speed slows down and deposits the snow on the hoar crystals which freeze instantly first forming a crust which builds up into a thick cake of slab. Although it is well-packed snow, it lies virtually like a bridge on top of the slippery hoar crystals with a space of air in between—this is a horrible, unstable situation as the slab has no anchorage. Should the skier walk across it, he hears a disconcerting hollow thump with each footstep; like as not, the slab will crack with his weight and the air is expelled through the line of cleavage, with a nasty "whuff". If the slope is steep enough the slab breaks up into large angular blocks as much as two or three feet in diameter and avalanches. It slides off the hoar crystals which act like roller bearings—in a way like launching a boat. A jagged overhanging wall of snow remains above at the site from which the slab broke away.

A short journey by 'bus took us to Juf; at seven thousand feet it is the highest village in Europe inhabited throughout the year. I had often looked down on it from the mountains above Bivio, and seen a remote little huddle of brown chalets in an isolated valley. Now I was there in reality. It too had not changed, except for a small drag lift for a few week-end skiers. The climb up to the Stallerberg Pass was easy and presented no problems and we were soon swinging our way down the slopes to Bivio.

Plate 65. View into the Bregaglia from Piz Lunghin (Bivio)

(Top) Plate 66. The print of the eagle's wing as it swooped down to a baby hare and flew off with it
(Bottom) Plate 67. The tracks of chamois and hare

I had visited the village many times over the years—Beryl, too, as she had not only learned to ski there but to tour as well, as the ski teachers prefer to tour in the mountains after the morning's lessons. I had run touring courses for the Ski Club of Great Britain—what better way to begin to learn ski-mountaineering than from a comfortable hotel, and returning to it at night! We had known the hoteliers since they were children and watched their small inns turn into hotels. Above all, the thing which remains in my memory of the Valetta Valley is its isolation, which encourages the presence of wild life, as Bivio is close to the Swiss National Park. The tracks of the chamois gambolling round bushes are abundant; the prints of a fox dragging his dinner home; the footmarks of a baby hare which cease beside the print left by the eagle's wing when it swooped down and flew off with its prey: these are stories of savagery in the struggle for existence, yet so near is the sophisticated life of humans—St. Moritz lies just over the pass, like Klosters, only a short distance away.

When we arrived at the hotel, the Torriani family greeted us warmly and the roadmender, the garage owner, the mayor and the carpenter all came in later and we celebrated with schnapps, schnapps and more schnapps, catching up with the latest gossip of the village.

Albula Alps to Upper Engadine Valley

The Julier Pass to Susch

A local taxi took us up the road to the Julier Pass to save time and we put on our skis and started to climb the Val d'Agnel. As old landmarks unfolded I tried to count up the number of times I had been there before.

A bitter wind was blowing on the pass and the snow was heaped up into little ripples and cliffs of *Skavla (Plate 6, Chapter II)*—a lovely-sounding Norwegian word simulating the scrape of skis sliding over the hard, irregular surface. "Snow devils" like dust whorls of the desert and Arabian Nights spun round and wheeled away in a wild kind of dance in front of us as we skied down to the Jenatsch hut. Although it was deserted, the baskets outside were full of provisions and gear, and equipment occupied every available corner: the Easter crowds had arrived in full force. How different from the last time I was there, when two Swiss from the Torriani's hotel had accompanied us in order to provide Beryl with her first experience of a mountain hut. Otherwise it was still the same and I wondered whether the stove still smoked abominably when the wind was in the west. It was a brute!

Beryl decided she had had enough for one day, and after a hasty lunch Richard and I set off for Piz Calderas in gathering cloud. The Jenatsch hut lies in a splendid position for short day tours—the really energetic may even roll two tours into one, as we did! As we climbed, a large party of skiers emerged from the greyness above us, like a herd of

Plate 68. The Fuorcla Mulix Bever: Piz Julier was peeping shyly over the billowing cloud

reindeer only the heavy tramping and forced breathing were missing. Some came down in skillful short swings, others bold—but attempting the impossible—culminated in a cloud of snow, while the cautious crossed and re-crossed in long traverses. We nearly turned back: finding a route through this mass of humanity was difficult, but eventually we did get through.

It was toilsome going, as there was nothing but mist, and mentally I wondered why on earth we did it. I gathered much later that Richard had had similar thoughts, but neither of us had wanted to be the first to turn back. As it was, we climbed until the slope fell away on all sides: we must be at the top. It seemed a curious sort of occupation. We shook hands solemnly and then ran down back to the hut. Beryl, cunningly anticipating our unrewarding tour, had stayed in the hut and made friends with the reindeer-squad and by the time we returned she was drinking their schnapps.

At night we were all packed tight in the two long multi-sex bunks, and poor Richard got little sleep as he was unable to turn over until late in the night, when the more angular portions of his neighbour had receded.

It was a clear morning and we made a start for Preda. I had slight misgivings over the route as the contours on the map looked intimidatingly close on the lower slopes. But they were not as steep as I had expected and the snow was hard enough for us to walk directly uphill on crampons, which gave us a sense of security. A side valley bounded by little peaks led to the Fuorcla Mulix Bever: our difficulties were over.

It was warm on the pass and well worth the excuse to pause and look back. The

Plate 69. Bergün: it was a case of "Sip it, drink it, and drain it"

Plate 70. Piz Kesch: the peak stood out like an islet in a fleecy sea

peak of Piz Julier, which overlooks the north side of St. Moritz, was peeping shyly over the billowing cloud which filled the Bever Valley. We were anxious to get down while we could see clearly, as the clouds were collecting in the valleys, but there was no evil. The Mulix Valley narrowed to a cleft where the slope steepened to forty degrees for a short distance, but once through it we were in warm sun and soon walking through woods to the road leading to Preda and on to Bergün.

Bergün is a typical Grisons (or Graubunden) village. The buildings have fine arched doorways decorated by attractive carvings and much use is made of wrought-ironwork in the windows. It had remained unspoilt—there was not much traffic and a flock of sheep wandered unhurriedly through the street, stopping at the trough to drink: it was a case of "sip it, drink it, and drain it".

In the lovely old inn the proprietress told us that she and her husband had given up their hotel in St. Moritz to come to a quieter life away from the bustle. She had an English waitress and although the proprietress had a command of impeccable English, she confessed that she found it impossible to understand the girl. When we spoke to her, the waitress replied with a broad north country accent, and our explanation of this considerably restored the morale of our hostess.

After a leisurely breakfast we walked up to the Kesch hut in uncertain weather. The path led through quite large deserted villages, many of the alp houses having been sold as holiday homes to new owners in the cities because fewer people worked on the land. Suddenly we heard a hiss of skis from above and a pleasant young man stopped and introduced himself: he was the guardian of the Kesch hut. He apologized that he would not be there to receive us, but he was a guide and had an appointment with clients in Davos. Nevertheless, his wife Erica would look after us. As it was snowing, this was welcome news as the hut would be warm.

The hut was perched up near the shoulder of the Funtauna Pass. This is not far from Davos and is a fine centre for a day or two's ski-ing yet it is strangely not much used in winter. Erica was reading in the kitchen. She seemed very young and like her husband she was a ski teacher in Davos during the season. She loved the peace of the mountains and watching the wild animals: only that morning she had found a weasel in the hut. Normally these creatures hibernate in a snow-hole until the warmth of spring, but this one had chosen the more comfortable quarters of the hut. Although spring was late in the mountains, he had come out of hibernation according to the date on the calendar rather than according to the weather conditions.

Erica invited us into her warm kitchen and allowed us to cook our own food which we had carried up not knowing that there would be a guardian. However, she also had wine and beer for sale, and they provided a good complement to our meal.

It was snowing hard in the morning and we returned to our warm blankets, getting up when our breakfast appetites became insistent, and postponing our attack on Piz Kesch until the morrow. Next day, it was still overcast when we went outside, but the layer of cloud was thin and patches of sunshine drifted slowly across the glacier. Quite suddenly the clouds began to disperse, revealing the semi-circle of jagged rocks piled up like spillikins which contained the head of the glacier. It was broken by a deep gash in the centre—the Porta d'Es-cha—which provides a route over to the Engadine Valley. A heavy white cap of cloud hung stubbornly above the peak and we dawdled over breakfast waiting for conditions to declare themselves. There would be no point in climbing the peak in cloud and if it did not clear we could continue our journey on to the Grialetsch hut. We had another look at the cloud, this time with animosity: and like a craven animal it began to slink away, revealing the snowy wedge of the peak. By eight o'clock we were away.

We climbed comfortably and bore right to take the peak in the rear. Clouds had been steadily filling the valleys below and the surrounding peaks stood out like islets in a fleecy sea, so aptly named in German *Nebelmeer*—cloud sea *(Plate 59)*. Although usually a fine weather sign, the clouds have a disconcerting habit of climbing the mountainside and enveloping the unlucky mountaineer.

Plate 71. Richard and I roped up and set off to climb the final peak

We were now in a steeper subsidiary valley, the cliffs at its head forming a fine amphitheatre—our final climb. It was sheltered and hot under the cliffs and already the snow was softening in the sun. We took off our skis and left Beryl lying under the lee of a little rock wall, as the climb would be steep and fairly difficult and she thought that Richard and I would enjoy it more climbing together.

We roped up and set off, with Richard in the lead while I carried the communal rucksack. The snow, though deep, was fairly well bonded to the deeper layers, and to save labour we climbed the rocks where possible. Our choice of route needed care, however, and we were glad of the rope as we were able to move faster because each anticipated the other's move. Wisps of cloud were steaming from behind the summit ridge, but fortunately they did not engulf us—and then we saw the summit cross: we were up. Beneath us, through holes in the cloud, we could see the green depths of the Engadine Valley. Anxious about the snow conditions for the run down, we did not stay long and we returned to the rocks where we roused Beryl from her sunbathing.

Two figures appeared from below—a man and a woman who thanked us for making the tracks, as they had come up from Zuoz over the Porta d'Es-cha, a long way. Leaving them to climb the peak, we started down and by choosing northerly slopes we succeeded in finding perfect powder snow, as the surface had not been attacked by the sun. It was another example of how our knowledge of snowcraft paid handsome rewards and we swung down the slopes with abandon. From time to time we paused to look back at the peak hanging above us in a thin veil of mist which gave it an ethereal appearance—but these joyous moments are over all too soon, and we were back at the hut.

A guided party had come over from the Grialetsch hut and were sitting outside, basking in the sun. They had had a narrow encounter with an avalanche in the Val Funtauna on the way, showing that the new snow had not completely settled. Then Erica's husband arrived with his party from Davos and we all got talking. They were amused at the long length of my skis—didn't I find it difficult to turn with them? Yes, perhaps I did, but as I usually had a whole mountain of untracked snow to sweep round on them, what did it matter? And they went much faster than the shorter skis. I only found them troublesome on mountain paths and pistes and the latter I never visited because I could not stand the moguls and crowds whizzing by. Erica's husband showed me his new equipment, in particular a new type of skins which he had been given to try. They were just the thing—like the old-fashioned sealskin but made of the plush fabric of the tie-on variety. What was more, they stuck on, as wax had now been replaced by a more modern type of glue. "You must get a pair," he said, and for once I agreed.

Someone produced a guitar, the wine flowed and we were all soon singing mountain songs. The Swiss were intrigued when I sang Italian opera—they seemed to think it somewhat unusual to find that I was an Englishman! In the course of the impromptu concert, the telephone rang—it was the guardian of the Capanna d'Es-cha—had anyone seen the couple we had met on Piz Kesch? They had stopped at the hut on their way up, but not called in on their way down. Nearly all the guarded huts have a telephone down to the valley—the newer ones are radio-telephones because the lines of the older variety frequently got buried and broken in the snow. Especially in Switzerland mountain people keep a close watch: not unlike a coast-guard watch on vessels at sea. The hut telephones provide a valuable link in mountain safety, though it is a pity that they are not available for emergency in the unguarded huts. It had been thought-less of these people not to report their return.

Plate 72. The freezing cloud of the previous night had covered the snow with frost crystals

We were up early next morning and left while the others were still snoring. An easy run in half-light took us down to a plain—the Alp Funtauna—where four valleys meet and by this time the sun had broken through the clouds. Old tracks led down from the left and were partly covered by an avalanche—they were clearly the tracks made by the party we had met in the hut. I could imagine their tensed fear, as the sharp crack of the pent-up snow masses fell on their ears, followed by the ominous, growing rumble of the avalanche. This one was unusual, as it had descended without warning from above; more usually, they are started by the passage of a skier cutting through the unstable snow and disturbing the finely-balanced state. But it was early in the day and still fresh, and there was no risk to us of other avalanches being loosened. Freezing cloud of the past night had covered the snow with huge frost crystals, which glinted like diamonds in the morning sun, their gilded blades contrasting with the limpid blue shadows beneath. Further up, beneath the stickle-back ridge of Piz Vadret, we could see across the Vallorgia glacier to the Grialetsch Pass and, beside it, lay the peak which was attractive enough to make an interesting diversion. We left our skis near the pass and soon climbed the peak, because we were lucky to find deep footsteps and these saved us much hard work. Although it was steep, Richard encouraged Beryl to come up, and we roped together and he gave her a helping hand. She was glad that she came, as an extensive view rewarded us. Far to the west was Piz Kesch—was it only yester-day we were there?

Plate 73. Frost crystals

We ran down from the pass in scintillating powder snow, pausing only to examine some ski tracks, curiously followed by the leaping tracks of what appeared to be a large dog. Before long, we saw the hut roof below us, and vociferous barking marked our arrival as a young alsatian came bounding out to greet us. The guardian, his ruddy face fringed by a fine beard, formally introduced us to her: she rejoiced in the name of Aphrodite—Afra for short—and although only eighteen months old, she was already in Category "A" as an avalanche-rescue dog. Whenever possible the guardian and Afra went off into the mountains together. He was a bachelor: so many of these solitary guardians have a deep love of the mountains, of which they never tire.

The Grialetsch hut is one of the older huts, solidly built of stone; its panelled walls and ceilings were dark with age and smoke. A fine tiled wood stove in one corner gave out a good heat. There is no doubt that they are a very efficient form of heating, but sadly they are being replaced by more modern oil stoves, probably due to the shortage of wood.

After lunch we sat outside to plan out our route for the next day, as we intended to climb Piz Sarsura and run down to Susch for Richard's last day. I felt the weather would hold—but perhaps too optimistically I disregarded the long banks of cloud cross-ing the sinking sun.

Alas for the optimism of weather experts! At 5.30 a.m. clouds swirled around the hut. Another half-hour ... patches of watery sun filtered through broken masses of low cloud, which promised no good ... then at last we could see up the glacier. We said a farewell to the guardian and Afra and set off. The clouds began to close in once more and the ridges and shoulders of the nearer mountains were a shapeless black against the dull white of the snow. Our peak soon became hidden and it would be pointless to climb it. However, the pass was just discernible and its passage would be enough. It was a featureless depression on a ridge. We peered over: it was worse on this side, nothing but blank whiteness. We looked at the map. The gradient was steep for the first sixty feet and then eased off. I stepped round a small cornice. But what were the first sixty feet like? Were there more cornices, wind scoops, little cliffs or small drops of ten to fifteen feet? An apprehensive prospect when you cannot see. I made a ball of snow and threw it down the slope. It rolled gently but disappeared in a flash as visibility was down to a yard, but at least the first step would not hurl me into space. Still, I was not taking any chances and roped myself to Beryl as Richard had the compass.

Standing sideways to the slope I stepped out into the void and searched around with my foot until I felt hard ground under me. Well and good. With each side step I warily tested the snow before transferring my weight and gradually, step by step, I edged my way down until the rope ran out. Then I waited and called to the others to join me. We continued down in this way until the slope eased off. It was now safe to take off the rope, as the visibility had improved.

Richard fished out the compass and we looked once more at the map. There were two valleys and we needed to travel north-east. One of the valleys was terraced with rocky cliffs but these should not prove difficult, as they ran parallel with the length of the valley. I skied downwards ahead of the others into the mist, until almost out of sight—fifty yards perhaps—Beryl followed, then Richard. Another fifty yards ... and another. Fortunately the gradient was now easy and I could check my speed by putting my ski tips together and snow-ploughing. The mist was clearing rapidly and we ran more freely down into a narrow stream bed choked with avalanches, some of them not so old. They were fun to ski across, as the snow had softened—all too often the lumps are hard, which leave the skier impotently fixed with one ski pointing at right angles to the other.

At the tree line the snow petered out and we rested on a bank covered with pine needles. The peaks were still trapped by a dark canopy of cloud, occasionally lit by a sinister orange glow of the sun. Woodpeckers were busy drilling holes in the trees and handfuls of wood chips fell to the ground. Across the Engadine Valley were the Ratische Alps and Lower Alps around the popular ski-ing area of Livigno, and the seventy square miles of the Swiss National Park lying to the west of the Ofen Pass. Here there is absolute protection from man for both plants and animals: no flower may be picked nor tree cut down, no shot may be fired; herds of chamois roam the rocks, roebuck and ibex graze and drink, but no cattle may be pastured.

We crossed a little summer alp and came down to the road running alongside the River Inn: we were now in the Lower Engadine Valley. Susch lay two miles up the road. It was an unpleasant walk, there was no snow and there was much holiday traffic; we were glad to arrive unharmed. In an old-fashioned inn we had a farewell lunch. I telephoned the guardian at the Grialetsch hut to tell him we had arrived safely. He was very glad and enquired about the snow conditions, to advise any other skiers should they arrive. He in turn told us that his hut was deep in cloud.

Sadly we left Richard at the railway station. We had climbed four wonderful peaks, been buffeted by storms, and covered a hundred miles together, always in perfect harmony. Whether he had another meal after he boarded the train I do not know, but Richard admitted later that whereas we lost our appetites in the mountains, he did not, and he was frequently hungry when touring with us.

We made our way up to Guarda, as it would be a good starting point for an unusual entry into the Silvretta mountains.

The Silvretta

Guarda to Ischgl

Guarda lay on a shelf some way above the railway station. In some ways it was a typical Engadine village and yet it had a distinctly Moorish air about it. The peasant dwellings are protected by Federal decree to ensure that the two-tone paintings of mottoes and prayers in Romansch are preserved. The walls are very thick and white, but the windows small and faced with grilles and shutters, reminiscent of harems and women closeted inside. There was an abundance of wrought-ironwork. Romansch was still being spoken here, although the people had allied themselves with the Swiss since the fifteenth century and had been members of the Confederation since the early eighteen hundreds.

In the inn that evening we met a student of architecture who explained how the Swiss mercenary soldiers travelled widely and having seen the style in Spain or North Africa, decided to adopt it on their return. The inn itself was a bit *chi-chi* for our liking, the hall being encumbered with spinning wheels and highly polished milk churns. The proprietors seemed reluctant to admit us, perhaps because of our scruffy appearance, and they were very surprised when we sat down to dinner clean and shaven. We had not expected to see other guests, as Guarda was rather "off the tourist map", but there was a sprinkling of smart visitors, many of them German. We soon made friends, for undoubtedly we were objects of curiosity. They were distinctly valley people, because one friendly family offered to take our "unwanted baggage" round by road! —not knowing that of course there were no roads where we were going and it must be difficult for the average holiday-maker to visualize countryside which is not accessible by car. Even the management thawed eventually, but all the same we were glad to leave for the Tuoi Hut next morning. We still had a few more days left and I felt that the Heidelberger Hut, in the Eastern Silvretta, would be a good place to end the journey.

I knew the Silvretta group well, but I had never approached it from the south side before. Steep and broken country on the Swiss side is separated by a chain of mountains which forms the Austrian frontier. On the north side, in Austria, a series of fine, gentle, undulating glaciers divided by subsidiary ridges, make a very popular area for ski-touring. We had the mixed feelings of curiosity and excitement as we set off, for it was like stealing up behind old friends and catching them unawares.

Crossing the green pastures dotted with purple crocus, the cry of the shepherd boy and the clanging of cow bells rose from the valley bidding us farewell to Switzerland and as we climbed back into the snow it was like walking back into winter. The shrill cry of marmots came from some way ahead. I looked up. Two small figures stood on watch on a large black rock. Suddenly they disappeared. Once again they popped up to look at the intruders: it was incredible that their valley had been invaded. We made a wide détour, to take them from the rear, optimistically hoping to photograph them. But what a hope we had! There were holes everywhere. We chose one and lay still for a full half hour, hoping that they would come up to investigate. Although we had the sense of being watched, they must have smelt us and were probably watching us from another hole. They are shy little creatures unless they live in a protected area, and then sometimes they become quite tame, but unfortunately only too frequently they are hunted.

The sun was scorching: it was time to move. Fortunately we found old ski tracks which were still hard. Many late spring avalanches—the *Grundlawinen*—had come off and cleared the slopes of their winter burden, stripping off every vestige of snow and carrying with them earth, grass, bushes and rocks, which lay piled up on the valley

Plate 74. The Grundlawine strips off the last vestige of snow

floor in muddy heaps. The two peaks of Piz Buin rose steeply in front of us, their height accentuated by fragmented cloud, and we had to crane our necks backwards to see them, hanging as though disembodied in the sky. A little to the right was the long and also steep flank of the Dreiländerspitz, where the idea of our adventure was born, and in between the two lay the Vermunt Pass. It would be a useful way of crossing to the north, but we would save a day by crossing the equally easy Jamjoch to the east. It was fascinating to see these old friends from this new angle—rather like being allowed in the kitchen when you had only known the drawing-room!

The Tuoi hut was built of stone and wood, and lay in a small open plain at the foot of Piz Buin. It was an old hut and very simple. The walls inside had been completely blackened by soot, testifying to one thing: the stove smoked! and previous occupants had made good use of their time drawing graffiti, some of them quite imaginative. The hut had been used more by Alpine troops than individuals, though it seemed very popular from the number of entries in the hut book. The stove worked well, there was plenty of wood, and piped running water from a nearby stream. What more could we want?

Plate 75. The Tuoi Hut: the walls were blackened and the graffiti imaginative

The morning was cloudless and fresh. The first rays of sun touched the mountains as we left the hut. Before long we could see the headland of Piz Tuoi and, further on, the slopes which led up to the Jamjoch; though at a rakish angle, they were not as steep as I had expected. As we neared the pass I could see a few figures on the Vorderer Jamspitz: they must have come up from the Jamtal hut. Even so I had no idea of just what was in store—for when we arrived on the pass, skiers were moving up to the Hinterer

Jamspitz as though on a conveyor belt. I had forgotten it was the first of May, a national holiday. We found a crawling ant-heap of bodies, encumbered by unnecessary ice-axes. We elbowed our way to the top without suffering too many bruises, though one good woman planted her ski stick on my foot—luckily it was blunt, but she showed no contrition. We forced our way to the summit and although the view was extensive, the clouds were collecting fast and there was little to stay for, and one might as well let someone else see the view, who had not been there before.

Whatever would the hut be like? I thought as we threaded our way down through the mass of skiers. Most of them had no rucksacks, I noticed, and a few had minute ones: I wondered how they would fare if there was a sudden change of weather or other emergency. Although to-day it was a frequented highway, a broken leg or a sudden white-out would catch the skier unawares and unprepared and he would have to rely on other more prudent mountaineers to provide protection. Though we were heavily laden and travelling at our usual sedate speed, curiously very few passed us. Indeed, coming towards us was a belated party still climbing the glacier. Suddenly a figure detached itself and came running towards us, waving his stick. I wondered if something was wrong, but no! it was the guardian from the Kesch hut come to welcome us and exchange news. Chance acquaintanceships in the mountains have extraordinary depths and long memories—but then I had rather an unusually thin face and goatee beard so perhaps these helped the memory!

As I had feared, the hut was packed out, but the guardian, Lorenz, remembered us from many years ago and greeted us warmly.

"There's always room for you," he said, taking us up to the dormitory; and he moved everyone's luggage up four feet on the large communal bunk.

When we went down to lunch there was a huge crowd milling around. In the midst of the hubbub was Lorenz, supervising meals, answering queries, quietly giving orders, cheerful and quite unruffled—he never seems to alter. That evening an old mountain friend, a guide from Grindelwald, recognized us and came over. He was with a small group of Swiss and had come over by helicopter to save time. He knew my dislike for this type of ski-touring because for me it broke the charm of nature and turned the mountains into the noisy playground we had witnessed on the Jamspitz.

"They can afford it," he said apologetically, with a grimace.

In spite of the crowded dormitory we passed a comfortable night. Fortunately the occupants nearest the windows had the right idea about fresh air, and kept the windows open.

We were up at 4.30 a.m., ahead of the crowd, although we had an easy day in front of us—over the Kronenjoch to the Heidelberger hut—which took us back into a small tongue of Switzerland. Despite a south wind the snow was hard and the sky was clear. A steep climb on crampons up the Breites Wasser brought us on to the Kronen glacier: it lies in a lovely isolated valley bounded by black jagged tooth-like rocks, appropriately named the Zahnspitze. Happily for us, all the other parties had kept to the main valley. We reached the pass by ten o'clock and, partly through laziness and partly because we wished to have the snow in good condition for the descent, we renounced the idea of climbing the peak. We were now on the frontier—it was wonderful to stand there in silence after the experience of the noisy rabble: we felt it was ours. Then to our surprise two Austrians arrived from the other side—it gave us quite a shock, for such was the isolation that I had the idiotic idea of going across to them and asking them if they realized they were trespassing!

Plate 76. The Zahnspitze: surrounded by jagged tooth-like rocks or "gendarmes"

We had timed the descent perfectly: steep at the top, and slope after slope on the most heavenly spring crust. We paused for breath as we reached the Heidelberger hut, and I said to Beryl "What a wonderful run for our last." For indeed it was. The next day it was snowing and we made our way down to Ischgl and back to England.

What memories we had to cherish. We had seen the wind hurling plates of ice through the air. We had met white void which underlined the advantage of a third person in bad visibility; we had climbed in biting wind to find it windstill on the peak; we had seen trees half bent by a blizzard and experienced a traffic jam on a pass. We had covered some one hundred and fifty miles—though it is difficult to measure on a map where a mountain two miles high appears as a hump of no distance—and we had progressed towards our goal. On the way, we had known the helpful kindness of the local people, who gave so freely without thought of reward; we had known the friendly concern of the hut- and inn-keepers. We had had the companionship of friends who helped us over difficult and lonely terrain and among yawning crevasses—their very presence made the party stronger—but companionship in the mountains goes deeper than individual memories. The tolerance and good humour of my friends and my wife were at times stretched to the limit in cheerless surroundings but never daunted. These invaluable qualities I shall cherish long after the events.

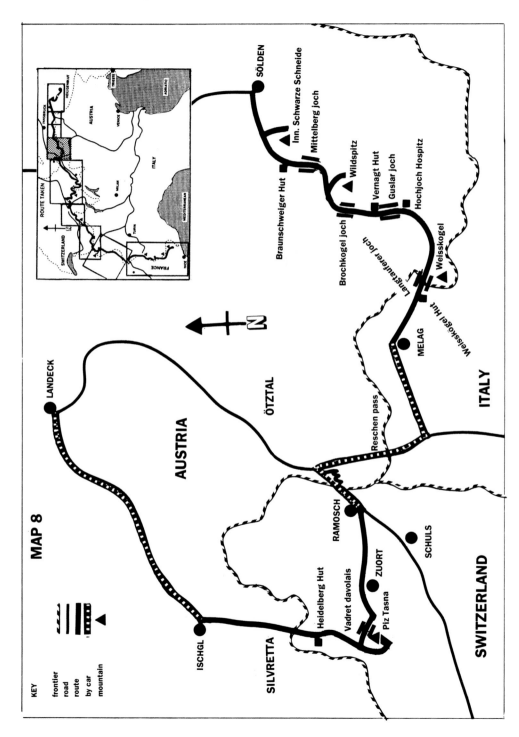

Chapter VI

1974: Year 5. The Year of Disappointment

The Silvretta Alps and the Ötztal

IF YOU consider that it is only about two hours by 'bus or car from Munich in Germany to Innsbruck in Austria, it is not surprising that the Germans have availed themselves of this proximity and made full use of the Austrian Alps, both for ski-ing and climbing, since they have but a few Alps of their own. Before World War II the Germans and Austrians had a combined Alpine Club, known as the *D.O.A.V.* or *Deutsches Österreiches Alpen Verein.* The wealthy and large ski clubs of some of the principal cities built and supported many mountain huts, as can be seen from their names—Wiesbadner, Heidelberger, Dresdener, Nurenberger etc. There are other huts such as the Franz Senn which was built by a philanthropic climber. Members of the *D.O.A.V.,* who did not necessarily have to be German or Austrian, had the privilege of receiving preference for the allocation of accommodation if the hut was over-crowded, and they paid only half price for it, and these funds went towards the maintenance of the hut. Nowadays, when the guardians of the huts are in residence, they make their money from supplying food and drink, though they are bound by rules to allow mountaineers to provide their own food and eat it in the hut without charge, unless the guardian has to cook it. Austrian huts, as a whole, have become more popular than the Swiss huts, owing to their accessibility, and as a result have provided more comforts and facilities; many of them have developed into varying degrees of mountain inns run by what is now the Austrian Alpine Club since World War II. The Jam Tal, Heidelberger and Rudolfs huts are good examples. The Austrian Alpine Club publishes a "Taschenbuch" which lists all huts, their accessibility, height and times when a resident guardian is likely to be there. But it is worthwhile checking in the valley beforehand, because if business is slack the guardian may have returned to the valley. The more remote huts are serviced by guardians who have other occupations such as carpentry. They will give you a key if it is your intention to return to the valley, but in our case we carried a "master key" which we obtained from the Austrian Alpine Club in Innsbruck as we were constantly on the move.

Needless to say, the guardians do everything in their power to increase the popularity of their huts, since their livelihood depends on catering, and many of them or their families run hotels in the valley as well. With this attitude of mind the guardians will now receive advance bookings for large parties, and for people who wish to stay for several weeks. Hence they provide "weasels" or motorized snow vehicles to carry up provisions, but they will also carry up extraordinary items such as suitcases. Regrettably, near a large hut like the Dresdener, ski-lifts have already made their appearance, so that the spirit of mountaineering is rapidly vanishing and is being encroached upon by the atmosphere of a ski-ing resort. This inevitably leads to a lot of overcrowding since long-stay visitors take the best accommodation and the weary mountaineer, who is but a ship passing in the night, is squeezed into what space remains, such as the *Matrazenlager* or dormitory; or maybe he is relegated to a place on the passage floor, without bedding, if the hut is full to bursting during times of public holidays.

The most popular huts are in the Silvretta and Ötztal, because the Silvretta provides an infinite variety of short day tours and it is an ideal area in which to learn about serious guide-less ski-touring: in the first place there are plenty of other people emerging from the hut to undertake the same excursion and one is not alone in the mountains; and in the second place it is a graduation from the type of ski-touring to which I had first introduced Beryl, where we returned at night to a comfortable hotel and a proper bed. Huts like the Jam Tal are a good introduction to the slightly sparser conditions. Many of the huts have two and four-bedded private rooms and sheets are provided except in the dormitory. Showers and flushing toilets have been installed to cope with the tremendous number of skiers using these huts—though at times these amenities freeze up, with unpleasant results!

After Bivio and the Silvretta I had later taken Beryl to the Ötztal. The tours there are longer and more ambitious, and there is an enormous number of huts within easy reach of each other, so that it is possible to spend one or perhaps three nights in each, climbing up and ski-ing down from the main peaks in the vicinity, and then moving on to the next hut over a mountain pass. This is one type of touring at its best because you can explore an entire mountain group. For these reasons Beryl and I knew both the Silvretta and Ötztal groups well, as they had given us our initial training ground. From these most of our holidays had been spent exploring mountain groups in the same way, and as our experience increased so we went to the Stubai, Ortler, Venediger, Bernina Alps, then Norway and even as far away as Kashmir. I suppose the idea of crossing the entire Alpine Chain was the logical development to link up one mountain group with another, as a purposeful journey, in the same way as the early Norwegians used their skis to travel from one place to another.

Ischgl to Sölden

Initially we had reckoned on four or five seasons, but we had no inexorable time-table other than our own limits of age and health. Nevertheless, resuming at the beginning of the fifth year we were only eight days' travel from Bivio—which had originally been our provisional goal for the end of the third year. We had enjoyed the trials and triumphs of the preceding years, we had made and renewed friendships in mountain huts and valleys, and we had had delightful companions for parts of our way. This fifth year, however, we decided we would travel alone and thus avoid committing ourselves to specific rendezvous. In the event, this was probably fortunate.

It was a Saturday afternoon. By the time we had bought provisions it was three o'clock and we were faced with the long walk of about five hours up to the Heidelberger hut. It was some six miles distant, and a climb of a thousand feet—it would help us to get fit. Cunningly Beryl found a place for her bulky sack on the weasel which took provisions up to the hut.

The lower path serves as a piste for downhill skiers as fortunately it is not steep; as they passed us, they looked astonished to see someone actually walking uphill. My repetitive greetings of *"Gruss Gott"* and *"Ski-Heil"* became monotonous: niggled when most of my salutations were ignored, I decided to save my breath and put their bad manners to shame by raising my voice to include all within earshot. But I need hardly have bothered: the old-fashioned habit of greeting fellow travellers is a courtesy disregarded by "battery skiers" and it was a relief when our paths diverged.

Through another of those boundary quirks the Heidelberger hut actually lies in a tongue of Switzerland which protrudes half-way down the valley. This is unusual, as frontier lines are mostly drawn along the peaks at the head of a valley.

Avalanche warnings were displayed beside the path, but the air was fresh and the snow held no menace.

The day began to ebb and darkness fell long before we saw the twinkling lights of the hut in the distance, and by the time we reached it we found it crowded with weekend skiers. As we entered, the guardian paused in what he was doing to look at the new arrivals. His face lit up as he recognized me. "Ah-ha! the Englishman!" he said with evident delight, and he managed to find room for us in the *Matrazenlager*.

We thought we would ascend Piz Tasna the next day: the climb would limber us up as well as give us the chance to spy out from a convenient summit our later route down to the Engadine Valley. As we left the hut the nearby peaks were halved by shreds of mist and the cloud was pierced by the disc of the sun—and the slopes were dotted with half the occupants of the hut, who all seemed to be heading in the same direction. Yet even so there was a pervasive stillness such as one experiences with the dampening down of sound in mist and fog—a silence suddenly broken by the raucous cry of a *Schneehuhn*. As we rounded a corner we saw the ptarmigan strutting up and down in an absurdly pompous way, his short furry trousers emphasizing the ridiculous spectacle. In spite of his cry he showed no fear, and circled us as though asking for titbits as any domestic bird would do.

In the flat light and poor visibility climbing was tedious and it was a relief to leave our skis and walk up to the false summit. Above us, on the true summit, one or two parties seemed to hover disembodied in the mist. We could feel the heat of the sun through the cloud layer, but from the top there was no view of our route and nothing to detain us. We made our way down the top slope carefully roped together, as it continued into the indefinable misty depths below and might prove dangerous. Emerging from the cloud we succeeded in retrieving our skis and to our joy we soon found our ski legs. There is always the hidden dread on the first day that the art has been lost. You stand on the slope—which is always steep at the top—wondering if you will fall and slide to the bottom. So it is every year—then a few tentative turns and with them comes the happy realization that nothing has changed. You have to be bold, and lean out down the slope just that little bit more. Neither of us was a stylish skier, because in order to balance heavy loads on your back you are forced to ski with your feet further apart, more so than style demands. The Eagle Ski Club, a band of ski-tourers and off-piste deep snow enthusiasts, had nicknamed us the "Hay Luges" because of the accentuated upturn of our ski tips and of course we were considered a joke when seen, beside a mountain train or a ski-lift, walking uphill to get fit.

Below Piz Tasna, all was well and to our joy the snow was in excellent condition—so excellent that all too soon we saw the hut round a corner. After a good lunch we lay in the sun dreaming of how nice it would be if all the tours on the traverse were like the one we had just enjoyed.

First away next morning, we were overtaken two hours later by a young Austrian. We all used this as an excuse for a halt, dumping our rucksacks in the snow and talking about our plans. The young man had an extensive knowledge of the Austrian Alps and as well as advice about sections of our route he was able to tell us that the Weisskugel hut would most certainly be open, so we could use it on our way in to the Ötztal.

Plate 77. It is worth making a small détour to visit the church at Ramosch

We crossed into the Val Davolais, but clouds were boiling up from the Engadine and as we met a party of Swiss coming up they utterly refused for some reason to believe it was Piz Tasna above us. Leaving the doubters and continuing our way, we met more parties from Fetan, in the Engadine valley, but then our path diverged eastwards to Zuort. A long path took us through the woods, green moss hanging from the branches of the trees, like an old man's beard, and after a wearying descent it really came as no surprise to find that once again the guide book had erred and the inn was shut. We sat beside deserted chalets and ate a beerless lunch. Ski tracks then led confusingly in all directions through the dense tree plantation, obviously trying to seek a way out between the trees. It was a considerable problem for us, too, until I found the trail of a single skier which showed us he was a man of determination. We followed it and before long it led us to a comfortable track which joined the path to Vna and our overdue glass of beer. Then we hurried down the grassy slopes to Ramosch, hoping to steal a march on time by catching a 'bus, but the last 'bus had gone. We found accommodation and almost fell asleep over our food: we were happy to turn into bed at 4.30 p.m.!

If you ever visit the Engadine Valley in Switzerland either by car or on skis, it is worthwhile making a small détour to visit the church at Ramosch, which has been panelled in pinewood and has the most unusual pews: they are like little armchairs strung together in a row.

The Ötztal

Ramosch is in Switzerland, very close to where the Austrian and Italian borders meet each other for the first time. At this point we had reached the end of the Silvretta range and would be entering the Ötztal, a region of large snowfields and glaciers. The Eastern Alps dominate most of Austria and quite a bit of north-east Italy, stretching well over two hundred miles in a welter of peaks. There are three roughly parallel chains, the chief one being the central one, and lying in the Austrian Tyrol with the Italian frontier along its crest. It is this chain which continues the line of the Alps into the Ötztal, Stubai and Zillertal groups. Whilst the spur of mountain thrusting sharply northwards falls away in the Engadine Valley, it creates a network of valleys either side of the main road across the Reschenpass, a lot of the land well below the snowline. When these circumstances were added to the frontier features, it was hardly surprising that route and 'bus services alike were complicated, and it seemed we should have to wait a long time for one of our connexions. We sat happily drinking our wine in the warm sunshine outside an inn, and watched lazily as the driver of a rather ramshackle motor caravan consulted a map. As the vehicle bore GB plates I wandered over. The man was a pleasant South African, meandering alone through Europe and he readily agreed to take us to Reschen. There we all lunched together and then went our separate ways.

Melag lies a short distance up a side valley but we had time before the 'bus left Reschen to buy provisions and stroll round. Two lakes had been combined by a new dam, and two villages submerged and re-built. There was a fine new church which we explored and which puzzled us because there was no offertory box—did they not need gifts of money? We were unable to make a contribution as we usually did—a customary but I suspect an almost primitive act of propitiation to God when physical danger is never far away. Certainly I hoped our inability to make the gesture would not bring down retribution on our enterprise: was it a warning? Who knows what causes luck to desert one?

We set off up a wild valley in the 'bus, the driver negotiating the bends with zest, on the assumption that nothing would be coming the other way. The only other passenger was a worried-looking woman clad all in black. She turned out to be the owner of the hotel to which we had written to book accommodation for the night, but she expressed total ignorance of the booking and added that the Gasthof was not open at that time of the year. For a brief moment her face brightened as she recalled that her daughter attended to all correspondence, but she soon relapsed into brooding gloom as she remarked: "We have no provisions."

The Gasthof was cheerless although recently modernized, and the daughter appeared witless—which probably accounted for my correspondence having been ignored. The husband was a guide and gave us unwelcome news: the Weisskugel hut would *not* be open. As his son was the guardian, this information was unhappily reliable: the hut was being prepared for Easter, but the son was returning home next day and could not leave us to lock the hut. Even with the most careful planning, with the latest maps and guide books, and despite enquiries made locally, one must never rely on any but one's self in the mountains. Traversing border regions has additional snags. In this case the hut was in Italy and our Austrian master-key was therefore of no use. Equally of only limited value was the old guide's suggestion that as we were to go on to the Hochjoch Hospiz, why not climb the Weisskugel on the way? This we had to rule out—it would mean climbing over six thousand feet from Melag to the summit carrying all our gear over unknown ground and still be ten miles from the Hochjoch Hospiz.

Plate 78. The Weisskugel on the left: we looked back at the Hintereis Glacier leading up to it and once more I felt cheated that I had been unable to climb the mountain

So we set off before five o'clock next morning, a feeble moon lighting our way and daylight catching us up as the hard going eased and our path was bathed in sunshine. We saw the Weisskugel hut as we rounded a shoulder and a young man answered my hail. We were given hot water for tea and we stopped for a second breakfast before the guardian closed the hut and returned to the valley.

Now the fine prospect of the Langtauferer Glacier led upwards, the last stretch steep as the icy river curved right, southwards, to the unseen Weisskugel, while our pass was straight ahead. Line after line of moraine stone shoots spread towards the glacier, but we found huge ice-blocks had fallen across our route from a hanging glacier *(Plate 32, Chapter III and Plate 93, Chapter IX)*, so we had to make a wide détour: ice avalanches are unpredictable and one takes no chances whatsoever with them. At one point we paused briefly to see the shapely snow pyramid of the Weisskugel and sighed for the splendid tour we might have had. Then, as I turned to help Beryl up the steps which I had just cut with my ice-axe, there was a thunderous crack from the hanging glacier below and great blocks of ice began bounding down the slopes away from us. I felt tremendous relief that I had not underestimated the hidden threat and that we were safely on the pass, with a lovely snow bowl at our feet. The Langtaufererjoch Glacier swept down to the even greater highway of the Hintereis Glacier and with our difficulties over once we reached this highway, we relaxed on a big rock in mid-stream. The run to the foot was a delight, but then climbing again, to the Hospiz, was a penance. We were not surprised to find the Hospiz full and although it was more expensive we had little regret that we had no choice but a room to ourselves.

Our next stage was short—simply over the Guslar pass to the Vernagt hut, and even after a late start we still had time to gaze at the Weisskugel Glacier unrolled like a carpet behind us and again we felt cheated. The snow was covered with frost crystals which glistened like jewels in the sun, creating all the colours of the rainbow through their prism-like surfaces.

The Vernagt hut was crowded and the staff unfriendly. They were ill-organized and surly, and our start next day for an ascent of the Wild Spitz was delayed by inefficiency in dealing with the ever-lengthening queue of skiers. The ineffective attempts to provide breakfast exasperated us all and we only obtained hot water for coffee through a friendly little man who got it included with his own order. Outside, the weather seemed equally badly organized, winds from north and south joining battle against each other and bringing the clouds down by the time we approached the Brochkogel Pass. Those skiers who had managed to get away ahead of us now appeared in the murk above like birds perched on a telephone wire, and for once we were glad of the tracks of others as visibility slowly deteriorated. Beryl was having constant trouble with her skins coming off and soon the parties ahead disappeared in the mist. Then suddenly figures began coming back down towards us, cries of dismay reaching us as the others gingerly felt their way down in the whiteness with an occasional sedate fall. How well I know that feeling: the impenetrable whiteness provides no horizon for the eyes, contours of the ground cannot be seen. There is no way of telling if the skis are moving forwards except by looking at the feet—and they may not be moving at all! All this produces a sense of giddiness which results in a person toppling over, even when standing still.

A number of skis planted in the snow told us there were still some skiers up the mountain and that we were near the summit. We followed their tracks and soon met them coming down. They greeted us enthusiastically—I could not understand why, but perhaps it is just nice to know that someone behind has yet to complete the toil. Before long, the summit cross appeared above us. There was nothing to wait for—no view, just cloud; we hastened down back to our skis. Tracks were fast being obliterated in the falling snow and I checked the direction with compass from time to time. Despite our care, we found ourselves too low, as the tracks were clearly crossing over to the Braunschweiger hut. Once more on course, it was with a feeling of relief that I recognized the pass which we had crossed earlier in the day.

It was just another niggle when we finally regained the Vernagt hut to discover that our hut slippers had disappeared—though normally mountaineers' equipment left in a hut is sacrosanct. My slippers were well worn and not worth taking, but ski boots are not worn inside huts—indeed, clogs are provided as hut slippers—and in any event one looks forward to a change of footgear—though not to clogs! A vociferous party of Frenchmen were obviously enjoying themselves at a nearby table, and a sudden burst of laughter drew our attention to them. Beryl stiffened.

"Look!" she said indignantly, "that man's got my slippers on!"

As we studied the feet of the party, Beryl spotted my slippers on another pair of feet. I crossed over to the group and claimed the restoration of our property. The leader, a Baron whose full title we failed to catch, most apologetically assured us that they had found our footwear with the clog slippers provided, and the peaceful restitution was accompanied by bottles of wine shared amongst us as we lingered to chat and swap mountaineering stories.

Our goal next day was the Braunschweiger hut on the edge of a glacier and we were to retrace our steps to the Brochkogel Pass. A broken glacier falls from the west side of the Wild Spitz, embraced by two rocky arms on each side of which is a convenient depression affording comfortable crossings. In contrast to the previous day the conditions were cold and clear, a little new snow had fallen and the ranks of cloud forming in the north were harmless. The climber's spirits and physical capacity are affected by the weather, and the climb which had been a dull slog in the mist the day before now became a pleasant walk enlivened by the play of sunlight and shadows on the peaks ahead. With the Wild Spitz to our right we crossed the glacier to the Mittelberg Pass and had a perfect run down in new powder snow. Occasionally we halted to look up at the Wild Spitz, now free of cloud, and while we rested, the Baron and his companions—also bound for the Braunschweiger hut—caught us up. They were unostentatious and steady runners and we continued on our journey together, enjoying the brief episode of ski-ing in their company.

It was perhaps fortuitous that we had met the French party. The Braunschweiger hut—not surprisingly as it is very near Sölden and easily accessible—was crowded when we reached it. It was still only early afternoon, but it was Easter and the hut-keeper had booked more places than accommodation provided. The Frenchmen had booked in advance and secured an attic to themselves, with the Baron having his own room, and by evening late arrivals were ensconced on the floors and in corridors without bedding: and this was all the guardian could offer us. In spite of a streaming cold, the Baron insisted on us sharing his room, although this provoked many jokes about his snoring, and then the hut staff were unwilling to give us food until the French

Plate 79. A broken glacier falls away from the Wildspitz

argued that we were part of their party. Though his cold showed no signs of abating, we and the Baron had a lively evening in the attic with the others, before turning in.

Once again we and the Baron's party were heading for the same goal—Sölden by way of the Rettenbach Pass. We had to contend with chaos at breakfast but managed to get away in reasonably good time, and when we reached the pass at the top of a very steep slope the French rucksacks were already stacked like bags of corn. Tempted by a gleaming shield of snow on our right we made a diversion to climb the Inner Schwarze Schneide as well and enjoyed the climb without our sacks. Completing the last stage we met the Frenchmen returning and we arranged to meet somewhere in Sölden.

We were rewarded with perfect visibility from eleven thousand feet up, which was most useful because we were able to see our route ahead. With the Ötztal peaks rising behind us, we were passing into the Stubai, and could just distinguish the Zillertal about thirty miles distant. It seemed a very long way still to go as we donned our skis once more; all too soon we reached the top of Sölden ski-lift and the horrors of the rutted piste. We had a continuous traverse on a left-facing slope and I wondered if skiers who spend a holiday in Sölden end up with one leg shorter than the other.

We spotted the French rucksacks, but no sign of their owners, so we lunched alone and then went outside the inn to consult the 'bus timetable. The Frenchmen must have been watching for us from somewhere, because one of the young men came running over to invite us to lunch, but of course it was too late—though we made time for a farewell schnapps and coffee.

Längenfeld was six miles down the valley and sitting beside the merry-looking 'bus driver, I admired a little figure of a cow perched on a shelf below the windscreen. The cow, whose head nodded gravely with the movement of the 'bus, had flowers in its mouth.

"Unfortunately," complained the driver, pointing to the plaster animal, "it doesn't give any milk."

Entering into the spirit of the conversation, I asked: "Why not?"

"Because it's in calf," was the rejoinder. Austrians have a very simple sense of humour.

I had known Längenfeld from years before and we were both delighted that it seemed to have remained unspoilt. There were some new buildings, but erected with tasteful concern and in keeping with the place. Zum Hirschen was still an attractive old inn, with heavily overhanging roof and paintings of Julius Caeser and Alexander decorating the outside walls. Inside, the rooms leading off a vaulted corridor were beautifully panelled, the woodwork dark with age. The reception was warm and friendly, with an understanding of our needs in the offer of hot showers—luxury indeed after the crowded huts.

Whilst we strolled around the village after breakfast, buying provisions, Beryl casually mentioned that she had awoken with a pain in her left shoulder, but apart from that she had no cough, temperature or fever and felt well in herself. There was no hurry to go up to the Amberger hut, as it was only a two-and-a-half hour climb from Gries, and we decided to wait until after lunch and see how she was. By lunchtime the pain was no worse, though in retrospect I have a shrewd suspicion that she knew it was more than a triviality, but she was determined to carry on—she did not want to disappoint me as there were only the two of us on this stage. It could be just a muscular pain from the heavy rucksack, or an odd position she had taken while asleep, and she thought that perhaps the climb up to the hut might work it off—particularly as she had no other symptoms.

We took the minibus up to Gries, a pretty little village with paintings on the walls of the houses. Men were working, still attempting to cut away a large, six-months-old avalanche which had passed between two houses, narrowly missing them both; and I thought what a close shave it had been, and how delicately life hangs on a thread.

There were many mountain-lovers walking up the valley on foot in the sunshine. For them, mechanical aids were not necessary to appreciate the wildness of the valley and it was refreshing to see their obvious enjoyment in the early spring: the cool fresh crispness of the air, the smell of pines. They stopped to gather a stray fir cone, examine some small insect or flower emerging from the melting snow, the sun glinting on pearl drops of water cascading over tiny rocks, reflections on pools, and listen to the restless sounds of turbulence.

Plate 80. Inside the Amberger Hut

We climbed slowly and reached the hut before dark, a dog barked and the guardian—at one time a guide—came out to meet us. It was one of the smaller huts and had not become commercialized as it was more isolated. There were about half-a-dozen skiers in residence and the whole atmosphere was different—it was friendly. In the day room, or *stuba*, was a large domed enclosed wood fire, decorated with green tiles, and one or two people sat reading, warming their backs against the stove, whilst socks, skins and gloves dangled to dry from lines above. We sat down at a table to drink some soup, but Beryl pushed hers away saying that the pain in her shoulder was now much worse and it was beginning to hurt her to breathe. In the mountains, away from common viruses and infections, one immediately thinks of the altitude being respons-ible for chest complaints such as pleural effusions and heart failure—even in fit people it is not uncommon—as the body tends to retain fluids. It is a failure to acclimatize quickly to height. This is why we usually spent a day or two limbering up on short tours with light sacks before tackling our goal.

However, Beryl had been a medical specialist and her main work had been confined to the treatment of lung disease when she was in Malaya. She decided that the pain in her shoulder was a referred pain from the inflammation of the pleura covering the diaphragm, and that its origin was probably influenzal—perhaps caught from the Baron's cold when we shared his room. It was now clear that we could not continue our journey and the next problem was how to get her back down to the valley; but it was useless to try until the morning. She had a bad night and the pain extended to the whole of her left chest. We discussed the means of getting her down with the guardian: he had a weasel and would take her rucksack down, but he did not recommend taking her in it as it would be a bumpy ride. She felt that her symptoms were not sufficiently severe for him to summon a helicopter and she decided to ski down. With frequent stops, we did, and took the first train back to England.

When we arrived at Victoria, I telephoned my old friend Professor John Goodwin at Hammersmith Hospital, who immediately cancelled his own plans in order to attend to Beryl. I was by now a very worried man, as it was difficult to know how much Beryl was concealing from me to stop me from worrying; and I was convinced that she had had a coronary thrombosis—after all, she was no chicken to be careering across the Alps carrying a heavy sack. It was a tremendous relief when John told me that her electro-cardiograph was all right and that her own diagnosis of an influenzal pleural effusion was correct.

The ward sister was slightly shaken to see me tramp into the ward with Beryl in a wheelchair, armed with skis, rucksacks and ski boots. I took the skis away with me, but put the rucksack and crampons under the bed—where else to put them? The cleaner hit them with her brush the next morning as she swept under the bed. She pulled them out and examined the crampons, wanting to know what they were. Beryl explained that they were the latest fashion in cannon-ball and chain to fasten around the ankles, and the good lady went away convinced that Beryl had been transferred to the hospital from prison! Yet perhaps she was the prisoner of The Wicked Baron!

The narrative is now taken over by Beryl

☆

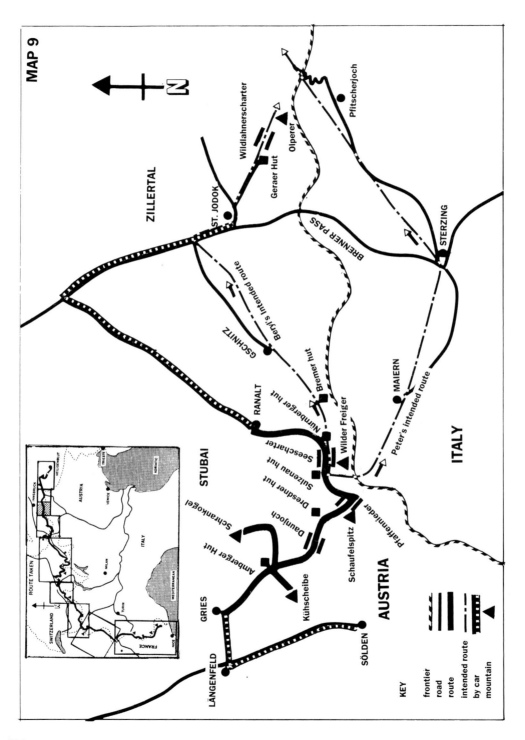

Chapter VII

1975 & 1976: Years 6 & 7.   The Years of Disaster

The Stubai

Längenfeld to the Dresdener Hut

FOLLOWING the pleural effusion which had brought our holiday to an abrupt end the year before, I tried to ensure that I should not do the same again, and I undertook training sessions during the winter and early spring of 1975. People in our Norfolk village got accustomed to me jogging round the quiet roads, accompanied by two low-slung dogs. Peter insisted that I had a check-up before we resumed our ski-touring, and I was put through strenuous tests at the hospital. I blew into balloons and pedalled stationary bicycles, wires were attached to me and to guages, and I was pronounced fit not only for a woman over sixty, but for an athlete even younger. This was a great relief to the dogs, who were thus excused further jogging round the village every day.

So we started 1975 with great optimism and enthusiastic plans, and we would again travel alone.

However, unusually little snow fell in the Alps during the winter months from October 1974 to February 1975, and then suddenly it seemed to fall all at once with pent-up intensity. In March, foot after foot of snow was deposited at an alarming rate, without intervening sunny periods to consolidate the layers. Conditions would be dangerous.

The steep and narrow road from Längenfeld to Gries was a potential avalanche trap if used at the wrong time of day, and the road was kept closed until the afternoon. The barrier was unlocked by the pompous *Bürgermeister* but it was Peter who raised it to let the cavalcade of cars pass through. We climbed into the minibus, launched on our second attempt on the Stubai.

We reckoned on a three-hour climb from Gries up to the Amberger hut, but the wild valley was safe enough and the walk particularly pleasant by comparison with my long-drawn-out struggle the previous year, with the added burden of pleurisy. The light would be fading, but we should be at the hut before eight o'clock. As we filed through a narrow rocky gorge just below the hut, a sinuous shape crossed the path ahead of us then merged into the rocks—a stone marten, unusually high up: what attractive prey had lured him so far from the density of the woods lower down? Soon we saw the bright lights of the hut and heard a dog bark, then a face appeared from behind a drawn curtain: the hutkeeper remembered us and we were quickly welcomed into the small group clustered round the wood stove.

One of the men allotted a bunk above us in the dormitory woke us by practising Yoga over our heads next morning. However, there was no hurry for us to get up; the weather was cloudy and unpromising. We had planned only a short tour southwards to the Kuhscheibe, but even this easy climb to the Cow Mountain was defeated: mist was accompanied by Föhn, that hot dry wind which descends the northern slopes of the Alps as a fore-runner of bad weather and which saps all one's energy. Back to the hut we had to go.

Outside the hut, the guardian was talking to his dog. The animal was a cross between an alsatian and something else, and had been trained in mountain usefulness. It was also a Grade "A" avalanche rescue dog, but more regularly worked as a post dog. He carried a small rucksack between his shoulders and our letters and postcards were strapped inside. On command, the dog bounded off down the valley to Gries post office, where outgoing mail was exchanged for hut mail, and the dog returned to his master—a service which he operated in all sorts of weather conditions, including deep snow.

Plate 81. The Post Dog: a small rucksack lay between its shoulders carrying our letters and post-cards

The following day we set off for the mountain dominating the valley from the east, the ten-and-a-half thousand-foot Schränkogel. Halfway up, unlike the dog who operated even in a snowstorm, we had to turn back: the wind was strong and snow was falling. Visibility of course was poor and another party also on the descent waited for us—a gesture which endeared them to us. This friendliness and concern for others in the mountains is frequently demonstrated by real mountaineers: and it is particularly shown in the case of a small party. Even as we arrived back at the Amberger hut three men appeared from the rocky gorge where we had seen the stone marten, and they told us that snow had avalanched into the gully and almost engulfed one of the three: he was mercifully unscathed, but relieved to reach the hut.

We remained in the hut for three days while the snow fell relentlessly. On the third day the snow began to ease and with others from the hut we decided to try climbing the Schrändele, a little further north up the Schwarzenberg Glacier from Schränkogel. We all shared the work of making tracks through the snow. On the peak there was thirty feet of new snow and this would take too long to climb, so we decided to turn back and make for the Schränkogel, an attractive rocky ridge on the other side of the glacier bowl, which provided an easier rock climb. Leaving our skis at the foot of the rocks we roped up and climbed to the summit through a little couloir; from the top we had a good view of the Ötztal with the Ortler group some fifty miles behind to the south-west. The peaks were clear of cloud. Bad weather tends to collect around these ice-massifs first, so they provide an excellent guide to the weather to come.

"Tomorrow," we thought, "should be fine and we can start our journey."

We were away by eight o'clock in cold and clear conditions which augured well. The snow, nicely packed by the previous wind, gave us an easy walk up the valley and through a gorge on to the Sultztal glacier. We had had warnings from the hutkeeper to stay to the right of the ice-fall and he emphasized the point with fearsome stories of skiers who had opted for a more direct route, ignoring crevasses at their peril. Legend had it that they had been claimed by dragons, but we saw none. A contour round the head of the glaciated valley brought us to the foot of the Daunjoch, a narrow snow crescent forming a pass on the rocky ridge. It was steep up to the gap, but the snow held, and toiling up the last hundred and fifty feet in hot sun was wearying as we kicked footholds in the snow. As we negotiated the narrow defile we were rewarded with the view of the peaks of the Wilder Pfaff and Zuckerhütl ahead of us some five miles to the east. The run down from the pass would have been perfect had not the ugly pylons of the ski-lift littered the slopes, but we were spared the sickening clank of the cable cars. There were periodic mystifying sounds of explosions though we saw no cause; they did not seem to be due to avalanches, nor did we see any signs of army manoeuvres.

Little did we know that it was to be the last time we would ski together.

Soon, however, explanations were given for the explosions. The Dresdener hut had been rebuilt since our last visit, several years previously, and it is now virtually a mountain hotel. Beside it was parked a helicopter, and inside we were greeted by a condescending pale-faced young man behind the bar.

"How did you get here?" he asked, obviously puzzled. "We've just had to fly out eighty guests by army helicopter."

"We've come from the Amberger hut," we told him, almost put on the defensive because of his manner.

"Well, you won't be able to go down the valley," he retorted, "the road to Neustift is blocked with avalanches. It's still unsafe—you can hear the Avalanche Squad are blowing them down."

Plate 82. The Schränkogel: at last the weather was clearing

Plate 83. The Daunjoch: once above the ice-fall a contour round the head
of the valley would bring us to the pass

So that explained the explosions, but we were not that dismayed.

"We're not going down the valley," we explained. "We're going to the Sulzenau hut."

"Not a chance," said the bartender. "It was destroyed two days ago by a large avalanche which came off the Wilder Freiger. The helicopter people saw it because they flew over the valley."

This was devastating. The hut had survived unscathed for fifty years; it was crucial to our plans. Only four days before some tourers had used it, and we were already a year behind because of my wretched pleurisy. Peter's plan had been to climb the Wilder Freiger and cross the Pfaffennieder the following day, thence either negotiate the Schwarzwandscharte or go down the Ebenerferner to Sterzing on the Italian side of the Brenner Pass. Neither route was easy and we would require two or three days of settled weather. Now the hut was gone, the weather had deteriorated, and the narrow lower valleys were potential death traps because of the avalanche conditions: we were snookered. Grasping despairingly at straws, we looked again at the barman. His pallid countenance surely proved he was no skier? Often these people come from the valleys and their advice is unreliable or aimed to scare skiers into keeping only to the beaten tracks ...   We decided to check for ourselves.

The ski-lift crews were assisting the Avalanche Squad by keeping in constant touch by walkie-talkie. Reports were grim: avalanches merciless everywhere, villages destroyed, and both the Reschen Pass and the Brenner Pass were blocked and people had been killed in their cars. The Brenner Pass is probably the flattest pass over the Alps, so there must have been an extraordinary accumulation of snow.

Plate 84. Avalanches were merciless everywhere

This avalanche which had destroyed the Sulzenau hut was obviously different from the wet snow and windslab avalanches which we had encountered on the early part of our journey. It was no ordinary avalanche: it was a dry snow airborne avalanche, one of the most destructive and devastating of all types of avalanche, which may involve up to a million cubic metres of partly-pulverized snow: it becomes a snow cloud which travels above the ground rather than along it, generating speeds of anything up to two hundred miles an hour, with such force that iron bridges and locomotives have been known to have been thrown into the air.

There was considerable speculation as to why the Sulzenau hut had been destroyed after remaining unharmed for fifty years. Some thought that it was the pressure blast which had initially destroyed the hut, as this type of avalanche is accompanied by an enormous pressure wave with suction behind, tantamount to an exploding bomb. The pressure wave overtakes the snow cloud and snaps off trees, demolishes houses, and hurls rocks in the air, destroying everything in its path—and it may travel much further than the snow.

Whatever the cause, all were agreed that it was a dry snow airborne avalanche, known in German as a *Staublawine,* because it had travelled the immense distance of four miles down a J-shaped valley to reach the hut. Fortunately these avalanches are rare, but then it had been a very unusual year with the sudden vast accumulation of new snow at low temperatures. During the snowfalls, the prevailing wind had been coming from the south and this must have lifted the very light, feathery snow, which was almost like down, on to the north side of the mountain. This would not have been able to consolidate as the weather was cold and there had been very little snow fall before March: what snow was already there could provide scarcely any anchorage as it was probably compacted ice. Moreover, the snow had had no time to settle, as the avalanche had fallen within a few hours of the last snowfall. This was a classic example of how new slopes are dangerous from the time of one hour after the sun re-appears until the third or fourth day, because it is during this time that the snow flakes are losing their interlocking plumes and when their central cores have no cohesion.

"What had started it off?" the discussion still raged. The sun coming out? A rise in temperature? Perhaps a small snow slide, a trickle of snow cascading off a rock as it melted in the sun, the widening of a rift already present in the snowfield—some small incident sufficient to upset the delicately-poised, unstable balance of the entire snow slope. The individual snow particles would roll and float over each other like a heap of feathers and peel off and produce a snow cloud, sufficient to suffocate any man. Yes, they finally agreed, the avalanche fulfilled the criteria of a *Staublawine*—cold, high altitude, north-facing slope, and occurring within three days of the last snowfall—but all this was poor consolation as we had planned to use the Sulzenau hut to climb the Wilder Freiger!

Two Germans had remained in the hut, hoping things would improve before their holiday was up, but we could only commiserate with each other. We did try the next day to find our way down to the valley, but had to give up after a few yards as the clouds lifted and then returned. Just before dark two Englishmen appeared outside the hut and for a fleeting moment our hopes revived. Where had they come from? But it transpired that they had come guideless from the Amberger hut and mistakenly taken the left-hand route through the ice-fall. Then in the mist they had gone down the wrong valley and had had difficulty getting back to the Dresdener hut—and, even more serious, there was a third man from whom they had got separated on the way up, but they did not seem to be in the least concerned.

I thought that Peter was going to explode with indignation. In his opinion they had broken the rules of mountaineering by abandoning their companion in the mist. It had not been many years before that three Germans had got lost from a hut in the Ortler where Peter was staying when he was leading a Ski Club party. These men had gone out in the mist against the advice of the guide, to climb Cevedale; they decided to turn back and could not find the hut, so wandered about until exhausted. One after another dropped with fatigue, and as each fell the other cut the rope and struggled on. They all died and the helicopters and dogs were out searching both in the snow and crevasses for a week to find the bodies.

It also made Peter angry if one of our companions, even if he were a particularly good skier, went ahead too far or took his own line down a mountain, because however good any one member may be the group must stay together. Even a good skier can break a leg and if this happens the other side of the mountain from where the rest of the team are, a lot of valuable time can be wasted climbing back to search for the injured member.

So it was with some anxiety that Peter and I set out to look for the third Englishman, as it was snowing hard and the ski tracks were rapidly becoming obliterated. The English party had already taken wrong valleys and it was more than likely that this lone man could get lost again. It was a considerable relief to both of us—to all three of us—when we sighted him.

Peter and I decided that we would return to the Amberger hut when the weather improved, and abandon the traverse for the year. We felt alternately castaways and caged lions: there was nothing to read, nothing to do—not a pack of cards nor even a set of chessmen which one normally finds, especially in unguarded huts; we prowled up and down in restless impotence. When the weather cleared half-heartedly next day we tried again to get away, but we were up to our knees in fresh snow and progress was impossible.

The two Germans, fearful of losing their jobs, were flown out of the hut by helicopter—they had to pay £60 each, but had they abandoned hope earlier and gone in the Army helicopter they could have travelled free. Meanwhile, the guardian, faced with this exodus of people and serious loss of revenue, had brought in the Avalanche Squad to blow down the snow from the unsafe slopes in the vicinity of the hut so that he could get his clients back and his ski-lifts working again. The men were fixing sticks of dynamite on poles and loading them on to their helicopters. The pilot, after consultation with the ski-lift crew about the best places to start avalanches, flew the craft close to the steep slope, the assistant primed the fuse and pushed the loaded pole out and into

Plate 85. The avalanche squad were fixing sticks of dynamite on poles

the snow, then the pilot flew the craft off as quickly as possible. Three minutes later there was a report and a puff of smoke, and the avalanche rolled down the slope like the crest of a wave on to a beach. Having done this, the Squad flew back to Innsbruck.

Plate 86. The helicopter takes off from the Dresdener hut to plant the fuse

There really was nothing to do. Without others in the hut to make a party, Peter did not seem inclined even to give a rendering of the Italian songs which he loved so much—he had a well-trained voice and his original inducement to learn Italian was his eagerness to enjoy Italian opera. He was, in fact, unusually quiet and I took myself off early to bed. At 2 a.m. Peter's prowling round the room woke me up. He was in acute pain and unable to pass urine. I found hot water in the kitchen and sat him in a hot bath, but this did not relieve his bladder, and not even a shot of morphia eased the pain or helped. I roused the hutkeeper, but he was not very responsive—indeed, there was little he could do. I insisted that we must get Peter out as quickly as possible as this was a surgical emergency, but a sledge to the valley was impossible ... the telephone wires had been torn down by the avalanches ... The hutkeeper said there would be a radio-communication to the valley at eight o'clock in the morning: he would try then, but it was unlikely that a helicopter could fly in as the clouds were too low—and that was the best he could offer. I could almost have hit him as he turned over in bed and went to sleep.

I returned to Peter. He had not been able to relieve himself and was still in great pain. There were four more hours to wait. It was worse than a bad dream. We must pin our hopes on the dawn—but it never seemed to come. The clock seemed to go backwards. I looked out through the window ... the dawn had broken, but all was white

Plate 87. The dynamite stick is planted high up and three minutes later the avalanche comes down

cloud. How many days would we have to wait before a helicopter could fly in? What was I to do if it could not come in? What would be the consequences on Peter if his bladder was not relieved? ... pressure on his kidneys, gradual coma—there seemed no chance that the bladder would overflow as it sometimes does. All these questions niggled my mind—and the worst part was being a doctor and being put in a position where I was completely impotent to help. Or was I? Where was my resourcefulness? I was not a surgeon, but if the helicopter could not fly in, I would have to do something: Peter was now in such pain that he was beyond caring. I looked at my penknife—it was pretty sharp. Our years together in Iraq and Malaya were now uppermost in my mind, when Peter had trained local surgeons to F.R.C.S. level in spite of the deficiencies and lack of surgical instruments; I thought of how his ingenuity and belief that difficulties were just inconveniences to be overcome had achieved remarkable results. No, I could not let him slide away through my own ineptitude—if the helicopter could not fly in and he went into coma, as a last resort I would have to make a stab wound in his abdomen to relieve the pressure in his bladder. Thus whirled the windmills in my mind.

At eight o'clock I was still glued to the window watching the clouds moving to and fro. They were far too low—one moment a complete white-out, the next the faint outline of the rocks on the other side of the valley; there was a faint hope ... then a gust of wind, a shower of snow and the clouds were down again. People were noisily walking along the passage outside our room, and I heard something clatter down the stair—or was it? ... was it? ...Yes! it was! The whirr of the Dragonfly ... and I saw it land. Somehow the pilot had got through, bringing a doctor. The crew were unconcerned for themselves, but the extra weight of the doctor as well as a patient was enough. Peter kissed me goodbye. I glanced at the hutkeeper—he would have problems with me on his hands, and almost in exasperation he called: "Have a try—take her too."

We left our gear in the snow, I climbed in, and the chopper hesitantly rose. It staggered with the extra burden, then lifted a bit more and we were away. We flew down the valley, just skimming the treetops, below the cloud layer, Peter clutching my hand. The scene opened and widened: help was now not far away, we were over the Inn Valley. Although there was a pad in the hospital grounds, our helicopter had to refuel at the airport, so we touched down to find an ambulance waiting on the tarmac. With sirens screaming we were whisked through the city to Innsbruck Hospital. The ambulance had not even stopped, it seemed, before all doors were opened, Peter was put on a trolley and wheeled into the surgery and a catheter was inserted. Over a litre of urine—nine times the normal capacity of the bladder—no wonder his pain had been intense.

We were both most impressed by the bravery of the helicopter pilot, and with the general efficiency—the timing of the ambulance meeting the helicopter, the trolley awaiting the ambulance, no preliminary waiting to go into the surgery, no bureaucratic formalities, no desire to take details of name and address until after the patient had been treated—it all worked with the precision of slick clockwork timing. Someone had given a great deal of time and thought to work out the system.

"Now you can go home," smiled the doctor, "but you will need an operation when you reach England."

Peter decided to stay and have the operation done in Innsbruck. They found a second-class bed where he shared a room with an Austrian with the same complaint.

After the operation, an orderly and a nurse made the rounds every half-hour checking the tubes and intravenous drips and this applied to all the patients in the same Genito-urinary block. The ward was run, oddly enough, by a sister who was also a nun and who wore a nun's habit. To Peter's amusement, he vowed her hand trembled when she pulled out his catheter before he went home!

While Peter was in the hospital we frequently watched the chopper fly in and land on the helicopter pad in the grounds; the patient was disgorged, often with an in-travenous drip already attached to the arm. It was no wonder that the hospital had a good reputation, and the patients were attracted even from Vienna and Italy. There was no charge for the helicopter service, nor was there a charge for a third-class bed in a general ward of six people, as there was reciprocity between the English and Austrian Health Services. In order to keep Peter amused, I went to the British Consulate and borrowed some paperbacks from a small library which they keep for the English in trouble.

I of course had to stay at a hotel. It was a pretty impersonal sort of place, and on the second evening, as I sat in the crowded restaurant having my meal, I noticed that more guests could have been accommodated if people had been prepared to share a table, rather than let one person sit isolated at a table for six. Diners came in and looked round, but they were disinclined to ask if they could take up the empty places, and they walked out. An elderly couple came in with a long-haired dachshund, which I made a fuss of, and I invited the couple to share my table. They were very happy to join me, as they had been looking for seats in several restaurants. We spoke in German and the conversation turned to what I was doing in Innsbruck. When I told them, they offered to find me accommodation with a family who lived near the hospital. Needless to say I moved in and the elderly couple came to fetch me on the Sunday and took me to the hillside around Innsbruck and then on to visit their family. They were just ordinary, working-class people, very lovable, kindly Austrians: I find they are particularly friendly if you can try to speak to them in their own language.

Within two weeks Peter was well and out of hospital, and we made our way back to England.

We had had two successive defeats with our traverse and we decided to smash a plate! Not our best one; but it is a Chinese custom to do this in order to break a run of bad luck. When we were in Malaya our Chinese cook had insisted on our breaking a plate when Peter and I had had two disasters within a week—Peter had narrowly missed a falling tree when he had been driving his car in a heavy rainstorm; and I had landed up in bed after being electrocuted by faulty wiring to the electro-cardiograph in the hospital. Then the customary third disaster did not happen after we had broken the plate, so we decided to try to end in the same way the run of bad luck of the traverse. Each of us held the edge of the plate, but Peter's hand slipped off the rim just before the plate broke. I said nothing, but wondered what the Chinese interpretation would be—I had a horrid feeling that it was a bad omen.

By 1976 we were both fit and well. In the summer of 1975 we had sailed as usual, in the autumn we had harvested the grapes in our small Norfolk vineyard and made our supply of wine for the coming year. I continued my amateur filming and Peter resumed his activities as President of the Norfolk Fencing Club and teaching fencing in the schools. Enthusiastically we discussed our next try. How I hated the Stubai, but with luck and good weather we should finish the entire traverse in four or five weeks—and we would stay out this time until we did finish it.

Discussing the weather, Peter thought the pattern had been changing over the previous three years, the bad weather occurring in March and early April. Perhaps we would go a bit later ... we fixed on the 15th April.

For my part I could not get this section of the traverse completed soon enough. I had an uncomfortable feeling that difficulties lay ahead and a small incident roused all my latent superstitions to an intolerable level. When we had been working in the Far East a grateful patient had given to each of us a God of Long Life and to my chagrin Peter's fell off its pedestal—the retaining wires had eroded through. I suppose we all have within us an element of superstition, particularly when faced with danger or excitement—how many people carry medals of St. Christopher in their cars? and I know of sportsmen who carry lucky mascots: indeed, regiments have their mascots. For three weeks I had a nagging sense of impending disaster—would it be an avalanche? an accident in a crevasse? a broken rope?

Peter seemed quite unaffected, and went to a Medical Enquiry in support of a colleague, so I started working in the garden, hoping that tidying up would take my mind off these primitive forebodings. Engrossed in my gardening, I glanced up and saw a village acquaintance approaching. She told me Peter was in the Intensive Care Unit ... somehow I knew in an instant that Peter was dead; and although the neighbour denied this, she drove me to the hospital. He had collapsed whilst cross-questioning in defence of his colleague and died immediately, despite all attempts at resuscitation. Although my acquaintance had not known of Peter's death when she came to tell me of his collapse, I have been told many times that premonitions such as mine are not uncommon. We had enjoyed thirty-six years of close companionship, in work and play, had shared our thoughts and ideas, had endured many difficulties and won through together: hardly surprising if our spirits were able to communicate at a moment of intense emotional stress.

Peter was buried on the 14th April, the day before we had planned to leave once more for the Alps. It was tragic that he died with his ambition unfulfilled, and the words of the Rev. Bob Bawtree in his funeral address were etched sharply in my mind:

> "Peter had achieved so much with all he did. He was a perfectionist, but there comes a point in life when we begin a task and fail to see it through."

Was this also Peter's last message? At that moment I knew the task was now mine: *I* must see it through. I would have no peace until I had done so. But how? When moments are low, but not soured by bitterness, there is always a hope or compensation to find. It was then that I experienced the third dimension—the power of friendship.

Chapter VIII

1977: Year 8. The Year of Endeavour

The Stubai

Dresdener Hut to the Brenner Pass

I CANNOT begin to describe how mixed up I was. There must be but few couples who have shared a life so closely as we had, both in work and play, and it was inevitable that we should take on some of each other's characteristics. A friend whom we had not seen for fourteen years had once remarked that I had taken on some of Peter's aggressive qualities while he had become more mellow like me. Although we had always preserved our individual interests, it was as though half of me had gone and I had to set about disentangling the real me.

All widows must experience the same problem: the loss of companionship, turning round to talk about something or to ask for advice—and no-one is there; the emptiness in the bed beside you and the knowledge that you will never be loved or kissed again; and my first problem was to disassociate Peter's physical meaning to me from the spiritual, for it was soon apparent that grief was sheer self-pity. The thing which helped me most was a card which I received from someone (I cannot now remember from whom, I received so many letters of sympathy) and on it were the words "He whom we love and lose is no longer where he was before but he is now wherever we are".

Perhaps this more than anything else made me determined to carry on life and do all the things we used to do together—regardless. I owe it to my many friends and acquaintances that I got going again. My house was visited by someone every day for at least a year, and I was even more determined not to carry my grief into other people's homes, and to keep a stiff upper lip.

I had never lived alone before. When I was a medical student I had lived with my grandmother, and when I qualified I was resident in a hospital right up to the time of my marriage. I had therefore to learn to live by myself and I found that I did not really like myself.

It was a challenge, but above all I felt that at all costs I must attempt to finish the trek across the Alps, as I was sure that that was what Peter would have wanted me to do. But just what was it that lay behind all this to spur me on? Would not most people have called it a day? I, too, was accustomed to setting myself targets throughout my life—in this respect Peter and I were very similar—but perhaps some of the success of our marriage had been due to my willingness to go along with Peter. He was an extraordinary mixture of perfectionism, purism and determination not to be beaten, yet he had an extremely soft, considerate and sentimental side, so concealed that only I and a few very close friends encountered it. He had an enormous variety of interests outside the medical profession, which made him very stimulating, and I seldom knew where we would go or what he would take up as a new interest—be it sailing, motor rallying, hill climbing, shooting or ski-ing—in which I would also join.

Peter had been invalided out of the army during the war because he contracted T.B., and, as there were no antibiotics at that time and he would not rest, an artificial pneumothorax was induced, but even that did not stop him from mountaineering after the war, because we took a little apparatus along with us and I removed some of the air before he went up the mountains and put it in again when we returned to the valley.

There were moments in our lives of complete upheaval, such as just after the War when I was settled comfortably in a Harley Street practice as a medical consultant. Peter was attempting to get a Surgical Consultant's appointment in a London hospital, but each time he was short-listed to the last two he had always been turned down on his past record of tuberculosis. That had settled it: he would go and work as a surgeon in Iraq, with far greater stress, because there he worked under tremendous pressure to maintain his standards—only the simple instruments for every-day surgery such as the appendix, gall-bladder or hernia were available, and he was trained for something better. As for anaesthesia, this was indeed primitive: ether was dropped on a mask and administered by a local G.P. If the instruments were not there, Peter must improvise, for always at the back of his mind was the need of his patient. His capacity to improvise was unique. I recollect the time when he removed part of a patient's lung. There was only one pint of blood available, so he did the operation using a high spinal and local anaesthetic—a hair-raising experience. As for special instruments, there were none, so he used the rib shears from the mortuary (of course he had them sterilized!) and clamped off the larger arteries and the bronchus with gall-bladder forceps. But his patient survived and loved him for it, for had he not carried out this operation, her husband would have divorced her—a serious situation for a Moslem woman.

While he wanted me to accompany him to Iraq, Peter left the choice open to me as he did not wish to terminate my career. But it was no sacrifice on my part when I packed up my practice and went out to join him, because I felt that if I was any good as a doctor it did not really matter where I practised, and I could be more useful in Iraq than in London where there were plenty of others to take my place—and in any case I had reached my target.

The rewards were great, for there are few wives who have encountered such a full and exciting life and I am fully aware of the privilege Peter gave me in asking me to be his wife. Yes! life would be very dull if I did not carry on—but how did I even start to finish the trek? I had lost my leader and it had always been part of the fun, for me a sort of game, that Peter never discussed our route in detail and I never knew exactly where we were going until we got there. He was the expert mountaineer, he loved mountains and even dreamed about them; far be it from me to challenge his ideas—I was just the passenger. It is true, though, that a great deal of his knowledge had rubbed off on to me, but would anyone have any confidence in joining a party led by an old woman of

65? I would need help with track-making; did I conscientiously feel that I could expect other people to trust themselves to my care as a leader of a guideless party when I had only led guided tours before? All these questions flashed through my mind, for the standard had been set very high. I had had far more trust in Peter as a mountaineer than in a professional guide. I had known him bring a party down from a peak in a complete white mist, find a way through crevasses and arrive at a hut with extreme accuracy—all done by "mountain sense", altimeter, map and compass. We never got involved in an avalanche except in the company of a guide, as Peter would bring out his spyglass (which guides never did) and study the mountainside carefully; and his knowledge of snow and its safety factor was indisputable.

Even after a year of widowhood I was still very emotionally mixed up and I felt that it might cloud my decisions. It would be better to find a leader who had more knowledge than I, if only for the safety of the other members of the party. In this I was fortunate, because Anthony Gueterbock, who had been with us on Year 2, rose to the occasion and agreed to lead; he also advertised in the Ski Club journals for people to join the party. He eventually assembled a small team: there would be five of us—Anthony, a newly-wed couple David and Marjorie Richardson, an anaesthetist Dr. Vanda Boyd, and me.

Meanwhile, I had to plan the route. I had a list of the huts which Peter had thought of using, which indicated the general direction, but there was little else to go on apart from our known proposed route when our journey had been cut short at the Dresdener Hut through Peter's illness.

Peter had planned to reach the Brenner Pass on the Italian side at Vipiteno (or Sterzing to the Austrians). From there he hoped to cross as much of the Zillertal as was feasible, entering from the Pfitschertal, but the traverse would be a zig-zag route because the general trend of the Zillertal range is north to south and of course our overall course was west to east. Alan Blackshaw, one-time editor of *Alpine Journal*, and writer of a near-bible on mountaineering, had omitted the Zillertal on his east-to-west traverse from Kaprun in Austria to Gap in France. What were my options?

The route from the Sulzenau hut down to Italy was complicated. Either of two valleys could be used, but unfortunately both were narrow and could be dangerous if the snowfall was heavy. I remembered that Peter had remarked that this part of the route would need three fine days. How far could I rely on the weather? Instead of going south and south-east through Italy, could I go east and north-east from the Sulzenau hut through Austria to the northern side of the pass? If the Bremer Hut could be used it would provide a direct route to Gschnitz and the Brenner Pass on the Austrian side and from there we would have an excellent entry to the Zillertal via the Wildlahner valley. How could I find out if the Bremer Hut was approachable in winter, or if it was only a summer climbing hut? It was all too obvious that I needed expert advice.

Then in February it looked as though any planning would be superfluous. I caught a cold which developed into a collapsed lung.

My doctor colleagues seemed equally as determined to get me well as I was, and they pulled out all the stops. They put a tube down my windpipe and sucked out my lung, and ten days later I tottered out to Kitzbühel to ski and get fit. The Alpine Ski Club had given me an introduction to Hofrat Friedl Wolfgang in Innsbruck (which was on my way to Kitzbühel) and I called to see him, to seek his advice. The fact that he did not know the district of my proposed route did not deter him: he called a conference of experienced ski-mountaineers who did know it. They agreed that the route I had outlined was feasible in uncertain weather. Furthermore, Hofrat Wolfgang's interest was not to cease at this point, as he took a keen interest right up to the time when I had finished the trek.

When I got to Kitzbühel I had planned to spend a week ski-ing on my own and trying to get fit before joining an Eagle Ski Club party led by Rosemary Sanderson around the Kitzbühel area, which would be a minor tour through deep snow.

In the first week I contacted the Ski Club of Great Britain (S.C.G.B.) representative and he invited me along to the weekly cocktail party. Whenever I was introduced to someone they replied: "Not *The* Wilberforce Smith?" This had the most catastrophic effect on me, for although Peter had been President of the Alpine Ski Club and Chairman of the Touring Section of the S.C.G.B. and had contributed articles to their magazine about each phase of our journey, I had never given a thought to the fact that he might be famous. The devastating reaction which flashed through my mind was that on no account must I let Peter down.

Yet that is exactly what I did do, for I was so keyed up and intense that I fell all over the place in the snow—I could not ski! When the week was over I set off, very humiliated, to find Rosemary Sanderson, wondering what I would be like in the presence of such a good skier who had a tigerish reputation. It appeared that she was equally nervous and had already passed me once in the street, recognizing me from photographs but too scared stiff even to approach this amazonian woman who was about to join her party! After a short preliminary tour she twigged my problem and we sat down and discussed it. Without doubt I owe it to Rosemary that I got going again, for the answer was simple: I was leaning in instead of outwards when I made my turns and this is why I fell over.

Cheered up, I returned to England, more confident to join our new party.

My friends were very amused when I set off from Norwich, with an O.A.P. rail ticket, to join Anthony at Victoria Station and, for the first time, to meet our little team. Anthony, of course, was an experienced ski-mountaineer, but the others had had limited or no touring experience—although they were all alike in being thoughtful and enthusiastic as well as eager to prove their worth, which indeed they did. I had received telegrams from Hofrat Wolfgang advising me of snow and weather conditions, and off we set, a curious, unknown team.

We had to resume the traverse from the Dresdener Hut and on our arrival we took stock of our gear and foodstuffs. Following Richard's complaints that he felt hungry with us, I left it to Anthony to make arrangements for provisions. With a young, unknown party it was difficult to guage their appetites and Anthony in turn had left it to David, Marjorie and Vanda to do the shopping in England so that rations were not duplicated. They had admirably researched the problem and provided several dried meat stews—ten meals weighing 1 lb. They had tried them out and decided they needed considerable titivation with dried onion and tomato to make them fairly palatable. It was impossible to find out in advance if there would be guardians in all the huts, and anyway some of them dislike cooking the skiers' own food because they make their profits by providing food and wine. For safety, therefore, we would have to carry enough food to last five people five days. Strangely, when we took stock in the Dresdener Hut of what they had bought, all the jams and honey were in heavy glass jars—we spent some time in trying to get the Jugoslav waitress to let us have some plastic containers. We were left with one jar of Rose's Marmalade, which we guzzled up because no-one wanted to carry it!

With experience and advancing age I have learned to reduce weight to bare essentials. Every article is weighed and if I end up with a choice between two blouses, the lighter one goes in the rucksack, even if the difference is only an ounce. A J-cloth is lighter than a flannel; a tube of toothpaste and tablet of soap will serve three people. I had a 100% acrylic Haase top and long pants which weighed only ten ounces but had three possible functions—useful to sleep in, wearable under ski clothes if it was cold and windy, and serviceable as a track suit if the ski clothes were wet. Ski-ing gear was as before, but I had at last bought Harscheisen to clamp to my skis when climbing on ice. With the weight of the rucksack, clothing, gear and my personal luxuries of sweets, camera and a book I was down to 17 lbs. without food. Not so the others. Anthony and I inspected their packs with meticulous care: they were far too heavily laden. Things like spare corduroy trousers for "evening wear" were definitely not essential: these were sent down to the valley.

It had been snowing for about a week when we arrived at the Dresdener Hut, but it cleared next day and we decided to set off, although we thought we might save time by having our heavy loads transported to the Fernerjoch. On learning that the cost would be four hundred Austrian Schillings for our journey, we decided to use the cheaper, bubble-car route south-west over the Schaufelferner to the Bildstockljoch. A short walk to the pass and then we were soon running down one thousand feet of the Gaisskar Glacier in the sun. I was relieved that my ski-ing technique had not deserted me again.

After a short traverse round a rocky cliff we were faced with a climb up the Pfaffen glacier. The snow was hard and icy and we began to slip going uphill. What a difference my new Harscheisen made, clamped under my skis—they were well worth the extra weight compared with the toil of putting on crampons and carrying the skis. Even so it was wearisome: Vanda, struggling behind me, thought my back looked a pillar of strength until I let out a groan. I looked ahead at Anthony and saw he, too, was wobbling a little. It was our first day out, our rucksacks seemed too heavy, and we were all suffering slightly from mountain sickness.

Worse was to come. Over the Pfaffen Pass the snow was such as I had never experienced. Under a foot of apparently innocent powder snow were patches of crust which suddenly broke into underlying soggy wet stuff. It gelled and incarcerated our skis, pulling us to a sudden stop each time. Only a snow shovel could extricate us. I felt I knew what a fly must feel when it lands on sticky fly paper. More difficulties were added: the glacier was heavily crevassed and clouds started to roll down with us as we descended. We roped up, and groped our way down, pausing occasionally to await a clearing. On reaching the foot of the glacier we came into sun and stopped for a well-earned lunch—though not for long: clouds caught up and engulfed us in a complete white-out. By map and compass under Anthony's leadership we arrived at the Sulzenau hut—safely—but the other three confessed they had had thoughts of having to dig a snowhole for the night.

By 1977 the Sulzenau hut was being rebuilt after its destruction by the avalanche and a temporary hut, with a guardian, was in service. We were able to lie an extra hour in our bunks next morning, as the clouds were still down—getting up in the dark to put on cold clothes is no more delightful in an alpine hut than anywhere else, and 4 a.m. starts are just as difficult for me wherever I happen to be, although I am normally an early riser. We all lay hoping that we would not have to go out and make tracks in the deep snow—but the sun came out and melted our alibis if nothing else. The weather was too uncertain for Peter's route, so it would have to be mine over to the Nürnberger hut. The Sulzenau guardian put in a suggestion that we went over the Seescharter—a pleasant way and seldom taken.

Plate 88. The seldom-used Seescharter on the horizon

We ploughed through the deepest snow Anthony and I had ever seen. Fortunately for Marjorie, Vanda and me the Sex Equality Act was not then law: we had to take it in turns to make tracks, agreeing on a hundred paces for the men but only fifty paces for the women! It took an hour to cover just a hundred yards or so; it was a joy to come out of the head of the tracks and let the others file by murmuring comforting words like "Well done!"

At the foot of the Seescharter there was an old avalanche and the snow was firm—what a relief! We went up it to the pass, from where we could see our future route to the Bremer hut lying over the Nürnberger Pass just opposite where we stood. But it was fairly steep and it was obvious that we would need more settled snow. In any case, we had had enough hard work for one day, the snow was heavy from melting in the sun and it was caking our skis. It was getting late—the avalanche hour—and we must make hot-foot for the Nürnberger hut to spend the night. We had a steep slope to cross and as a precaution we loosened the bindings on our skis and spread out, because if an avalanche should come down it would be better to involve only one person in the party rather than all of us. The chances of freeing one's self and getting out are greater, too, if unhampered by skis.

Plate 89. The route to the Bremer hut lay on the opposite side of the valley.

The approach to the Nürnberger hut from the valley is narrow and as we had confirmed to ourselves, it was avalanche-prone; hardly surprising, then, that it is seldom used in winter. For the avalanche year of 1975 there were no entries at all in the book, and no-one had crossed to it in winter for a very long time. However, it was comfortable and would be warm with the good wood stove and bunks in the same room. One additional amenity was, sadly, not working: the Victorian telephone operated by a torch battery. The battery was flat.

None of us regretted the snow next morning. We all needed a rest and just the mere thought of bashing out a track as far as the moraine was uninviting. Besides, we felt we had too much food and competition was keen to eat some of it. Vanda unpacked. Despite our attempts to jettison extra weight, she had a cache of luxuries—shampoo, short nightdress (was she hoping to meet the German of her life?) and two bikinis (one for the valley and one for the mountains). We ceased teasing and chiding when she produced the Scrabble.

We told each other stories of our escapades in the Alps, and the conversation turned to crevasses. We had roped together on the Sulzenau glacier as a precaution against falling into a crevasse in the bad visibility, but Marjorie and David wanted to know more about crevasses. I explained that since glaciers were rivers of ice wide open crevasses could be expected on the domed part of a glacier and they could be spotted by the convex curve in the snow's surface, which should alert the skier to the imminent proximity of a crevasse. A concave curve followed by a depression signified that the crevasse was choked with snow, but it might be just a bridge which could be very thin. This prompted my memory of the story told to me by the guardian of the Casati hut in the Ortler, who had previously been a guide. He had skied across a glacier alone and a small snow bridge had given way and he dropped into a fairly narrow crevasse— fortunately, with his feet down. He fell twenty feet and became wedged on a shelf. He was able to remove his skis and he sat on his portable wireless set, which he had in his rucksack, for five days, until a search party found him.

This story, of course, raised the question "How did the search party get him out?" and Anthony and I thought that it would be a good idea and an interesting occupation to teach them what to do.

We all went outside the hut, where there was a tower of small balconies, one above the other, and Anthony climbed up to the top one and threw down three ropes. Vanda was the first "victim". and so we tied one of the ropes around her waist. We tied a loop, about a foot long, into the ends of the other two ropes and Vanda put one foot into each loop. Anthony was now in control of the other

Plate 90. Practising getting out of a crevasse at the Nürnberger Hut

end of the three ropes from above, and he called out the instructions:

"First, bend your right knee," and he shortened the righthand rope.

"Now transfer your weight to the right foot," and he shortened the 'waist' rope. Vanda was now suspended above ground, with a foot in each loop. Anthony's next order was "Bend your left knee," and he shortened the lefthand rope. "Transfer your weight to the left foot," then he shortened the 'waist' rope again. In a brief space of time Vanda had 'walked' up through mid-air to join Anthony on the top balcony.

Plate 91. Descent from the Nürnberger Hut. Thick wads of snow bent branches half double against a grey ominous sky

It continued to snow. We read all our books, practised tying knots and more knots. A ski stick planted in the snow showed that the snow was accumulating at the rate of eight inches a day, and that was falling on top of all the recent snowfalls, which, from the depths we had already waded through on our way to the hut, had certainly not settled. By the third day I was worried—clearly we could go neither forward nor back on our traverse, though there remained the narrow valley to the north. With growing concern I watched the snow piling up on the peaks above it: if we tried that escape route just one blast of wind could lift off the snow and deposit it on and around us. It was ironic that from feeling we had too much, I now knew we could be trapped without food. We would have to take a chance: we would go at dawn, when the snow was frozen, by way of the valley to the north.

With a forlorn gesture we placed an ice cube as a spring tonic for a pathetic little pot plant and left the hut, to walk into cloud. We roped together and trailed an avalanche cord. Although now largely superseded by "bleeps" or "Autophones" which emit signals even if buried under snow, our red cord tied around the waist and trailed as we moved would have provided a means of tracing us if we had been trapped under an avalanche.

We had to feel our way cautiously as we descended, as we knew there was a precipice to avoid, but we could not see far ahead. Having then safely negotiated a difficult gorge we were able to ski down the valley to a wide summer alp. Respite! There was time to linger in this photographer's paradise, marvelling at the scenic effects of branches bent double under thick wads of snow against the background of a grey, ominous sky. There were switchbacks made by bowls of melted snow under trees, and we skied light-heartedly over them, down the summer path to Ranalt. Day tourists with their cars watched us skirt the avalanche barrier across the road.

"Why have you been up and ignored the barrier?" they asked. They obviously thought we must have gone up the way we had come down.

The weather in the Alps is often regional and it was possible that there had been less snow in the Zillertal than in the Stubai. We took a taxi down the valley, the ridge on our right falling away as we joined the trans-Alpine road leading from Innsbruck up to the Brenner Pass. We branched off from St. Jodok about six or seven miles eastwards, up to the Geraer Hof. This is the local mountain rescue centre and on the western edge of the Zillertal. A taxi, we thought, could take us to the snow either up the Wildlahner valley or the Kaserer valley. This suggestion produced glum faces. There had been even more snow here and avalanche warnings were broadcast over the radio: we could not go.

We debated. Why not try the last section of the traverse and come back to the Zillertal the following year? We could resume from the Rudolfs hut, some fifty miles east, perhaps. We rang the Rudolfs hut—yes! they were ski-ing. We caught the train from Innsbruck, and then travelled by 'bus to the cable-car with a heavy black cloud following us all the way. We arrived at the hut, still enveloped in cloud. Yes, they were ski-ing ... but the Rudolfs hut is very much a mountain hotel and all the ski-ing was on the piste. The mountains, they told us, had been obscured for days.

For two days we waited idly, helplessly watching the snow fall, and deriving no hope from the weather forecasts. We decided to return home.

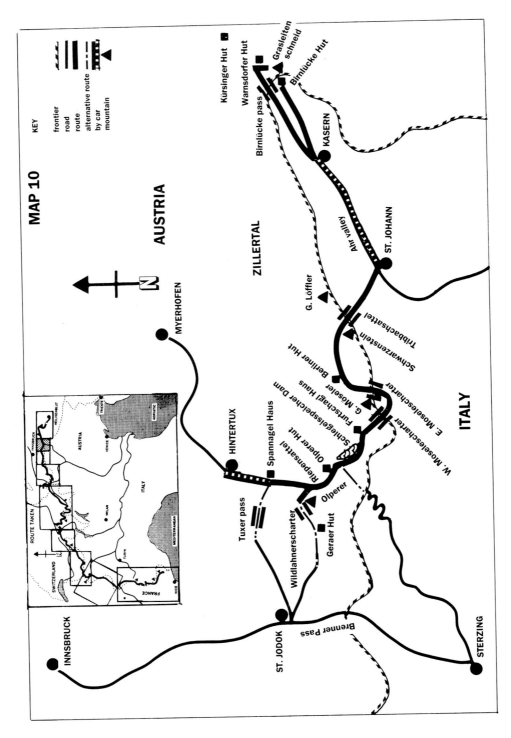

Chapter IX

1978:   Year 9.   The Year of Fulfilment

The Zillertal

THE DISAPPOINTMENTS of the previous year were still with me as I tried to take up Peter's task once more. At least I had proved myself to myself with sufficient justification to pursue the goal. Yet there was still a month's journey and I would need two teams. All Ski Clubs seemed interested, and I was able to recruit from the volunteers who were eager to join.

As Anthony Gueterbock was not available, I asked Richard Brooke to lead one team. He had been with Peter and me on the fourth year and was, more importantly, a particularly experienced mountaineer who, furthermore, had been with Sir Edmund Hillary's Antarctic Expedition of 1956-58. The first part of the tour, the Zillertal and Venediger, would be difficult; Richard chose that one, as he could only be with us for a fortnight.

Fred Jenkins was another volunteer, whom I accepted but with some apprehension. At the age of 64 he was still an avid and active mountaineer; being 65 myself I did not feel his age was against him—what concerned me was that he was not only a retired schoolmaster, but a retired army padre as well. I did not know him, and the reports that he was reserved raised doubts in my mind—I am inclined to swear if I fall over in the snow, or get annoyed: how would Fred take it? It was a relief to discover that his functions as Army Padre had included keeping his troops happy and fit, and he did this by teaching them to climb mountains. He set my mind at rest when he told me the story of setting off to climb five thousand feet with his troops fully equipped. Being a Sunday, he held a brief service in the valley first, and then led his men upwards. After a short distance he heard a voice from behind: "We've just sung the psalm 'I'll turn mine eyes unto the hills', but what about my bloody feet?"

Fred was to be with us all the way—indeed, he led the second section after Richard had gone home—and promised to "sit it out" until I finished the traverse even if all the others went home.

The Brenner Pass to the Val Aurina

We were to be joined at the Geraer Hof at St. Jodok by Jonathan Wallis, a medical student then 23, and Robin Chapman, an Orthopaedic Surgeon in his early thirties: it would certainly considerably reduce our average age! Furthermore, as three of the team were married but had left their wives behind, it was not long before I was known as "The Other Woman!"

They were a wonderful team and seemed determined to get me across the mountains even if they had to carry me on a bier. I knew that I *had* to finish the journey this year—it would be impossible to keep up for yet another year the standard of fitness necessary to cope with a ten-hour day.

Flaunting providence, I had bought a new pair of skis—my third pair since the occasion fifteen years before when a salesman had told me the pair he was selling me would "see me out". This latest pair were short skis—much lighter; we were starting in mid-April and expected spring snow so there would be less likelihood of the skis digging in. Nevertheless, when we assembled at St. Jodok it was snowing and we met the same stubborn refusal to take us up either of the two valleys by car to the foot of the climb. The street was barely covered, yet we repeatedly met the woeful remark: "There is three feet of new snow," and to prove it they would dial for the weather report: "Avalanche warning!" We could not argue: the hotel was the avalanche rescue centre.

There was nowhere to ski in the vicinity—indeed, the snow was beginning to thaw in the ski resorts lower down the valley. However, two valleys lead up eastwards from St. Jodok to a ridge, and from these the Olperer Glacier, our starting point, could be reached. On the eastern side of the ridge, the Tuxer Tal leads south-westwards up from Mayrhofen to the little resort of Hintertux and we could reach the Olperer Glacier from there. Fearing boredom, Richard and I decided we would go round to Mayrhofen, up to Hintertux at the head of the valley, and on to the privately-owned Spannagel Haus close to the top of the cable-lift. Richard was determined not to be hungry this time and when we climbed into the cable-car, the attendants were puzzled by the eight loaves of bread we were carrying in a polythene bag. "Were we going to eat it in the snow?" they wanted to know, they were so accustomed to carrying piste-skiers who lived in the valley, that it never occurred to them that anyone might want to live in the hut, barely a few yards from the top of the lift. When we arrived, everywhere was enveloped in total whiteness: for once, the locals, whose minimum measure for new snow was always three foot, were correct.

The winter room of the hut was open, but it was a chaotic shambles. Damp, dirty, sleazy bunks; hardly any blankets—it was obviously used as a store-room for empty beer bottles and cartons. There was no cooking stove, but here Fred came into his own. I had already commented that his rucksack was heavy—I could hardly lift it—but it proved to be a veritable Pandora's Box from which he frequently performed the miracle of the loaves and fishes—you name it, he had it! Like a Boy Scout, he was prepared for every emergency.

As we looked round the Winter Room, Fred produced a calor cooker and proceeded to melt snow. Leaving him to his ritual, we trudged back to the Restaurant at the ski-lift. Here was warmth, food and comfort, but no bunks. Yes, the Manageress told us, the Spannagel Haus *had* a guardian but he had gone down to the valley—our only course was to go back to the valley as ski-touring was out. I argued with her that we could not afford such a course, and that the hutkeeper must come back. I added that a Ski Club of Great Britain party, led by Terry Hartley and a guide, and also including Jonathan's father, was expected. This clinched the matter, and the guardian soon returned to open up the hut beyond the Winter Room. It was comfortable and soon was warm as well, and the guardian allowed us to cook our dried food.

Fred, working wonders with a packet of Protoveg (dried soya bean) suggested it might last five days, and was staggered by the quantity of food we had provided. But with young appetites as well as Richard's, there was no doubt that we should need it all. We distributed our provisions to spread the weight, but Richard felt the weight of my sack every day and always took something out.

"There are younger people than you in the party," he would say, silencing my protestations. I was grateful for his thoughtfulness—though it strengthened my conviction that I must complete the traverse this season.

Both parties set out in brilliant sunshine next day, blue shadows slanting across the snow and the temperature was well below freezing. We were all carrying light sacks, but even so dodged grudgingly the caterpillar tanks as they belted down the piste flattening the new snow. At the Gefrorner Wand our ways parted: the others intended going over it to the Geraer Hut and St. Jodok—just the way I had wanted to come. However, we went to the Riepensattel to inspect our own route southwards. We could trace out the journey for the next three days.

Here we were in silence, well above the ski-lifts. Silky white glaciers blended imperceptibly into magnificent deep blue valleys, between parallel ridges of mountains; the Schlegeisspeicher Dam, with its frozen lake, stretched far in the valley below. All

Plate 92. The Riepensattel: our route for the next three days spread out before us

Plate 93. At the top of the picture is a hanging glacier which has overflowed down into the valley

round us was peace and quiet. I took a deep breath and mentally thanked God that I was still able to enjoy it all.

Turning back, a short traverse below the Olperer Peak brought us to the Wild-lahner Pass, where we joined the others. I was curious to see what it was like, although I was denied a glimpse of the Geraer Hut itself because the route lay below a huge hanging glacier which had strewn bright and gleaming chunks of ice over the snow.

When we got back to the piste, people looked with amazement at our rucksacks. They questioned us about our ascent to the glacier— "the Gefrorner Wand, the Frozen Wall?" —marvelling at what seemed to them such a venturesome departure from the path of the snow cat.

"Did you make those tracks we can see on the other side of the glacier?" they queried; "Was it nice?"

The clank of the ski-lift grew louder as we approached it, and I felt a deep sadness for these people: their pleasures were cramped and confined because no-one had introduced them to the wide open spaces beyond the cable-car, to the silent, serene, beautiful unbroken snow and the exhilarating views from the ridges and summits.

Yet not all development is bad: on the fairly deep snow my new short skis had run well, needing far less effort to turn, and I was glad of the advances made through new materials and modern design.

Next day the Austrian pennant hung majestically from the flagpole, the red and white bands gently stirring in the breeze, while wispy clouds picked up a tint from the red of the rising sun. It was cold—a good sign. We soon got across the Riepensattel and launched ourselves downwards. Sun the previous day had melted the snow's surface but the night had turned it into a light crust. Time and again we broke through the crust on our turns, our bodies littering the snow, but we learned to listen to the scrape of the skis and to distinguish by ear the harder patches of snow on which it was safer to swing round.

We allowed ourselves only a short rest at the Olperer Hut. We had made good time, but had a long day if we were to reach the Furtschagl Haus. We got to the Schlegeis-speicher Dam, close to the snow-covered road from the Pfitscherjoch. I looked at it with a degree of sadness: that was the way Peter had wanted to enter the Zillertal. I turned before emotions got too strong, and we started on a tedious track upwards past trees and silent houses, clambering over old avalanches, the snow getting wetter and wetter in the sun. It balled under our skis and skins until Fred had the bright idea of waxing the skins. Gladly did we pause for lunch in the shade of some trees at the farther end of the valley, and then the snow improved on the gentle north slope. Choked with snow, higher up the summer path rose steeply, in full sun, over twelve hundred feet to the hut. A few sprigs of grass showed here and there on the slope, but the snow would be safer here than at the head of the valley, where it was deeper.

Richard and Jonathan set to with zest and a determination to get me across the mountains at all costs. Yet even they soon found track-making exhausting and they frequently slumped in the snow for an unscheduled rest. With the Furtschagl in sight I sat down and was joined by Robin, sweat pouring off his face. I remembered the small bottle of malt whisky I had bought on the boat to use up loose change. We each took a swig. It had a miraculous effect: we started off again, trying to catch the others, but even so I arrived last. Robin was waiting for me with a cup of tea in his hand, while Richard and Jonathan were collecting drips from the eaves to make unlimited quantities of lemonade. As we quenched our thirst we looked round: we had company! There were footprints of a hare round the hut and as I followed them they led to a snowdrift engulfing the roof, the hole to the hare's lair going down beside the eaves. We had no sight or sound of the animal, and we settled in the Furtschagl hut for the night.

We had a good day the next day, to the Grosser Möseler and the Berliner Huts. We took full advantage of an early start to climb in shadow when it was cool, and we did not feel the heat of the sun until we reached the séracs of the ice-fall near the top. The slog uphill had been monotonous, and looking round my imagination was fired by the vision of icicles in the shape of boar's tusks which scored grooves in the snow, and slid down the steep slope, like a giant shedding his milk teeth. I began to fantasize on what he looked like and as the gradient eased and we gained the West Möseler Pass I saw my ice-plastered Andean Giant, still left with some little icicle teeth—the peak of the Grosser Möseler looming above us.

The Grosser Möseler guards the frontier. It is a complicated peak about eleven thousand two hundred feet high, and to round it we had to carry our skis down the steep south face into Italy, work across a hot sunny plateau, and then slog back up again to the East Möseler Pass into Austria.

The Waxeck Glacier stretched down ahead of us. It was going to be a beautiful run and I could sense the impatience of the others to get started.

"It's all yours," said Richard with a gentlemanly bow. The others drew back respectfully. Touched by their gallantry, because they had done all the hard work, I swept off down ... and fell flat on my face! Getting up with as much nonchalance as I could muster, I chose a central line down the crevassed glacier. It was more challenging than the normal route above the broken sections, but the crevasses were visible. We may have been a little late, as the skis ran slowly, but that gave us the chance to linger on the unsullied powder snow. We were surrounded by gleaming blue séracs and yawning crevasses, and descended nearly four thousand feet through one of the finest ski runs in the Alps.

The summer path ahead was marked by a cairn on the left-hand moraine, but that way would take us below the Berliner Hut. Our map showed a path on the right-hand moraine—we decided to take that and save height. Alas! The glacier had receded since the map was drawn: the path became steep at the snout where the glacier had melted, and there were great slabs of slippery rock covered with a thin layer of snow. They were a menace. We strung out in a row, quite unable to turn round for fear of sliding, and we had to shuffle backwards in our tracks until a steep couloir offered a way off the dangerous surface. Shouldering our skis, we walked down to the valley floor—we had not saved height. I wonder how many, many times we all try unsuccessfully to save height in the course of ski-touring!

We then had to slog up to the hut, and I cursed—but inwardly. Why are mountain huts invariably perched up on promontories? That last climb is always a chore.

The guardian was digging out the door of the winter room, which was an outbuilding of the very large summer hut. He had watched our antics through binoculars and berated us for our choice of route off the glacier. From the hut the correct way was all too obvious: down the summer path on the left-hand moraine. Our valley approach, we

Plate 94. The Waxeck Glacier: we descended four thousand feet—
one of the finest ski runs in the Alps

were told, was only safe before 10 a.m. and late in the evening: we had been extremely lucky!

Having dumped our packs and had some food, I went outside. The guardian was lying in a deck-chair in the sun, his eyes closed as he listened to the radio. However, we chatted and he told me he had visited the hut from the age of two: his father had been guardian for fifteen years, but he had now taken over. The guardian sighed. He had hoped to be a summer guide, but now he was a ski teacher in winter and in the summer season the hut took all his time. In the precious few intervening weeks, he toured the mountains alone on skis, self-sufficient, happy and at peace in the silence of the snow.

We had had two consecutive days of eleven to twelve hours, and we were all tired. I felt we could do with a day's rest. When I learned that the guardian was to return to the valley at dawn, I bought from him a large quantity of beer which I thought we would all appreciate. My warm glow of satisfaction was dissipated, however, on retiring. The bunks were cold, and in a separate room from the kitchen with its comforting stove. Despite seven blankets, extra pullovers and a woolly hat, I spent most of the night shivering, dozing fitfully. I was woken eventually by a cup of tea brought to me by Jonathan—what luxury, morning tea in a hut!

It seemed we were all suffering in some way. Our faces were blistered from two days' sun, but in addition Richard had tummy trouble. Was it the dried foods? We had had some of Fred's pernicious concoctions resembling "Fillatum Chunky Pet Food": could that have blown us all up to uncomfortable proportions? Fred was suffering himself, even though he had seemed to like the stuff—which surprised me because I knew that in the valley he had a gourmet weakness similar to mine.

Richard definitely suffered most, and I added to the problems by giving him some tablets to which, we discovered, he was allergic. He was very tolerant and did not say much, but I remembered similar situations when Peter had enjoyed quoting the Bible: "He that sinneth before his Maker, let him fall into the hands of the Physician!"

We all returned to bed.

Later, after dark, two Germans arrived. We exchanged brief greetings and they too went to bed.

The next day was warm and windstill, and snow began falling. The Germans left us the remainder of their fresh meat and bread, deciding to go back. We remained for another night, but by morning Richard was much worse, and my feet were badly swollen. It was time to go down to Mayrhofen and see a proper doctor!

It was a shorter and more direct run down, through a narrow gorge, which crossed many avalanche heaps. Two railway-line ruts formed in the snow by the passage of previous skiers made things even more precarious, and they were now icy in the early morning snow. Once launched on the "rails" there was no holding back. I set off, rounded a corner ... and there was Fred blocking my path, because he had taken a toss over a cattle grid. Having no anchors or brakes to apply, I swept Fred away in my headlong descent, but fortunately no harm was done.

Practically everywhere in Mayrhofen was shut: the expensive-looking Neue Post seemed our only choice. It is much to their credit that they batted not one eyelid when five decidedly shaggy people, hardly a wash between them for five days, walked into the hotel and asked for beds. Later that evening we were even included in the celebrations of the head ski teacher for a good year's takings. He was swaying slightly on his feet as he pulled a loose piece of skin off my peeling nose and placed it over his heart, inviting me to drink schnapps with him. It was like old times with Peter—a party was under way.

Two nights in the valley, three enormous meals—we seemed completely different people and were all ready to go back to the hut. We talked to local inhabitants and were advised to wait till late afternoon before setting off, as the snow would then be hardening and avalanche risks lessened. A lot of snow had melted since we had come down and the advice proved sound. We saw this for ourselves when, having passed two skiers on their way down, we found an avalanche had crossed and obliterated their tracks.

It was dark when we got back to the Berliner Hut but we knew where to find things and cheerfully dined by candlelight.

We reckoned on five-and-a-half-hour's climbing to start our next day, and this could be a challenge. We were awake and up by 3 a.m. and left the hut by moonlight, planning to cross the Schwarzenstein Pass into Italy. This route means a long day and is seldom done, but it is an intriguing way out of the Zillertal. Clouds were gathering behind us to the north, but we hoped we could count on six or even eight hours for the climb before the weather broke. Time was an important factor and so we did not stop for a second breakfast, but after nearly three hours we all had some Kendal Mint Cake to save precious minutes. This cake has a wonderful and immediate energising effect, but about ninety minutes later the blood sugar level falls rapidly—a state of hypoglycaemia may develop. We were almost at the top when suddenly I became drowsy, practically falling asleep on my skis, and sweating. Richard, already on top, dumped his sack and came back for me, as I had slowed down, but meanwhile I had recognized the problem and the cause, and had eaten some more Mint cake. By the time Richard got back to me the cake had done the trick and in a short time we joined the others on the Schwarzenstein Pass. Clouds had collected and cleared away, so perhaps the battle with the meteorological cold front had also been temporarily won. In sunshine we climbed to the top of the Felsköpfl and there we sat for lunch.

Plate 95. The Schwarzenstein: the advantage of the early start
is the climb In shadow when it is cool

We were at a height of well over ten and a half thousand feet, but beside us, to the south, the massive Schwarzenstein peak towered above us almost dwarfing us with its extra four hundred and fifty feet; while way, way below us luscious green valleys lay in the depths. We were again on a frontier line, looking down to what used to be the Ahrntal when South Tyrol belonged to Austria but what is now the Val Aurina in Italy. This, for some, is ideal walking country—a valley rich in flowers, fifteen miles long up to Pratomagno, the most northern village in Italy. For us, the Schwarzenstein and the Gross Löffler were the visual attractions, the highest peaks at the eastern end of the Zillertal rising either side of us.

We were lunching on the small Felsköpfl which lies between the peaks. It was only nine o'clock—we had made very good time: five hours. Consulting the map, the best way off was not clearly shown and we chose to descend the slope to reach the Tribbach Pass. We had not been able to foresee the incredible steepness. For the first time we had some spring snow and the run down the Tribbach Glacier was unforgettable. It certainly flattered our ski-ing abilities: we descended nearly five thousand feet scarcely pausing for breath! Although we later saw that the best way off the Felsköpfl would have been to have descended the south face, I for one did not regret that five-thousand foot ski-descent when I looked back from below the glacier.

We were then confronted with narrow snow gullies and rocky bluffs, just the terrain for the deer and her kid which we glimpsed as we reluctantly shouldered our skis. We then either glissaded—that is sliding down on the heels but keeping the body upright—or ploughed through thigh-deep wet snow until we reached a path leading us over green pastures, thick with crocus and stable muck. We threaded our way through wooded glades scented with the lovely aroma of pine cones and we reached the village at St. Johann, some seven thousand five hundred feet below our lunch site.

It was early afternoon, blisteringly hot. The village sprawls beside the River Aurina and our thirst misled us into thinking the first house looked like a pub. It was a home for the mentally handicapped. An inmate came out and, conveying that we were not considered eligible for admittance, he made wild noises and gestures sending us up the road. We were tired and thirsty, but shops, pubs, everything was shut: all in honour of the local Saint's feast day. Getting warmer and wearier we trudged back and forth, finding no-one helpful and twice we met yet another seeming village idiot. The Saint had little reason to be proud of his flock—or was I just getting tired and irritable? In fact the Saint had kept the best for himself: there beside the church was a pub, and inside kindliness and help. Large glasses of beer and a platter of cold meats put us at peace with the world again.

We had a short sleep indoors then, refreshed, we celebrated our crossing of the Zillertal with spaghetti, wienerschnitzel and wine.

The Venediger

We were poised to enter the Venediger group to reach a point from which Peter and I had already crossed part of the range. The first time, we had gone in from the Salzach Valley some fifteen miles northwards, in Austria—a diabolical eight-hour slog up the Ober Sulzbach to the Kürsinger Hut but known as "the normal way". Peter, however, was always in search of a new or unusual route and the second time we entered from the Virgental ten miles to the south, and traversed the Venediger group as far as Kaprun: a very worth-while route. Why bother to do it again? Well, "the mountains were in the way", for one thing, and for another from St. Johann to the head of the Val Aurina was a direct line presenting a new way in. We would go out of Italy over the Birnlücke Pass to the Krimmler Valley and Warnsdorfer Hut, then up to the Krimmler Pass and the Kürsinger Hut.

The grandmother at the Ahr Gasthof was cheerful even at 4 a.m., when she presented us with an enormous breakfast. Obviously, by now, we had earned a reputation for good appetites. The old lady also sold us provisions for the journey and—thank God—a bottle of Slibbovitch, because the shops had all been shut the day before. A sleek Mercedes took us to the snow line, just past Kasern at the head of the valley.

The first part of our route was a long gentle climb up a narrow valley. Clouds were hanging about everywhere, but it seemed worse looking down than up, although the sky was generally overcast. We reached a plateau, had a drink in a stream, and then struck up to the left into a narrow defile which led up to the Birnlücke Hut.

It becomes an automatic reaction to assess the safety of all slopes before climbing them and many factors have to be taken into consideration. Steepness is one, bearing in mind that any snow slope can avalanche above a gradient of 20° given the right conditions. This slope was fairly steep but it was bordered on both sides by a rocky ridge which should hold the snow. Its contour was flat, and there was nothing to suggest that it was a snow-filled gulley—which is always a notorious place for an avalanche to fall, as the curve in the ground acts as a chute. Anchorage of the snow to the underlying surface is of prime importance, because it is well known that snow can slide like a blanket from a slippery grassy slope. But here we were high up in the mountains, where, seen in summer, the terrain would be rough and strewn with small boulders which would provide a good anchorage for the snow.

As for the snow, we expected to find good spring or "firn" snow as it was late April, the slope lay full south in the sun, and there had been no recent snowfall of any consequence for ten days. Yes, the slope should be safe enough to climb, and so we set off upwards. We spent an hour and a half traversing from side to side making innumerable kick turns as the passage was narrow; this is always a laborious process and tiring as well. About three quarters ot the way up I noticed large air holes in the snow.

This was not only alarming: it was also dangerous. It was obvious that the heat from the rocks nearby had begun to melt the snow, and because melt-water trickles down to the deeper layers until it finds an impervious barrier such as ice or even the ground, it flows along this layer loosening the bond with the snow above. In this way the melt-waters act as a lubricant on which the surface snow avalanches. At this moment, so early in the day, the snow and melt-waters were frozen, but by noon or later it would be suicidal to attempt to climb such a slope. I did not like it, but we were too near the top to turn back, and it would be safer to continue upwards as the bonded spring snow lower down was probably supporting it from below. Nevertheless, I worried lest the ageing process in the snow had indeed developed a stage further: when these melt-waters vaporize under the snowholes to form cup crystals or deep hoar frost crystals which are loose and do not bond together, they are aptly named *kornschnee* (corn snow) by the Germans. They provide no anchorage under the surface crust and if this fractures the whole surface will slide off on what is equivalent to ball bearings. I plunged my ski stick into one of the air holes but to my relief no crystals came out.

At the top of the couloir we saw the Birnlücke Hut standing on a spur to the south of us and surrounded by murky grey cloud. Richard suggested that we made a détour to inspect it, in case the weather drove us back, as it would be unwise to return later in the day down the slope which we had just come up.

The hut stood on a man-made platform surrounded by a low stone wall on which was mounted a large wrought-iron crucifix. Under different weather conditions this platform must have commanded a wonderful view down the valley. We tried the handle, and the door opened into a small but very sparse winter room lit by two large windows: it was little more than a shelter. The concrete walls were about eighteen inches thick and whitewashed with a sort of pebbledash. It would be a "port in a storm". There were two canvas slung bunks and two wooden beds with only the boards to lie on, as there were no mattresses. There were three stools and three blankets—nothing else. There were no cooking pots, no stove, but we did have Fred. Just to prove it, he brewed us up some coffee and we had an early lunch before setting off up a ridge which led to the pass.

The pass was now visible in sunshine, but cumulus clouds continued to hover above it and around the peaks. It was not far to the pass and Jonathan and Richard, who were in the lead, reached it in time to gain a view of the far side before the clouds closed in on us once more. All of a sudden there was a complete white-out and it became cold and very windy. I looked ahead—I could not see the others—only whiteness. I looked back—there was no hut—only whiteness. I looked down—the wind was streaking across the ski tracks and already in places they had been obliterated by the swirling snow. I must hurry forwards before the tracks had gone forever, because it is so easy to get lost in cloud and I had not got the map. Even if they called to me I might not hear in the wind. I turned my skis uphill, found the tracks, lost them again, then the ground eased and began to fall away, I must have crossed the pass. For a moment the clouds cleared and I looked about me and saw the others sheltering from the wind under a rock, waiting for me—just where I expected them to be. I think their relief was as great as mine.

After a brief consultation we decided to walk down from the pass until we could see, and to do so, we formed a line with Richard in the rear steering by compass while I went on in front. By keeping us in a line ahead Richard could correct our course: this was just as well, because in the cloud, with nothing to focus my eyes on, I kept veering to the right. As I am right-handed I wondered if left-handed people veer to the left—it is an interesting thought! It is well known that in these conditions it is possible to turn full circle, as we did when crossing the Col du Palet near the Val d'Isère.

We were soon below the clouds and I could see down the Krimmler Valley. Two parallel moraines of heaped-up stone and tilth deposited from the Krimmler Glacier ran along the sides and above the far one was the Warnsdorfer Hut barely half a mile away.

We were very near to our goal when suddenly Richard shouted: "Look out!" He had seen a ripple of snow in front of us. It was an avalanche coming off the Grasleiten Schneid on our right. I looked up to see a curious heaving movement in the snow on a shoulder, but it was strangely silent. This was a typical wet-snow slab-avalanche. Colin Frazer describes it in his book: "Wet-slab avalanches have a characteristic form of motion for the first few yards of their run. A crack appears in the snow cover and then, quite slowly, the cleft yawns open. Below this rupture, the snow, which is of course warm and plastic, forms waves and creases as it begins to move. It may heave itself up into folds like an enormous cloth or carpet. Then once it has gathered speed, the snow slab breaks up and the movement becomes similar to that of a wet loose snow avalanche, with the typical formation of snowballs and boulders."*

We turned away from where it had stopped short, and continued down on foot. The weather cleared and it became remarkably hot. Suddenly more avalanches began to

Colin Frazer: "The Avalanche Enigma"; John Murray, 1966

fall from the Gasleiten Kogel but these had a rustling sound as they swept down the slopes below us; the nearest stopped within twenty yards. First one fell, then another, and then another on top of them. This shook us all, particularly as some of the avalanches were coming from north-facing slopes despite the absence of a snowfall of any consequence during the last ten days.

The possible explanation was that the snow on the north face contained a high proportion of cup crystals, or as Seligman calls them, deep hoar crystals. Following the "firn" stage in the ageing of snow there is a constructive phase when the "firn" crystals in the lower layers vaporize into upper layers of the snow due to a temperature difference, and in these upper layers the cup crystals form. They grow to as much as half an inch in size, since they form at the expense of the snow crystals in the deeper layers. They do not bond like the "firn" crystals, and a sudden temperature rise, or melting of the ice round a small rock, even an icicle falling into this unstable snow, could cause it to avalanche. When the weather has been cold it is possible for the snow on a north face to be composed entirely of cup crystals.

Whatever the cause, we were standing on a very dangerous slope. With dry snow avalanches, once they are down it is usually considered safe to walk over them—but not these. Not only had they covered the slope down which we wanted to walk into the valley, but also we did not know how many more avalanches there were to come. We stopped to look at the map to see if we could find an alternative route, but the slopes below us leading into the Krimmler Valley were steep and craggy. Even under better conditions they might not be safe, and it would be madness to attempt them now. Richard made the correct decision—we must go back to the Birnlücke Hut.

Robin started upwards, making a new track by kicking steps in the snow to avoid the fallen avalanche. Suddenly there was a loud "Vrrumpfh", of escaping pent-up air, another large avalanche was belting down towards us.

"Keep going and move to the right," shouted Richard. This Robin did with alacrity, and we were all lucky not to be engulfed, as the avalanche fell over a previous one and did not travel far. This was obviously a wind-slab avalanche, and it was an extraordinary experience to witness three different types of avalanche on one slope; but it was an experience that I never wish to repeat. I was now even more convinced that the date of one's death is predetermined!

We climbed back into the cloud and the wind funnelled through the pass blasting our faces; on the far side Jonathan and Richard managed to pick up our old tracks here and there, and lead us back to the hut without resorting to the use of the compass.

We decided to stay in the hut as the slope down to the valley would now be very dangerous at this time of day, and we had tempted providence sufficiently. We were "locked in", as it happened, in more ways than one. The hut was cold and we put on all our clothes and spare pullovers. Richard pulled a balaclava over his head and as he sat down a dreamy look came into his eye—he was loving it, he was back in the Antarctic! We took off our sodden boots and socks, and replaced them with dry socks and covered our feet with polythene bags.

Fred in the meantime kept a constant brew of tea going on his "Camping Gaz"; needless to say, the tea was heavily laced with the contents of my bottle of Slibbovitch. We emptied our sacks of our remaining food and rationed it around, one helping of curry chicken and a helping of Fred's protoveg-goulash, and Fred even managed to rustle up three containers and spoons for us to use. The atmosphere was very cheerful, and as darkness fell we decided it would be more romantic to have our after-dinner coffee by candlelight.

Robin decided to go out and piddle.

"Just a little smell of gas," murmured Fred as he changed the gas cylinder. We were all used to this ritual patter by now, as Fred seemed to delight in doing most of the cooking.

Suddenly there was a violent flash of flame and Fred jumped back with singed eyebrows, dropping the gas cylinder on the floor. It rolled under one of the wooden stools near the door and flames leapt into the air. My first thought was that they were going to burn the bloody hut down and that would be the end of a perfect day!

Our retreat outside was barred.

"Take cover," someone called out, "the cylinder may explode."

We all cowered behind the wooden bunks while Fred stepped valiantly forward to cope with his Brocks' fireworks. Robin returned to the door at this moment and seeing our retreat cut off, shot outside to fetch a shovel of snow, which he handed to Fred. The snow subdued the flames temporarily, but any attempt to cast the cylinder outside only made the flames shoot up with increased vigour. There was nothing else the rest of us could do except cower behind the bunks and enjoy the pantomime of Fred wielding the shovel and shouting to Robin to get out of the way, while Robin danced about in the snow outside shouting "Mind the skis!"

Eventually Fred managed to throw the cylinder outside and anticlimax descended on us all. Nevertheless it had warmed up the hut! There would be no more tea or Slibbovitch, and none of us expected to get any sleep because of the cold, but gloom was soon dispelled when I remembered that I still carried my small solid meta fuel stove for emergency. Strange to say that had I known beforehand that Fred carried so much equipment with him, I would not have put it in my ruck-sack. We settled down to discuss how the incident happened, and it was Richard who pointed out that we had all forgotten the lighted candle on the windowsill, which had probably sparked off the flames when Fred changed the gas cylinder; and he recounted an even more dramatic event when a petrol stove and can caught fire in the confined space of a bivouac tent when he was in the Antarctic.

Bedtime came and Richard and Fred shared one of the canvas bunks, sleeping head to tail. Jonathan and Robin shared the canvas bunk above, and I spent an uncomfortable night on the hard wooden bed with one of the blankets. Richard was probably the lucky one, as Fred managed to produce the added luxury of a Karry-mat to put on the bunk and this stopped the draught coming through the canvas. Owing to the cramped space, however, they all had to lie on their backs and it was not long before I was lulled to sleep with loud snores in symphony. I awoke with daylight, and Robin saying that it was half-past four.

We had very little food left, as we had only anticipated spending one night in the Warnsdorfer hut before passing on to the Kürsinger hut, which had a guardian. In addition, we had not been able to top up our food supply on account of the shops in the valley being shut. The weather was far too warm and still overcast; even at 5 a.m. the snow was sodden on the slopes. After a quick breakfast we decided to go down to the valley and back to St. Johann.

On the way down we heard an avalanche fall, but we did not see it, and when we reached the couloir we carried our skis making a veritable elephant track.

At times I looked into the snow air-holes; they were bright blue from the high water content, and I plunged my ski stick into the hole: this time there were the dreaded cup crystals which came out with the stick. I really think that the Patron Saint of Lost Causes, whom I believe to be St. Jude, must have been with us as the snow held firm and showed no signs of avalanching during our descent, but all of us were very thankful to knock the snow off our skis when we reached the road.

On our way down we had met three young students going up. We warned them of the conditions but they said that they would carry on for a while. They had left their lady friend in a Dormobile, as she had a blister on her foot; needless to say, Jonathan and Richard soon struck up an acquaintance with her, and she offered to run us all back to St. Johann. They were German students, and she told us that she wanted to get some meat from the "botcher".

It was 8.30 a.m. when we arrived back at the Ahr Gasthof in St. Johann, and they asked us if we wanted breakfast. But we said we wanted *lunch,* and our young friend joined us when they produced large plates of cold meats and jugs of steaming coffee.

All except Fred and I had to return to England, as the others had been away two weeks. The journey back to Innsbruck was very complicated, because we had first to take a 'bus down to Bressanone (still called Brixen by the Austrians). We stoked up with beer whilst waiting for the 'bus, and then at Bressanone we had to change our Austrian Schillings into Italian lire while we waited for the Brenner Bahn train; as we had to do this in a café, we consumed more beer. On the Brenner Pass we had another wait for the train, as it was the frontier back into Austria, and the Italian and Austrian trains only run as far as the pass. To while away the time we consumed two litres of red wine, and it was not surprising that we nearly missed our connexion. We dashed down the platform, but the customs officers wanted to examine our passports. However, Fred swept by, calling out "We're British!" and I got away with it, too, as my camera got entangled with my rucksack and I ran past them saying "I'm *eingelockt*" —my translation for "I'm locked in!" The customs officers laughed so much that they let us through, though with the remonstrance that we should have come earlier.

What were my thoughts as I sadly said goodbye to Richard, Jonathan and Robin on Innsbruck station? "I was glad that I had been one of the few privileged people to have so many good friends."

The Gross Glockner Group

Although disappointed, I was not particularly upset by our failure to cross the Venediger on this occasion, because Peter and I had already done it previously in 1968, and in a way it provides a second or alternative ending to this book, and for this reason I have left the description of the Venediger traverse to the last chapter. Peter decided to cross it again on the "Little Walk on Skis" because it was a logical continuation from the Zillertal and Ahr Valley through to the Gross Glockner group and the Rudolfs Hut.

In addition, he was always looking for fresh routes, and although we had been to the Venediger group twice before, we had never entered from the Krimmler Pass via the Warnsdorfer Hut.

Had we not been plagued by bad weather and avalanches on this occasion, we had planned to cross the Venediger taking the same route as Peter and I had done in 1968, and when we reached the Rudolfs Hut, Richard and the others would have returned to England, leaving Fred and me to pick up Eric Farnsworth to continue the journey through to the Gross Glockner, Sonnenblick and Ankogel groups of mountains, hopefully ending the journey at Mallnitz, which was what Peter had wanted to do. But he himself had said that the eastern end of the High Alps trails away sadly and it was difficult to know where they *did* end, for parties have been known to ski along Low Level hills as far as Vienna in winter.

Yet what are the High Alps? They are generally regarded as snow-capped mountains in summer, which means that they are higher than seven thousand feet. Not all of the High Alps are skiable in winter, because some of them are very steep and rocky, and these are regarded by mountaineers as Alps to be climbed in summer on foot with ropes and ice-axes. Hofrat Wolfgang had told me that people skied around the Gross Glockner, though the peak itself is only regarded as a summer climb, and for this reason I asked Alan Blackshaw why he started his east-west traverse of the Alps from Kaprun. In his opinion the High Alps began at the eastern end of the Gross Glockner area. So what of the mountains beyond, were they skiable in winter, or summer climbing Alps?

Amongst Peter's papers I found maps and a list of huts which he intended to use, but there were no details about the route except for an odd note here and there. However, it was clear that he planned to cross the Odenwinkel pass on to the large glacier which surrounds the Gross Glockner, and then traverse along its south side using various huts and passes to reach Heiligenblut. Anthony Greenwood, who had skied with us on past expeditions in Norway, confirmed that the route was feasible; I am also greatly indebted to Tristram Pye, who worked out all the details for me. However, it left me in some doubt as to the practicability of the route beyond.

After Fred and I had seen Richard and the others off at Innsbruck station, we went along to the Austrian Alpine Club to get more information. They knew very little about the mountains east of the Gross Glockner in winter, and referred us to the Reisebureau. There, a sun-tanned elderly skier, who knew the district well, told us these were regarded as "summer mountains" and it was not possible to traverse them in safety during the winter, as the valleys were narrow and the avalanche dangers would be too great. I found this hard to believe, but decided to act on Hofrat Wolfgang's advice and consult the chief guide when we reached Heiligenblut.

In the meantime, Fred and I hurried round to the Rudolfs Hut, where we had arranged to meet Eric Farnsworth, who would make our team up to three to continue our journey. However, when we arrived he had gone down to the valley, leaving his 'phone number as he had been tired of waiting for us. Neither of us knew him. He had applied to join the tour through the Ski Club of Great Britain. All we knew was that he was aged 58 and a retired bank official who lived in Switzerland. He had had some experience in ski-touring with Philip Andrews, but among some two hundred people milling about in the hut—which is virtually a mountain hotel—what did he look like?

While we were awaiting his return, I speculated with Fred on every male who entered the room. As each one looked more decrepit, I repeatedly said: "That's Eric!!" With Fred aged 64 and me aged 65, it would complete a geriatric trio!

It was cloudless and sunny so Fred and I decided to explore the Odenwinkel Glacier in preparation for the next day, as the way down to it was said to be difficult. It was a steep slope which had to be traversed along an icy ski track, but once on the glacier it was a gentle walk up to the ice-fall. To our left was the Hohe Sand, a steepish climb up to the Odenwinkel Pass. Way above our heads a group of people was making easy going and we knew that there would be no difficulties given good weather—what a pity we were unable to continue then! We both felt lazy and as we turned to go back to the hut, we heard the peal of bells. It was Sunday, but there was no church near the hut—surely it must be an echo from the valley. What curious mountain shape or freak of wind could invoke it, as we were seven thousand feet up and in a valley well set into the mountain ranges?

The snow was soft when we returned to the steep slope near the hut, and avalanches had fallen obliterating our tracks—but once these small avalanches are down they are unlikely to recur. We looked unhappily at the sky; cirrus was building up and bad weather was not far away. Eric had arrived, and despite our speculations he was slim and wiry and looked almost young!

That night there was a terrific blizzard. Although the hut is solidly built of stone, it lies on an exposed promontory, and it caught the full force of the wind. The banging of doors and shutters echoed through the stone corridors and we had very little sleep. By

Plate 96. The Kalser Tauern. We crossed between the two peaks in thick mist

4 a.m. it was time to get up and make a start, but we looked outside and the clouds were still low in the valley. We went in search of an Austrian and his wife who had asked if they might accompany us over the pass, and found him wandering about disconsolately; we all agreed to abandon the journey for the time being. Throughout the day it rained and sleeted; large puddles of water collected on the terrace, and we sat glued to the television for three days watching the weather reports—low troughs moved in constantly—while clouds obscured the whole valley. The Austrians went home. As there seemed little prospect of the two or three days' fine weather which would be needed to cross the Odenwinkel Pass and traverse the Gross Glockner, we decided to take the lower level route down the Kalser valley.

Next morning we could see the rocks on the far side of the valley and we agreed to make a start. The clouds were coming and going by the time we reached the Weiss See, a lake below the hut. There is a dam at its north end distinguished by a small tower, aptly named the pepper pot. We took a compass bearing on it and set off to find the mouth of the valley which led up to the Kalser Tauern Pass. Eric, who had been a gunner, took charge of the map and compass; he was in the rear, while Fred led off carefully counting his steps to measure the distance. Suddenly I noticed that the slope which had been on his left was now on his right. We re-checked the compass and found, much to Fred's indignation, that he had made a complete U-turn in the whiteness. Setting him back on course, we now steered by compass, all the time climbing in cloud, and we reached the pass without difficulty. On the far side the low clouds had cleared and we were rewarded with good visibility as we skied down to the valley. Ice crystals were plastered on the south side of the rocks—a legacy from the storm, but the snow

Plate 97. The storm damage. Trees had been broken, branches and fir-cones
were strewn in the snow greyed with moraine

was in wonderful condition, an inch of powder on hard crust. But once on the valley floor it became treacherous.

It was a wild rocky place, dotted with a few larches stunted in their struggle for existence, and lower down a small wood had been partly decimated by the blizzard. Fir trees were broken off at the base. Branches, twigs and fir-cones littered the snow, already greyed by moraine dust which had been carried down from the rocky ridges above us.

Passing a deserted summer alp, it too was dead. A bleached jawbone of an animal lay on the brown grass. Uncleared rabbit droppings still littered the floors of the cages let into the walls of the chalets, which told a story of the quick departure of the inhabitants to the plains in the previous autumn. It was like the valley of death—until I heard the cuckoo and saw the tracks of an Ibex with her young.

The Kalser Tauern Haus, a summer mountain hut for walkers, was shut, which was not surprising as the only access to it from the valley below was through a narrow gorge, the Daber Kamm. There was a narrow, cramped pathway hollowed out of the smooth granite rocky mountainside, with a sheer drop on one side into the river bed below. This was partly choked with snow, and the consoling handrail had been removed for the winter. Fortunately the snow was soft and we were able to make our way down by kicking a path through it, but it was not pleasant, as we were fully laden with rucksacks and skis on our backs; whilst watching where we put our feet we had at the same time to take great care that the skis did not catch on the rock wall and disturb our balance. Our feet were precariously poised on a soft slippery bed, about a foot wide, above a drop of some one hundred and fifty feet. Eric soon confessed that he did not like heights, but it did not worry me as the drop was only on one side. However, Eric carried on nobly, turning his face to the rock wall as he dared not glance down, but he looked very sick. We passed behind a small waterfall cascading from the rock above, rounded a corner, and came to a halt. The entire path was filled in by a snow wall about twelve feet long—there was no way round it with a rock wall on our left and a precipice on our right.

We had a consultation: there was only one thing to do—attempt to tunnel through it. Fred set to with the snow shovel and ice-axe, and gradually disappeared into his hole as far as his knees. Suddenly he gave a grunt and wriggled out backwards: he had encountered a frozen waterfall, and had been chipping at it with his ice-axe but could make no impression on it, and, what was more, there were still another eight feet to negotiate.

What was the alternative? We peered down into the gorge—the snow wall was flush with the rock cliff which fell sheer down to the river. Could we cut foot- and hand-holds in the snow wall and climb round it on the outside? We looked around for a boulder or rock spike on which to tie a rope, as we could only undertake this task if belayed—but there was nothing suitable. I must confess that I was not keen on the idea, and Eric even less so as with his dislike of heights, the prospect would have been hazardous. We looked at the map. We would have to retrace our steps for a mile and a half and try to go over the shoulder. However, on our way back through the gorge I noticed a tunnel, unseen from the other direction, blocked by a wooden door, which opened to my touch. Armed with candles and torches Fred and I plunged into the darkness. The tunnel was wide enough for a jeep. Water poured down in places from

Plate 98. Fred in the Daber Gorge: the pathway was hollowed out of the mountain side and partly choked with snow

the roof,and after about five hundred yards we saw daylight. We were once again on the gorge path, but this time below the frozen waterfall. What luck!

We went back and collected Eric and our gear, and soon came out on to a wide open plain above Kals, and by good fortune the hotel there had just opened for the season.

Plate 99. A snow wall blocked the path, and we would have to tunnel through it

After a large plate of goulash the others lay on a grassy bank studded with crocus, while I went in search of a taxi to take us above Kals in readiness for our journey over to Heiligenblut the next day. A rather drunken Austrian presented himself and he agreed to take us to the Groder Hof some five thousand feet above the Kals valley where we could spend the night with his sister. He was obviously accustomed to driving in this condition, as he negotiated the hairpin bends with great skill. Next morning he kept up his strength by drinking wine while we ate our breakfast, as he was going to give us a lift up the road as far as the snow line, which would save us two hours' walk.

We set off for the Glorer hut at 5.30 a.m. The sky was overcast. It was not inappropriately Ascension Day, I thought, as I put on my skis at the foot of the climb. We took it in turns making tracks through breakable crust and gradually climbed into the clouds. Although there was a silent ski-lift, its pylons were no help as a guide, for (higher up) they spanned a steep cliff. We found a snow-covered road which contoured round until that too disappeared, leaving us with frozen downhill ski-tracks to follow in the complete white-out. At times we lost the tracks and had to retrace our steps, but we comforted ourselves with the thought that they might lead us to the Glorer hut.

Eventually we found the hut beside the top of the ski-lift, on an exposed pass. We had been assured that there was a winter room, and as the clouds were right down, we decided to stay there because the route beyond was complicated and required some degree of visibility. The door was covered by a deep snowdrift and Eric and Fred dug down to find it. After an hour's hard work they had cleared a space sufficient for the top half of the door to open, but to our dismay there was another door immediately behind it and our master-key did not fit the lock. What now? Apart from a shed, which obviously was not the winter room, there was no other building. We could not see to navigate over the pass, nor could we see the tracks of the way we had come. Somehow we would *have* to get inside the hut. We wandered round it, and found one of the window shutters old and brittle, and a gentle lever with the ice-axe managed to prise it open. A tap on the glass window, and we climbed in.

It is not recommended to break other people's windows; however, we could neither retrace our steps to the valley nor continue forward on account of the bad visibility, and, in the mountains when weather conditions are bad, it is better to be prudent and seek the shelter of the hut rather than freeze in a bivouac outside.

Furniture was stacked everywhere. We would have to light a stove which was large enough to cook for forty people. There was plenty of wood, good bunks and blankets, and it would at least give us shelter, but it might be uncomfortably cold with the broken window.

After lunch we looked outside and caught a brief glimpse of the lower rocks of the Gross Glockner: the weather was clearing. Should we make a dash for it, as we might otherwise be marooned here for several days? Yes, let's go we thought. We stuffed up the hole in the window, and left a banknote on the table to cover the damaged pane. We set off down towards Heiligenblut, as it was clearer on that side. Carefully I led the way through soft crust; the main difficulty was to avoid a sudden invisible drop on a steep slope, but as we edged our way down we were below the cloud and we could see how three valleys joined to form one. High up to our left was the Saml hut and chamois were prancing across the stream below us. The snow was wet and soggy and we walked and waded downhill, alternately taking our skis off to cross grassy patches and then putting them on again. The valley narrowed and the sides steepened, and I paused for an avalanche to settle before crossing it. It was an unpleasant place and the distance along the valley far longer than we had anticipated, but we would have made short work of it had we been able to ski.

Lower down the snowfield was spattered with the muddy holes of hare and marmots, and we caught glimpses of several well-fed ones silhouetted against the snow. I felt inwardly that my journey must be near the end, for these attractive little animals were there to greet us when Peter and I first started our journey, and here they were to bid me a nostalgic farewell.

We stopped for a bite of chocolate. It was now getting late but we had only just over a mile to go: we were nearing the junction with the main valley and we would soon be in Heiligenblut. We crossed the stream, climbed up a shoulder, rounded the corner and thankfully saw a notice board— "Heiligenblut 1" —but one what? Was it one kilometre? one hour? or something else?

A steep slope fell away to our left into a rocky ravine. We would have to traverse a shelf above it, but there was no path, no signs nor dabs of red paint on the trees to indicate summer paths and the way off. We traversed, dropped down, found an impassable couloir, climbed back again, crossed back and forth, each time encountering a rocky ravine. It was maddening. Darkness was beginning to fall, and we could see the lights of Heiligenblut twinkling in the valley.

"I can't go another step further," Eric said suddenly.

It was now 8 p.m. —fifteen hours since we had started. There was no question—we must bivouac. But how? There are several kinds of shelter which can be built out of snow, assuming that one is not carrying a tent, and Peter and I had learned how to build them when we attended a ski-touring leaders' course run by the Eagle Ski Club. Undoubtedly the most attractive is the igloo, built out of snow bricks, such as the Eskimos use for their permanent homes. But they are not practicable in times of emergency, as they take too long to build. Alternatively, if there is a bank of deep snow, a J-shaped tunnel can be excavated and enlarged at the end to form a small "room". Better still, on a flat surface, a five-foot-deep trench can be dug, with ledges to sit on, and this is roofed over with skis, and then snow "slates" are piled on top. But for all these shelters we needed deep and well-compacted snow, and here we were standing on a fairly steep slope, which held only about two feet of soft wet snow, near a little waterfall; at least that would save us melting snow for water, and as for the bivouac, we must improvise.

I cast round and saw a natural snow seat under a fir tree. That would do if I built up some sides. While Fred brewed up some soup, I built two walls and laid the skis on top, and covered them with fir branches, finishing off the roof with slates of snow. On the "seat" we put the rope, more fir branches, Fred's Karrymat (a waterproof mat used for camping), and lined it with my foil blanket; to cover the front, we hung Eric's polythene sheet. It looked more like the back seat of a car, but at least it was a shelter and would keep out the wind which is the "killer", as it cools the body rapidly and produces a state of hypothermia—not an unpleasant death as the person goes into a long sleep.

To Fred's amusement, I told Eric to go off and piddle as I did not wish to be disturbed during the night. Our boots, socks and gloves were wet and Eric's windjacket sodden, and so he removed it. We changed into dry socks and insulated our feet with polythene bags, and all climbed into Fred's Zdarski sack which was a waterproof nylon bag about two yards square. As Eric was minus a windjacket, we put him in the middle between Fred and me, and I put my arms around him to keep him warm, at least on one side, but Fred remained aloof on the other! We settled down to a fitful sleep.

"I'm sitting in water," said Eric about an hour later. We got a torch and had a look round—sure enough there was a large puddle—it almost looked pleased with itself as the socks, which we had taken inside the bag to dry, floated around on the surface. The foil blanket had channelled a small tributary from the waterfall into the Zdarski sack. We mopped up the water, squeezed out the socks, and rearranged the foil blanket to prevent the tide from coming in again, and settled down once more.

We slept a little, but the next rude awakening was a cold "plop" on our faces as the snow slates began to melt with the heat from our bodies.

Despite having put on all my spare clothing and a kagool, being on the outside I was now quivering with cold. Did Eric mistake it for emotion? He snuggled a bit closer saying "It's years since I snuggled down to my wife like this."

"Well, you had better get some practice and surprise her when you get back," I retorted. I was far from amused, because the others were obviously warm—at least until 2 a.m. when it began to freeze. We stamped our feet and comforted ourselves that it would only be two hours until daylight—and I have never been so glad to see it come. Nor have I experienced anything more unpleasant than putting on sodden boots over wet socks, with the feet too swollen to wear more than one sock. But Eric, having no dry socks, put his gloves on his feet.

Before starting off. Fred and Eric consulted the maps, comparing the 1:25,000 which Eric had been using, with the 1:50,000 which in our fatigued state the day before had lain forgotten at the bottom of Fred's rucksack. Had we used the 1:50,000 map we might have found the way off the mountain, for it was now clear that we had to traverse the shelf to its full length where we would find a steep summer path leading down to the road. We found the way without difficulty, and literally fell into the first Gasthof on the outskirts of Heiligenblut. Every bit of our clothing was wet and we hung everything out on their clothes-line to dry while the proprietress lent me a pair of shoes. I fell asleep while Eric was talking to me over a well-earned meal, and after a luxurious hot bath dropped into bed in a dreamless haze.

By evening we were refreshed. The chief guide was away but his deputy came to see us. Was the remainder of the journey a summer expedition as we had been told in Innsbruck? We could climb the Sonnenblick and return the same day, but a traverse to Mallnitz even by direct route via the Duisberger hut was out of the question at that time of the year. Would he be prepared to take us over? In summer yes, but not on skis. Our journey was ended. Although we had gone south, we were only just a little bit further east of Kaprun—where I like to feel the journey really finished.

Back at my home in Surlingham, I am often asked why I ski across mountains. Perhaps it is difficult for people to understand what lies behind it—how some magical force links two lives together and drives them into the spirit of adventure—where the challenge of danger provides a desire and discipline to survive.

Time is always an enemy, for moments have to be spent with excitement to squeeze every ounce out of life and live it to the full. There is always something round the corner—when my World crashed around me, there was Peter's last message—I must arise from the morass of self-pity, there was a task to complete, a reason to go on living. This has taken me into a new life amongst a world of *real* people.

As Peter said: "What purpose the journey without memories?" There is a silence amongst snow-capped mountains, at moments tinged with pink and gold, and the vision of deep blue shadows creates the realization of man's insignificance, and there is something greater than self. There is the privilege of knowing that the warmth and kindness of mountain people still exists in an era of degraded morals, the companionship engendered by the closeness of living in the mountains. Yes! it has been an unbelievable experience. A journey impossible without Peter—and those who so readily stepped in in his place—for I was merely a passenger with a through ticket, and but for the "Little Walk on Skis" I would never have lived.

Chapter X

Epilogue

The Venediger and the Hohe Tauern

I WAS often puzzled about why Peter referred to the Venediger as the Hohe Tauern until I looked at the map.

The Hohe Tauern is a regional name given to the middle range of the Eastern Alps, which is comprised of four mountain groups. It is sandwiched between the Kitzbühel and Pinzgau alps in the north and the Dolomites, Carnic and Julien alps in the south. The four mountain groups take their names from their principal mountains—the Venediger from the Gross Venediger, the Glockner from the Gross Glockner, and, at the far eastern end, the remaining two groups are the Sonnenblick and the Ankogel. The groups have been separated by Tauern, which are grooves running north to south across the west-east chain. The name *Tauern* probably means watersheds; for example, the Krimmler Tauern, which I have referred to as the Krimmler Valley in Chapter IX, runs northwards from the Krimmler Glacier to the Salzach river, a tributary of the Danube, which it joins west of Vienna. The Krimmler Tauern separates the Zillertal from the Venediger. Likewise the Velber and Heiligenblut Tauern separate the Venediger from the Glockner, and the Glockner from the Sonnenblick and Ankogel groups. These two Tauern run from north to south to join the river Drau, also a tributary of the Danube. The better-known Gross Glockner Pass which connects Zell am Zee with Lienz has been built through the Heiligenblut Tauern. The numerous passes called *"Tauern"* are snowless.

In Chapter IX we failed to cross the Krimmler Tauern to enter the Venediger group, and to complete this story of traversing the Alpine Chain on skis, I must fall back on an account of a complete crossing of the Venediger which Peter and I made in 1968—two years before the "Little Walk on Skis" was started. At that time we little knew that we would be finishing it before it began. But does consecutive time matter, since we did the journey across the Alps in stages, and the story in this book is one of traversing the Alpine Chain from end to end. In 1968 we covered exactly the same route across the Venediger, in the same direction, as we had proposed to do on The Walk, had we not been turned back by the avalanches in the Krimmler Valley. The only difference was that in 1968 we entered the Venediger from the Virgental in the south, instead of by the Krimmler pass; then we climbed more peaks, whereas on the later occasion we had only intended to climb the Gross Venediger in passing.

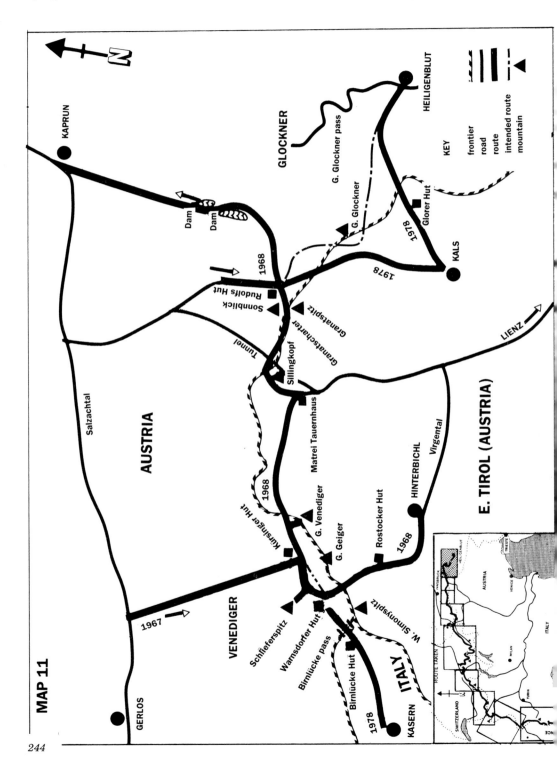

MAP 11

The 1968 tour also highlights the difference between a mountain traverse and ski-touring from mountain huts, an exercise which all prospective ski-mountaineers should undertake before attempting a lengthy traverse because on a traverse there is a need for greater fitness and endurance, as the skier is under constant pressure to reach his goal—a shelter for the night. A traverse entails being in the mountains much later in the day, and at a time when the sun has affected the snow, to an extent which lessens the safety factor, and this calls for a greater knowledge of mountains, snow and glaciers.

My second reason for including this traverse at the end of the book is because the 1968 journey ended at Kaprun, which, seen on the map, is almost as far east as Heiligenblut. What is more, I feel that this account provides a second ending to the book: one which I much prefer, as the closing pages are written by Peter and have been taken from a reprint of an article which he wrote for the Ski Club of Great Britain in the autumn of 1968. I am sentimental enough to think that the architect of the traverse was with me at the end—as he was with me at the beginning—and he only missed a little bit of the Stubai and Zillertal on our "Little Walk on Skis".

Hinterbichl to Kürsinger Hut

We were joined by Archie MacKenzie, a business man and part-time faith healer, and Geoffrey Buckley, an engineer (who accompanied us on the second year of the "Little Walk").

Part of Peter's notes of this tour are missing; nevertheless, I have managed to revive my memory by the use of Archie's notes and my photographs.

When Peter announced that we would be exploring the Venediger Group once more, I groaned, for on our previous visit we had been driven down from the Kürsinger hut, which lies on a windy shelf, by a terrible storm. The vivid memory of being blown flat on my face as I walked outside the hut and having to crawl on all fours with my rucksack and skis until I reached the lee-side of the mountain, was uppermost in my mind. Nor was this memory mitigated by the thought of an eight-hour climb from the Sulzbach valley to the Kürsinger Hut—not all that *again!* But No! he had found a new way—the Rostocker hut had been rebuilt. We would travel through the Tauern tunnel by 'bus from Kaprun to Pragraten at the head of the Virgen Valley, then it would be a short walk up to Hinterbichl.

Hinterbichl was unspoilt, and while we were waiting for Archie and Geoffrey to join us, we wandered round the village; the fields were already green, and although it was spring, barred frames were dotted about in readiness for drying the autumn hay. The old water-mill still worked, and the church sun-dial clock needed no winding—it was a place far from jets, juke boxes and pistes. We had already stocked up with a few lunch provisions, not needing to carry much food as there would be guardians in the huts.

Geoffrey and Archie were waiting for us in the little inn when we got back, and after a quick lunch we set off for the Rostocker hut contouring round the mountain to

Streden, at the foot of the Maurer Valley. After half-an-hour's climb along an easy wooded path, we came to a small clearing. I could hardly believe my eyes—there was a service lift up to the hut! Without any questions, I dumped my sack on it, for I dislike carrying an unnecessary load, particularly on the first day (even if I *had* been climbing on the mantlepiece at home to get fit). Peter demurred, as he spurned anything to do with wires—they spoilt the mountains—and there was no point in encouraging them, even if they *were* there! The others followed my example, and Peter reluctantly gave in. We pressed the bell, and watched our sacks sail off up the valley.

It was just as well, as we had nearly two thousand three hundred feet to climb through wet snow which clung tenaciously to our skis. It would have been a good deal more trying with heavy rucksacks, and we were glad to reach the hut. Although newly-built, it was disappointing from the outside, and it looked more like a public lavatory, but at least it was functional and comfortable inside.

We unpacked our rucksacks; this was the great advantage of using the hut as a base for when we went on tours we only needed a light sack with essentials for the day. It certainly adds enjoyment as carrying a heavy sack day after day on a traverse is very wearisome.

There was a party of reserved Germans in residence, but two of them were friendly and we rapidly got to know them. They had already been there a week, as the hut is ideally placed for a wide range of ski-tours. We could grade our tours according to the fitness of our party, and by making an early start we could time the descent to capture the best snow conditions. After a late lunch we hoped to lie in the afternoon sun and for a change watch the avalanches pour off the rocks, in safety and comfort. It promised to be a comfortable life, without the sense of pressure or endurance. But it did not pan out that way!

Our first day, to the Regen Torl, entailed a two-thousand-four-hundred foot climb which took us three hours, but it was sufficient to "limber up". It was followed next day by a four-thousand foot climb of four and a half hours, to the Westliches Simony Spitz, as it is important, if possible, to lengthen the distances and heights each day in order to acclimatize. Both of these tours were considered easy and on each occasion we had to turn back before reaching the summit as we were deep in cloud and snow began to fall. Whether it was a peculiarity of the Venediger glaciers, or just the snow conditions of the year, I never found out, but the crevasses were treacherous. We would be walking along a flat snow surface and suddenly see a small jagged black hole, perhaps only nine inches across, which if prodded would become considerably larger. There were no warning signs to indicate that a crevasse might be there, which was quite contrary to my previous experiences. When crossing a glacier on skis one does look at the map first, and one chooses a line which looks to be free from large crevasses by the lack of cross-hachuring in blue. In the concave hollows of glaciers the small crevasses are narrow and choked with snow, and quite safe to ski across, and usually this applies to a flat surface as well. Once the glacier is seen to be *slightly* convex one starts to look ahead for wider crevasses spanned by snow bridges. If there has been a lot of snow these bridges are usually deep and firm, but if the snowfall has been light the crevasses can often be seen as transverse ridges and grooves in the snow, rather like the swell in the sea, the crests being the snow-covered ice and the troughs being the snow bridges covering the holes. If there is any doubt as to the thickness of the bridge it is better to stop and prod it, but in any case it should be crossed at right angles as the ski spreads the skier's weight.

Where the glacier becomes convex, as it falls down into the valley, the ice splits open and one *expects* to find large, and sometimes wide open, crevasses especially where séracs or blocks of ice have been pushed upwards, but here one is wary, because the upper lip falls away downwards and one knows that it is not always possible to see the lower lip of the crevasse and it is better to stop and have a look round if the curve in the snow starts to fall away.

One of the most dangerous mountains I know of is the Alphubel in the Saas area in Switzerland. It is not so far from the top of the ski-lift, and many inexperienced piste skiers are tempted to go up and ski down. This glacier is constantly on the move, and the snow bridges are often loosened and poorly choked with snow. The crevasses there have sadly claimed a number of skiers in terms of lives every year, when they have dropped into a void of some three hundred feet, never to be seen again. Here in the Venediger, the wind had been blowing across the crevasses and thoroughly masked them, and it was very disturbing. The next day Geoffrey suddenly disappeared in a crevasse to his waist when we were on a gentle slope. He shouted and Peter turned round and told him to spread his arms out and keep perfectly still, for should he struggle—which would be his natural reaction—he might sink in further; by spreading his arms he would be checked from falling deeper if the slit in the ice was not too wide. Peter threw him a rope which Geoffrey tied under his armpits and we all pulled. It was like sucking a person out of quicksand, he suddenly gushed out and made a most spectacular fall downhill.

With this caution in mind, we roped up to ski back, though it was not very successful as none of us was accustomed to ski-ing roped together. As the first man set off, the rope pulled tight, jerking the man behind off his feet! Nevertheless, it would check the distance of a fall, should another of us break through—possibly into a really deep crevasse.

Peter and Archie both fell on their turns, and twisted their knees, which gave Archie at least some successful practice with his faith healing. However, the onset of a blizzard confined us to the hut, where we played chess and cards, and practised jump turns when the weather cleared. Such was the life of the many people whom we met in the huts during our "Little Walk on Skis"; some of them toured from hut to hut exploring a region, but we encountered people making a real long distance journey only twice on the whole traverse.

After a week, it was time to move on to the Kürsimger Hut, where we had arranged to meet Peter Capps, because we all wanted to climb the Gross Venediger, from which the district takes its name. As we set off, the two Germans ran after us to say goodbye, full of promises to send us photographs—which indeed they did—but they failed to include their address and we were never able to thank them. I browsed through old ski note-books at home searching for it among the many names and addresses of brief friendships, and chance acquaintances met in huts; sadly memories of faces dissolve only too quickly into the haze of time, and I wondered what some of them looked like and whether they would recognize us if we called on them in their homes. Yet on occasions, a joyous slap on the back, in a mountain hut in a completely different district, heralds a reunion to be celebrated by music, and an evening of wine,

Plate 100. The Gross Geiger from the Kürsinger Hut

Plate 101. The Gross Venediger seen from the Schlieferspitz. The Venediger can be seen from all the surrounding peaks

for such is the fraternity between people of all classes whose common interest lies in the love of mountains.

It was a gentle easy climb to the Maurer Pass, which would take us over to the Obersulzbach glacier. We left Archie on the pass with our rucksacks and contoured round to climb the Grosser Geiger, as there are superb views of the Gross Venediger seen from all the surrounding peaks. At eleven thousand feet on the peak, we shook hands with each other, as this time, although it was enveloped in clouds, we actually saw to the north-east the summit of the Gross Venediger.

Joining Archie once more we ran down to the Krimmler Pass and looked over. I think that even then Peter must have been planning the "Little Walk" as he was anxious to see what it looked like. We did not see much, only clouds boiling up from the valley, like a steaming cauldron, and the narrow couloir leading down to the Warnsdorfer Hut was bounded by dark black cliffs. It looked a sinister place and might be unsafe except under good snow conditions and little did we know at the time that we would never be able to use it on the "Little Walk on Skis".

Timing is an extraordinary thing in the mountains, because, as we arrived at the head of the Obersulzbach valley, there was Peter Capps—straight from London! He was to join us for the next part of the trip, when Archie and Geoffrey had to go home. Capps had all my sympathy, he was hot and sweating hard. The eight-hour climb had taken him ten hours, and we still had another three hundred feet to climb to reach the Kürsinger hut on its windy shelf. It was not so windy this time, but not unexpectedly it was very cold. The guardian allocated Peter and me a room to ourselves, normally a luxury, but it was in an isolated part of the building. Instead of undressing we put on all our spare clothes, took the six blankets from the two beds, and lay closely huddled together with the two duvets on top of the six blankets, and still we were cold. By next morning the water in the jug had frozen solid and we had to go down to the kitchen to find thawed water to wash in!

It was a fine sunny morning as the five of us set off to climb the Gross Venediger, but we paused outside the hut to look across the valley at the fine row of mountains: the Grosser Geiger, the Kleiner Maurerkees Kogel and the Maurer Pass on the extreme right, which we had crossed the day before. The path from the Kürsinger hut loses very little height down to the rather flat Obersulzbach glacier, and it did not take us long to reach a rocky ridge which falls from the peak on the north side of the Gross Venediger. But clouds started to come down as we contoured round it to reach the broken glacier which leads up to the peak.

We threaded our way through the ice-field of crevasses near the shoulder—which could at least be seen—and we decided to rope up, on two ropes for safety. But three hundred feet below the summit of over twelve thousand feet, the mist got thicker and we could only see each other. There was a wide *Bergschrund* to negotiate and a big cornice on the summit: the view would be nil. Was it worth it? No. We turned and retraced our steps and even then had to use a map and compass to steer our way back to the hut, as our climbing tracks were hard to find.

Next day Geoffrey and Archie had to go home, and Capps, Peter and I climbed the lower peak—not quite eleven thousand feet—of the Schlieferspitz, to the west of the Kürsinger hut. It is approached up a narrow couloir from the main glacier and the glacier above sweeps up to an impressive knife-edge ridge leading to the summit. The

Plate 102. The knife-edge on the Schlieferspitz—mountains have no business to be so sharp!

passage of many feet, I was told, had made a pathway, though it did not look like that to me! I jibbed at the last few yards—I did not mind one side of the mountain falling away nearly vertically for a thousand feet, as I could look away—but both sides ... well, the mountain had no business to be so steep! No! It made me feel sick. There was nowhere to look. If I looked at my feet I could still see the intimidating drop out of the corner of both eyes. I was offered a rope, but as Tartaran said in his *"Climbs in the Alps"*, what use would it be if we both fell off, one on each side of the ridge—to cut the rope?! But I suppose I could have walked along it had it really been necessary.

Kürsinger Hut to the Rudolfs Hut

Next day it was time to move on. We had climbed the best peaks, and we might make a second attmept to climb the Venediger, if it was free of cloud, on our way over to the Matreier Tauern Haus. We were now embarking on the route across the Venediger which Peter had planned to take, and which later failed us, on the "Little Walk".

It was an easy gradient to the Untersulzbach pass, which was wide, flat and characterless. As usual the Gross Venediger was in cloud; there was no point in climbing it, so we continued down the Viltragen glacier on breakable crust. The valley narrows at the end of the glacier, and we hurried on as it is reputed to be avalanche-prone. However, there was no excitement and we reached the river on a wide open plain, where we decided to bathe. We started to undress behind a very large rock, on the edge of the river. There was an ominous rumble. We peered round the rock—a huge avalanche was sliding off the Kessel Kogel; large blocks of snow, tumbling and churning like a tidal wave twelve feet high were most inconsiderately making straight for our rock! There was nowhere to run, as the rock was blocking our way. We crouched behind it hoping it would split the avalanche in two. Then silence. Cautiously we looked round—it had stopped thirty feet short of us. What a place to be caught in with your pants down! Needless to say, we hurriedly dressed and pushed on quickly down the valley.

Reaching some chalets where the valley broadened, we paused for a rest, but no bathe! There was a similar large rock to the one which had sheltered us, but it must have had a natural cave, as someone had ingeniously converted it into the body of a small church. At the entrance, a typical church front had been built of stone, complete with belfry and a door. Putting a donation in the box in gratitude for our safe delivery from the Venediger with its crevasses and avalanches, we pressed on to the Matreier Tauernhaus.

The Tauernhaus was a mountain hotel, and although full of German school-teachers, a room was found for us as the owner had an enormous sympathy for ski-tourers. He warned us that they were noisy, and this was no understatement! That night they were having a farewell party, and seeing we were the only other guests they "sucked us in". Wine flowed and before long alpine songs echoed up the mountainside. After a while they looked at Peter—why not an English song ... Clementine ...? But they had to settle for Italian Opera, which floored their guitarist. We ended up singing

Plate 103. The little chapel ingeniously created out of the rock

outside in moonlight while one of their party tolled the bell of the little chapel nearby.

In spite of the night's gaiety everyone was in fairly good shape the next morning. The Germans left early, and for each departing car load we tolled the bell in farewell.

We were late by the time they had gone, but despite this we set off for the Hochgasser for a day's tour. It was a tedious climb and I kept thinking of an English General whom we had met on a ski-tour. He was a heavy whisky drinker and every day a ring of icicles formed round his head as he sweated uphill—it looked like a tonsure. It amused me to pretend it was the alcohol oozing out—but of course it could not freeze—perhaps it was the exertion of the climb which eliminated mine! We finally came to the Grüner See, a little lake still some distance from the peak. It was swelteringly hot, and I was tired. The weather looked uncertain, and as we had a long distance to travel over to the Rudolfs hut the next day, and were not quite certain of the route we should take, we turned back.

It was a cloudless morning and too early for the ski-lift to be working, so we climbed the lower slopes to the Regenalm carrying our skis over hard-crusted snow. Above the ski-lift we traversed to the right of the rocky headland of the Daberkögele, and crossed slopes which fell away steeply to the stream bed. It was a great strain on the ankles. Our goal was the Sillingkopf, and from there we might be able to see a reasonable way over the next valley to take us to the Rudolfs Hut, as the usual way is to go up the Landeck Valley.

Presently we saw a lake below us, and we entered a broad valley bounded by a ridge which swept up on the right to an imposing shattered rocky pyramid—the Glockenkögel—and beyond it lay our peak. A two-terraced glacier led up to it with a steepish climb between; our way lay to the right. We looked back for the last time at the Venediger peaks: the Kristallwand stood in the foreground, a triangular smooth fold in deep blue shadow with the Schwarzwand and Gross Venediger staggered behind in the far distance.

It was hard work climbing the steep part of the glacier, but a fresh breeze kept us cool. We were now confronted by a short sharp slope which led to a ridge; it was the obvious way as it curved up to the peak of the Sillingkopf. The snow was icy and crusted, but not hard enough to bear our full weight. We removed our skis and carried them while Peter kicked steps—at first forty steps before a rest, then thirty-five, then twenty, until we were up. Heavily laden as we were, it was not easy even for Capps or me as we followed behind, but our interest was sustained by the ever-changing view—as we approached the top of the ridge the peaks appeared as if they had been waiting to surprise us.

The summit of the Sillingkopf was incredibly small and had an overhanging cornice, but it gave us a chance to look round. The mountain fell away steeply to the Landeck valley in the south-east, and it was flanked by a line of nondescript mountains, dominated from behind by the impressive wedge of the Gross Glockner. Towards the south were the jagged black teeth of the Lienzer Dolomites. Across the valley to the north-east we could see our next pass—the Granatscharter—and we now looked round for a way off the Sillingkopf into the valley. The ridge which we had climbed to the summit was broad and led down to a steep pass; it would afford a practicable way. Our main worry was now over, and we traversed round the valley on a terrace below the Karl First hut: a grand-sounding name for something little better than a sheep pen, but it never aspired to be anything more than a refuge in bad weather.

A short climb up the glacier brought us to the Granatscharter. We were soon running down the terraced Sonnenblick glacier in the most atrocious breakable crust to the Weiss See, which lies below the Rudolfs Hut.

The hut, although part of the Austrian Alpine Club, was no less than a mountain hotel—complete with cable-car from the valley, an anathema to Peter. The way down to the valley was now a piste. The churning mass of bodies fighting for food in the dining room, only concerned for themselves, drove Peter outside. In his characteristic way he was planning to make us work harder—and this is how he did it.

Rudolfs Hut to Kaprun

"An Odd Way Down from the Rudolfs Hut"*

"...a crossing rarely undertaken and scenically beautiful. Only advisable in good snow and weather conditions. A much more beautiful route ..."

I was lazing in the afternoon sun outside the Rudolfs Hut at the finish of three weeks' interesting touring, often frustrated by weather. One member of the party had bitterly complained that we always seemed to be climbing uphill and never running down. I took his point.

The words of the ski-guide leapt at me from the page. Why not spend our last day doing something new, instead of scraping down the rutted piste to Enzigerboden in the more customary way? The guide-book emphasized the steepness of the final slopes, but it seemed all right on the map and there was a convenient hut on the far side should we be too late to reach Kaprun in the day.

Our intended early start was frustrated by the (dis)organization of the hut, in which early starts were subservient to hangovers after a late night. It was not until after seven that the dining-room was opened by a sleepy-eyed girl. We were to suffer from this delay for the rest of the day.

The morning was fresh, and a clear night had hardened the snow well. After a few minutes' climb from the hut, we could see into the valley floor three hundred yards below. On the far side steep slopes rose up towards a wild and lonely-looking side valley, which would take us to the Kapruner Törl. I looked at the lower slopes critically. They were certainly steep but still lay in shadow and should be safe enough.

Putting on our skis we set off. A pleasant run in the early morning sun was marred by patches of *faulschnee* (or wet sodden snow) beside the bushes which were already emerging with the approach of spring. Our little *scherzo* of a descent was accompanied by a series of curses in counterpoint as one or other of us sank in knee-deep.

Despite all, we were soon down, and started to climb up the far side. The snow was still hard, though not hard enough to bear our weight on foot, and prolonged edging of the ski soon became tedious. I was a little way ahead. Quietly rounding a corner, I spied two marmots on a table of rock, playing in the sun. The valley must surely be rarely visited, for they took no alarm and it was only when I was very close that they lazily lolloped off. It was a pity that there was no time to stay and entice them with food, for they had little fear.

We were now well lodged in our side valley, though the pass was still hidden from view. We rounded another shoulder and my heart sank. Away across the other side of the valley ran a steep rock ridge without any sign of an actual pass. Snow slopes of impressive steepness ran up from the glacier to its base. Presumably the lowest part of the ridge constituted the pass. The slopes lay full in the morning sun but I took heart that despite the last few days of warm sun no avalanches had yet fallen. Also slopes always look steeper seen face on, don't they?

Rallying ourselves, we skirted the lower glacier slopes, which were liberally strewn

---

*Written by Peter Wilberforce Smith and reprinted from the Autumn 1968 edition of *"Ski"* by courtesy of the Ski Club of Great Britain with fallen rocks from a steep ice-cliff above. Sometimes carrying our skis, sometimes wearing them, we got above the steep moraine. There was sudden consternation. Beryl had lost a climbing-plate somewhere. Those damned new-fangled contraptions. It must be below, where she had taken off her ski. To our relief a cry came that she had found it.

Now came the really steep bit. Fortunately some rocky spurs enabled us to scramble straight up, handing our skis up from one to another and we were soon on easier ground leading up to our pass. It really was a pass—just a narrow cleft in the ridge, which was soon reached; so narrow that we could easily touch the sides with our extendced arms. What was in store for us the other side? I remembered more references in the guide book to steep slopes requiring care. To our relief they were not really so steep, and we could see right down into Mööserboden—our next objective. It was a good place for lunch: all our difficulties were over. Or so we thought.

Plate 104. Above the Mööser lake and looking back to the Kapruner Torl in the centre

The run down in good spring crust was delightful, though with heavy sacks we were ski-ing with care. Our little valley soon joined the Karlingerkees, with its splendid ice-fall. A last schuss* and we were on the valley floor—Mööserboden. A frozen lake lay in its lower bowl, with a high dam rising from the far end. The ice was riven with large cracks caused by the falling water level, and we skirted the right-hand side. Up and down we went interminably, the dam approaching with tantalising slowness. Old avalanches had crossed our route, and at one point forced us down to lake level. A cry

*Schuss—running fast on skis in a straight line without turns

from Capps— "I'm in a crevasse". So he was: a lake crevasse. Fortunately, it was very small and he was out in a moment.

A steep little climb took us on to the dam. All our troubles were now over, and we would soon be strolling down a mountain path on the far side. We peered over the dam wall and received a rude shock. A second dam had been built below. There was another crevasse-split lake, with steep slopes leading down on each side. What was worse, the hut which I had mentally reserved as a refuge was somewhere beneath the water. It was four o'clock and although the weather was fine some of us were distinctly weary. We were in an uncomfortable position. We walked along the dam wall a trifle despondently. Work of some kind seemed still to be in progress for there were a number of workmen's huts still about. The noise of an engine broke the quiet and a Jeep approached from around the corner. Beryl put on a fine show of exhaustion, not entirely simulated, and asked the driver if he would take us as far as possible down the mountain road, for it was no longer feasible to ski. He willingly agreed and off we sped, down and down. Suddenly the road entered a tunnel; our Jeep stopped and the driver dismounted. "End of journey," he said laconically. I wondered where on earth we were. A bunch of workmen eyed us curiously. One of them took us in charge and shouldering our skis we walked further into the mountain

Suddenly we came to what can only be described as a subterranean cliff-lift. Our guide handed us over to its driver, the gate clanged to, and we shot straight downwards. There was a strange air of unreality about it all. We stopped. We were instructed to walk along the tunnel for about half a kilometre, when we would find a second lift.

Our footsteps echoed along the dimly-lit tunnel, and from time to time our skis clattered against the low and dripping roof. Were we really awake, or had we been involved in an avalanche and was this a state of suspended animation?

Our second lift was a splendid two-coach affair. We felt rather disappointed that there was no dining-car. A number of troglodytes were already ensconced, apparently awaiting us. Down and down we went. There was a pause as we edged past another lift on the way up. After what seemed a long time, we reached the bottom. Another tunnel, longer still, and this one had a miniature railway: but the little locomotives were still and the carriages empty.

At last there was a glimmer of daylight which steadily grew stronger as we neared the iron door at the end. As I unlatched it, it clanged open with a blast of compressed air. We emerged into the daylight and looked round us curiously. The little terminus outside even had a booking office, though it was shut. To our surprise there were large wall maps showing our underground route, for now that the dams are built the underground system is also used as a summer attraction for tourists.

The air was balmy, for Spring had already come to the valley, and flowers were already thrusting through the damp earth. The rush of a nearby waterfall fed by the melting snows broke the evening stillness. It all seemed a rather odd, but perhaps fitting, way in which to end our tour.

A final word from Beryl:

For me, "A Little Walk on Skis" ends with Peter beside me, for although he is no longer here, his Spirit lives in the mountains—for what purpose the journey without the memories?

Plate 105. His Spirit lives in the mountains